Want to Play by Ear?
A Step-by-Step Approach

By Ron Sprunger

Ashland Theological Seminary

With a Chapter on Hymn Improvisation by Kathy Smith

Mid-American Nazarene University

Second Edition, Revised and Expanded
© Copyright 2004 Ron Sprunger
Original Edition © Copyright 1998
All Rights Reserved

Note: This teaching manual includes several copyrighted songs that are complete: "Give Thanks" (Example 80), "Lord, Be Glorified" (Example 83), and two of the songs included in Appendix J. The copying of these for use in the classroom, worship, or other setting is not permitted under what is considered "fair use." Also included are several short excerpts of 2-4 measures each, the duplication of which is also prohibited in that each constitutes more than ten per cent of the complete song (see Examples 142-146, 182-183, 186-189, 198-199, 202-203). Under copyright law an entire chapter of a book may be duplicated, provided it does not constitute more than ten per cent of the total number of pages. If chapter six were to be duplicated, Examples 80 and 83 would have to be deleted, unless a print license were secured from copyright holder. Likewise, if chapters nine or eleven were to be duplicated, the excerpts of copyrighted songs would have to be deleted. The author should be contacted if there are questions (drsprunger@aol.com).

ISBN 0-9665956-1-0

The text with CD and floppy disk are available from the author (see e-mail address above and street address which follows):

> Ron Sprunger
> 408 Keen Ave.
> Ashland, OH 44805

TABLE OF CONTENTS

DEDICATION	vi
INTRODUCTION AND ACKNOWLEDGEMENTS	vii
CHAPTER	Page
Chapter 1. GETTING STARTED	1-8
• Five Finger Melodies	1
• Melodies with a Range of Six Pitches	3
• Melodies with a Range of One Octave	3
Chapter 2. DARE TO BE SIMPLE	9-32
• Guidelines for Selecting Basic Chords	10
• Tonic and Dominant Drone Accompaniments	14
• Tonic and Dominant Chords Linked by Common Tone	15
• Non-Harmonic Tones	16
• Independent Accompaniment Styles	19
Broken Chord Pattern	20
Tuba Bass	21
Walking Bass	21
Twelve-Bar Blues	23
Calypso	25
Arpeggiated Chord Patterns	25
Chapter 3. HARMONIZING SCALE FRAGMENTS	33-48
• Melodies That Include Scale Lines	33
• Scale Fragments	
Do (1) Re (2)	34
Do (1) Re (2) Mi (3)	36
Do (1) Re (2) Mi (3) Fa (4)	37
Do (1) Re (2) Mi (3) Fa (4) So (5)	40
Do (1) Re (2) Mi (3) Fa (4) So (5) La (6)	42
• Scale Fragments in Sequence	44
Chapter 4. HARMONIZING THE COMPLETE SCALE	49-60
• Descending Scale	49
• Ascending Scale	55
Chapter 5. SUBSTITUTE CHORDS: THE CHANGING FUNCTION OF A TONE	61-72
• The Submediant Chord (vi) as a Substitute for Tonic (I)	61
• The Mediant Chord (iii) as a Substitute for Tonic	65
• The Supertonic Chord (ii) as a Substitute for Subdominant (IV)	66
• Hearing Changes in the Function of a Given Pitch	68

Chapter 6. SCALE HARMONIZATION: USING SEQUENCES   73-94
- Descending Scale from So (5) with Succession of Fifths   73
- Succession of Fifths in a Minor Key   77
- Key Signatures Listed by Succession of Fifths   79
- Descending Scale from Mi (3) with Pachelbel Canon Sequence   80
- The Alteration of Chords in Sequence   90

Chapter 7. HARMONIZING A MELODY: THE PROCESS   95-114
- A Six-Step Approach a la Forte   95
- Selecting Chords on the Basis of Chord Outlines   103
- Harmonizing on the Basis of Underlying Scale Lines   106

Chapter 8. MODULATION   115-138
- Definition and Purpose   115
- Guidelines   116
- Half-Step Modulations   116
- Whole Step Modulations   121
- Minor Third Modulations   125
- Major Third Modulations   129
- Modulation Down a Perfect Fifth (up a Perfect Fourth)   133
- Modulation to the Dominant (down a Perfect Fourth or up a Perfect Fifth)   134
- Tri-Tone Modulation   135

Chapter 9. IMPROVISATION   139-164
- Introduction   139
- A Good Way to Begin: Improvising Pentatonic Melodies   142
- Creating Melodies Using Basic Rhythm Patterns   144
- A Fun Way to Do Dictation   145
- Embellishing Melodies and Harmonies with Non-Harmonic Tones   147
- The Use of Suspensions   150
- Exploring Modal Harmonies   151
- The Subtonic Chord   151
- Bi-Modal Harmony   152
- Combining Binary and Ternary Rhythms   156
- Renaissance Dance Rhythms   157
- Chords That Never Made the Hymnal   157
- Tri-Tone Substitutes   157
- Altering the Chord Used for Notes of Anacrusis   159
- Altered Deception   160
- The Values of Improvisation   162
- Nurturing the Growing Process   162

Chapter 10. READING FIGURED BASS   165-170

Chapter 11. IMPROVISING ACCOMPANIMENT TO ENHANCE
           PRAISE AND WORSHIP (Kathy Smith, Author)   171-190
- Why Embellish the Voice Parts?   171
- Melody Doubled with Full Chords   172
- The Movement of Inner Voice-Parts   175
- Melody in Octaves   176
- Outlining Chords with Scales   177
- Full Right Hand Chords with Octave Movement in Bass   179
- Descending Scales as Fill   180
- Chord Substitution   181
- Chord Inversions   183
- Broken Chords   184
- Antiphonal Effect and Imitation   187

APPENDICES   191-211
- Appendix A - Common-Tone Chording with Basic Chords   191
- Appendix B - Diatonic Triads of the Major Scale and Their Inversions   193
- Appendix C - Common-Tone Chording with Basic Chords and V7 of V (II)   195
- Appendix D - Major, Minor, Diminished, Augmented Chords   196
- Appendix E - Diminished Chords   197
- Appendix F - Adding Suspensions   202
- Appendix G - Changing Function of a Repeated or Sustained Pitch   204
- Appendix H - Chords That Didn't Make the Hymnal: From Simple
      to More Complex Harmonies   207
- Appendix J - Lead Sheets   209

REFERENCE LIST   213

INDECES
- Index of Musical Examples   215
- Index of Recorded Examples   217
- Topical Index   219

WORDS OF DEDICATION

As I offer this material to the reader, a deep sense of gratitude wells up within me for the contributions of those who have taught me though word and example. For those who are mentioned in the course of this writing, there are many others whose names could have been included.

My education began in the days of the one-room school house. It was in this setting that I experienced the joy of learning through the teachings of one who enjoyed his vocation and loved the children he taught. With several different grade levels in the same classroom, he was able to challenge the gifted students and, at the same time, provide encouragement and help to those for whom learning was more difficult. The activities of the day included what are considered the basics, but learning was enriched by singing, drama, athletics, and generous doses of humor. This book is dedicated in memory of his great example to me and many others whose lives were impacted during his thirty-five years of elementary teaching. The more I teach, the more I realize my indebtedness to one who was not only my teacher for four years, but also my dad. His love for singing permeated both classroom and home, where Mother's singing and playing of the piano was another source of joy and inspiration. Her creativity in sewing and other areas of homemaking, coupled with Dad's creativity, provided a climate for growth and nurture. Clinton and Verena Sprunger left a rich legacy to me, my brothers Bob and Curt, and our extended family. Their influence continues to this day.

I also want to express my gratitude for Linda, my lovely wife, whose encouragement and help in this project have been invaluable. Proofreading and editing have taken hours of her time. Her musicianship and understanding of music theory enabled her to read the material with keen perception, and her suggestions have been most helpful.

I feel that I have little more than scratched the surface when it comes to understanding the order and beauty of God's creation, of which music is an integral part. It is to Him that I dedicate the contents of this book, with the prayer that it will serve to equip keyboard musicians to use their God-given musical gifts for His glory, and to do it with a greater sense of freedom that comes through understanding.

Ron Sprunger
Professor Emeritus, Music and Worship
Ashland Theological Seminary

INTRODUCTION AND ACKNOWLEDGMENTS

The background of those who will use this instructional method is likely to be varied with regard to keyboard skills, knowledge of theory, and experience in playing without music. I suspect many, like I, learned to read well, but without any encouragement to play by ear.

I was fortunate to have a dedicated teacher who taught me not only to read, but also to hear the printed page. Alberta Berg, with whom I began the study of piano and continued through high school, encouraged me to sing the letter names of the notes as I learned them. Singing what I played helped me to internalize the sounds. Although I was not encouraged to play by ear, I received an excellent foundation for later development.

A considerable amount of ear development during my formative years came through the "faking" of vocal harmonies, as our family sang hymns and barbershop songs around the kitchen table after the evening meal. It was many years later that I realized I could learn to "fake," or improvise harmonies at the keyboard, as well.

As a student at the Oberlin Conservatory of Music, I had three separate learning experiences that would later come together in a significant way. The synthesis of these experiences, coupled with other insights gained through continuing study, led to a breakthrough in learning to play by ear.

One day Dr. Wesley Smith, Prof. of Music Education, said that anyone who diligently practices solfege will eventually be able to sing familiar melodies with syllables without referring to the music. I was a bit doubtful at first, but trusting his judgment, I proceeded with the task of learning solfege. To my delight, it wasn't long before I could sing many songs with syllable names, as if they were additional stanzas to these familiar melodies. Soon I began to transfer this to the keyboard and was able to play these melodies in different keys simply by thinking the syllable names. A few years later, in a methods class taught by Earl Lehman at Bluffton College, this concept was reinforced as I was shown how children can be taught to master the tones of the scale. Syllable names, or numbers, were arranged vertically on the chalk board, and the children watched and listened as the teacher pointed to the numbers while teaching a song. Soon the children were leading this activity.

The other learning experience that was to be extremely valuable was the study of scale harmonization in Prof. Robert Melcher's theory class at Oberlin. We were required to play an ascending and descending scale with a supporting chord for each scale tone. The bass line was sung as it was played in all keys, and the Roman numeral analysis served as lyrics. The breakthrough came when I discovered that I could combine the understanding acquired through solfege with the chords that I had learned through scale harmonization. Further development came as I began to explore other possible harmonizations for each tone of the scale. Another insight was gained several years later as I studied theory pedagogy with Prof. Hugh Glauser at Kent State University. I observed that Mr. Glauser would drill his students in determining the feeling or function of both the soprano and bass pitches of isolated chords. In my work with Roman numeral analysis and the singing of bass lines, I had not given much thought to which chord tone (root, 3rd, 5th or 7th) was in the soprano voice.

Learning shouldn't cease when we complete our formal study of music. For most of us, commencement marks not only the beginning of our musical careers, but also the beginning of the process of life-long learning. Some of the people from whom we learn may have less formal training than you or I. This is especially true when it comes to playing by ear. Along with "picking the brains" of these people and listening to them play, I have also gained much from graduate-level study. For example, in a graduate course in keyboard harmony taught by

Dr. Walter Watson, we revisited many of the concepts learned in undergraduate study and were challenged to build on them. This study seemed particularly relevant to my work as a choir director, organist, and public school music teacher.

For me, personally, a strong motivation for the development of a command of keyboard harmony has been my desire to be able to accompany singing without reference to the printed page. I found a most helpful approach in reading Allen Forte's *Tonal Harmony in Concept and Practice*, particularly his discussion entitled, "The Six Steps in Soprano Harmonization" (Forte, 1879, 227-233). Dr. Forte's systematic approach helped me to see the value of moving from simple to more complex harmonies. As I progressed, a la Forte, from the use of basic chords (I, IV and V) and their inversions to the use or secondary chords (iii, vi and ii) and other possible harmonies, I became more aware of chord function. I learned to hear the different chords that could be used to support each tone of the scale.

The most recent development leading to the writing of this material was the study of Schenkerian analysis with Dr. Anne Marie deZeeuw at the University of Louisville. My interest in Heinrich Schenker's work was kindled by Robert Melcher's inspiring teaching, in which he repeatedly called our attention to the underlying scale-wise movement that served as an undergirding of phrases and even larger sections of a composition.

Although Schenkerian analysis is too complex to be a part of an instruction book such as this, some of the insights gained through my study of his method will be included. Hopefully, the emphasis on the scale-like structure of some melodies, along with continued emphasis on scale harmonization, will make this course or instruction valuable for the student of music theory and for those whose primary goal is to play by ear.

Through the analysis of many of the progressions that I've heard and played, my ear is now better able to sift through the tones of an unknown melody to find the basic scale-like structure, as well as harmonies implied by chord outlines. As an artist is able to sketch that which is seen, we who are musicians ought to be able to "sketch" the lines of music at the keyboard and other instruments. All too often teachers of music approach the teaching/learning process visually rather than aurally. We forget that sound should precede symbol in the process of learning.

As I use the phrase, "playing by ear" or "without music," I am reminded of an experience I had as a student in Austria about forty years ago, an experience that was interesting, amusing, and instructive. A friend and I were shopping for music, and he said to the clerk, "Ich möchte Musik kaufen" ("I would like to buy some music."). The clerk, obviously amused by the request, said, "Sie können nicht Musik kaufen. Sie können nur die Noten kaufen" ("You can't buy music. You can buy only the notes."). The German language, which is most precise, distinguishes between sound and symbol. Music is sound, not dots on a page!

For the person whose music-making has been restricted to translating symbols (notes) into sound, it is nearly impossible to reach a point where one operates solely on the basis of what is heard. However, I am convinced that all of us can learn to operate in the realm of sound more than we have in the past. This will come through the analysis of the sounds we hear and use. Of equal importance is the conscious application of that which is analyzed, in different keys and in different musical contexts (styles).

This course of instruction is written, first, for the person who has the desire to play by ear and is willing to spend the time needed to develop both the skill and the understanding that it requires. Second, it is written for the keyboard instructor who would like to make the development of the ear an integral part of teaching, along with the study of repertory and technique. Those who teach children will be delighted to discover how quickly they learn.

Perhaps those of us who are older learners would, likewise, have progressed rapidly, had we been encouraged to play by ear when we were young.

This material can be used effectively in class or private instruction. Although the musical examples have been selected with the needs of the church musician in mind, the principles are equally applicable to the work of the teacher in public and private schools. The materials could also serve as a rich supplement to the study of functional harmony in traditional theory courses.

Specific assignments have been included in each chapter. However, the teacher should feel free to augment or delete at his or her own discretion. It is not necessary to complete every exercise. The interest and ability of the individual should be considered.

A final word of encouragement is needed. Although the principles outlined here may be covered during the course of a year, it may take years of practice and application of these principles is order to gain proficiency. I trust you will enjoy the adventure of exploring the world of sound through keyboard experiences.

In the above words of introduction, I have acknowledged numerous people who have contributed to my understanding of music. I would be remiss not to mention others who have aided the progress of this writing project. A special blessing was the provision of a place to write without interruptions. Robert and Naomi Loukinen's home in the woods of upper Michigan was just perfect. I am indebted to Dr. Frederick J. Finks, President of Ashland Theological Seminary, who encourages the creative efforts of faculty members. I have wanted to write this material for years and the school's provision of a computer and music software were just what I needed to get started. Ken VanDuyne helped me takes my first steps with notation software, and the world of MIDI was opened to me by Nancy Daley and Rich Messenger. Most recently I've been helped by Carolyn Daugherty of Ashland University, who consistently comes up with solutions to all my problems related to computer technology. A last hour blessing was the help of Jim Frado who converted the MIDI files to audio CD. This list could go on and on, but it's more important to get on with the exciting work of exploring sounds at the keyboard. Let's begin!

Abbreviations and Additional Resources

Frequent reference will be made to *The Worshiping Church* (Hustad 1990), and will be indicated - **TWC**. Reference will also be made to *Songs for Praise and Worship* (Barker 1992), and be indicated - **SPW**. The pew edition of SPW is particularly useful in the development of the ear, because it includes no chord symbols. Another collection of tunes and texts without chord symbols is: *Great Songs for God's Kids* (Haron 1991). For practice in reading a "lead sheet," an excellent resource is *The Best of the Best in Contemporary Praise & Worship* (Zehnder 2000). If help is needed in interpreting chord symbols, the **Accompaniment Edition** (Zehnder 2000) could serve as reference, for it includes chord symbols above the written accompaniment for each song. Other collections that include chord symbols with written accompaniment are: *Songs for Praise and Worship: Worship Planner Edition* (Barker 1992), *Sing to the Lord: Accompanists'/Pulpit Edition* (Bible 1993), *Maranatha! Music Praise Hymns and Choruses* (Vegh 1997), and *The Celebration Hymnal: Accompaniment Edition* (Fettke 1998). Kathy Smith, the author of Chapter Eleven of *Want to Play by Ear?*, makes frequent reference to *Sing to the Lord*, for which the abbreviation **STTL** will be used. Occasional reference is made to *The Hymnal for Worship & Celebration* (Fettke 1986), for which the abbreviation **TH** is used. For more information on the above resources see REFERENCE LIST, p. 213.

The usefulness of this material is not contingent upon the availability of the above supplementary resources. Nearly all of the hymns that are included are found in other hymnals. The choruses, likewise, are included in other collections of praise and worship music.

Frequently, the abbreviations **MIDI or CD** appear with an assignment. Many of the musical examples are recorded in Standard MIDI File (SMF) format and on compact disc. If neither MIDI nor a CD player is available, you are permitted to have a cassette recording made from the CD. The visually-oriented learner is encouraged to *listen* first, then study each written example (see **INDEX OF RECORDED EXAMPLES**, p. 172). **Please note**: When using the MIDI file with different equipment, there might be a slight change in the order of songs. For example, when using Roland MIDI players the last file (**60.mid**) might appear first, in which case the succeeding files are changed. MIDI file **01.mid** is actually **02.mid** and **02.mid** is **03.mid**, etc. If there is a question about the title of a given song or exercise, refer to the selection as recorded on the enclosed CD, where the songs occur in the correct order (see pp. 172-173).

Chapter One

GETTING STARTED

Playing tunes by ear can be great fun, if you can stand a few mistakes. It's not only fun, it's foundational, for it is the starting point for the improvising of supporting chords, rhythms and "fills." Attentive listening to the succession of sounds is important, for one must learn to hear where each pitch is leading.

The first exercises begin with the eye, but the ear must do the work of completion. Through continuing practice, the rise and fall of a melody by steps, skips, and even larger intervals can be played with increasing ease and accuracy. Some people seem to have an invisible tape measure that guides the ear. Those who don't have this intuitive sense will have to work a little longer and harder to learn to hear melodic leaps (large intervals). The process could be described as tracing with your fingers what is heard by the inner ear. Hopefully, the successful completing of a few tunes will convince the student that "playing by ear" is a skill that can be learned.

To assure some measure of success, the initial melodies will involve only movement by steps (2nds) and skips (3rds) within a range of five pitches (Do Re Mi Fa So, or 1 2 3 4 5). The first few pitches of each melody will be given for those who need a little help in getting started (see Example 2). After listening to the first recorded song on MIDI or CD, play the tune. For those who do not have access to MIDI, a CD is included, with more than one recording of some of the examples. The melody, or other part deleted on the succeeding track, is to be played by the student. The accompaniments are intended to serve as enrichment and as a challenge. A few key changes will not only keep you "on your toes," but also prepare your ear for the chord progressions and modulations to be studied in later chapters. Those who use MIDI files can delete parts as well as transpose the accompaniment to different keys for added challenge.

Five Finger Melodies

The following procedure is suggested: Play the first five pitches of the scale and the tonic chord (the major triad built on the first note of the scale), then the tune (see Examples 1, 2 and ASSIGNMENT 1). For a review of the five-finger pattern in all keys, listen, then play each pattern with the sound of supporting chords, beginning with C major (**01.mid** or **CD 1**).

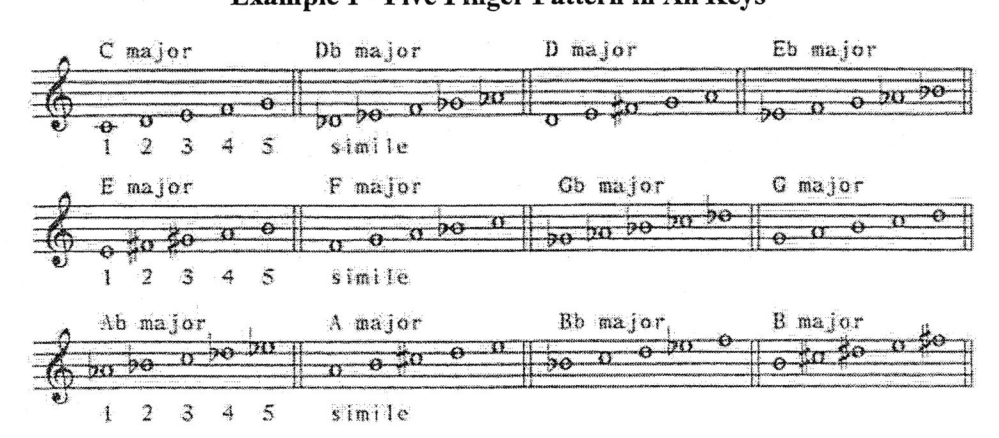

Example 1 - Five Finger Pattern in All Keys

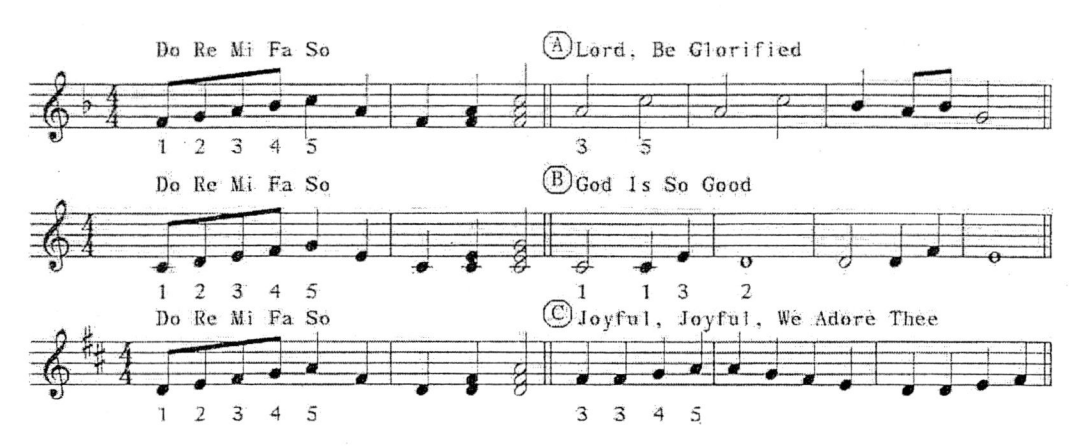

Example 2 - Preparatory Exercises with Starting Pitches

©1978 Bob Kilpatrick Music. P.O. Box 2383
Fair Oaks, CA 95628. Adm. by the Lorenz Co. Used by permission

Another effective way to determine the first pitch is to sing the whole song, then compare the final pitch with the beginning pitch. Note: Most songs end on Do (l).

ASSIGNMENT 1

1. Play the following melodies in the keys indicated (see Example 2 for starting pitches). **Remember, if a song begins on the third note of the scale in the original key, it also begins on the third note of the new key.**

   - Lord, Be Glorified (TWC 537 in F, D and Eb) - **02.mid** or **CD 2**
   - God is So Good (TWC 75 in C, Db, D, Eb) - **03.mid** or **CD 3**
   - Joyful, Joyful, We Adore (TWC 20 in D, F, F# and G) - **04.mid** or **CD 4**

   Note: For the basic left hand accompaniments used on the recording, see Examples 13 and 15.

2. Select two songs below that are familiar. Sing the tune, then write the scale numbers in the gray box on page 3. After the numbers are written, check for accuracy by playing the tune.

   - Lightly Row (5 3 3, 4 2 2)
   - Mary Had a Little Lamb (3 2 1 2 3)
   - Bind Us Together (3 3 3 3 2 1) (TWC 690 or SPW 140)
   - What Can Wash Away My Sins? (1 1 1 2 3 5 3) (TH 195)

Abbreviations: TWC = *The Worshiping Church* (Hope 1990), SPW = *Songs for Praise and Worship* (Word 1992) and TH = *The Hymnal* (Word 1986)

Chapter 1 – Getting Started

```
1 3 4 5    1 3 4 5
1 3 4 5 3 1 3 2
3 3 2 1 1 3 5 5 5 4
3 4 5 3 1 2 1
```

Songs with a Range of Six Notes (1-6, or Do-La)

In playing the tunes that follow (Example 3), you'll find that it works best to play the tonic (I) chord with the fingering - 1 2 4. This extension of the basic hand position facilitates the smooth (legato) playing of a wider range of pitches.

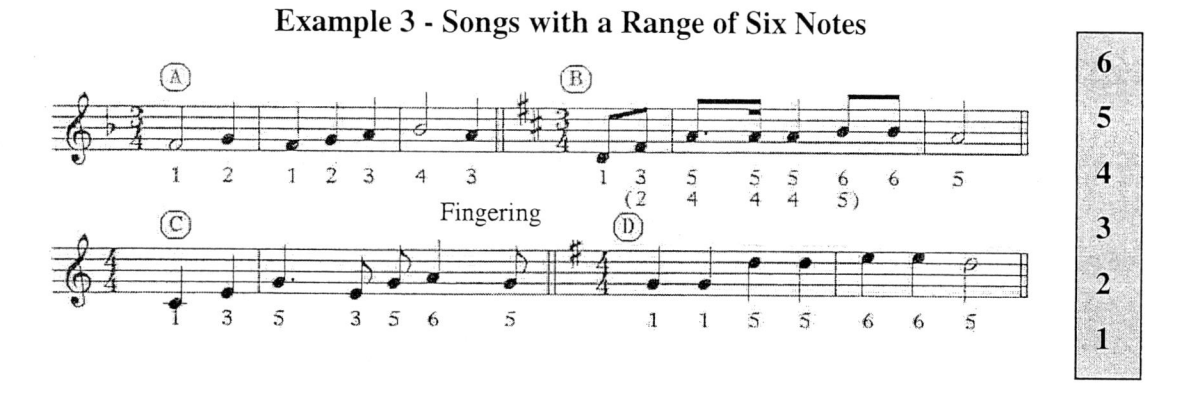

Example 3 - Songs with a Range of Six Notes

ASSIGNMENT 2

1. Complete each of the tunes in Example 3.
2. Transpose each of the tunes to the keys indicated in parentheses below.

- Come, Thou Long-Expected Jesus (TWC 135 in Gb and G)
- Kum Ba Yah (TWC 630 in Eb, E and F)
- Michael, Row the Boat Ashore (Db and D)
- Twinkle, Twinkle, Little Star (D, F and Eb) - **05.mid** or **CD 5**

Songs with a Range of One Octave (1-8, or Do-Do)

The first two melodies in Example 4 are rather easy to play by ear because of their scale-like (conjunct) movement. The tunes that follow are a little more challenging because of their skips and leaps (disjunct movement). One of the melodies climaxes by going one step beyond the octave range. The need to hear altered scale tones (accidentals) also increases the challenge.

Chapter 1 – Getting Started

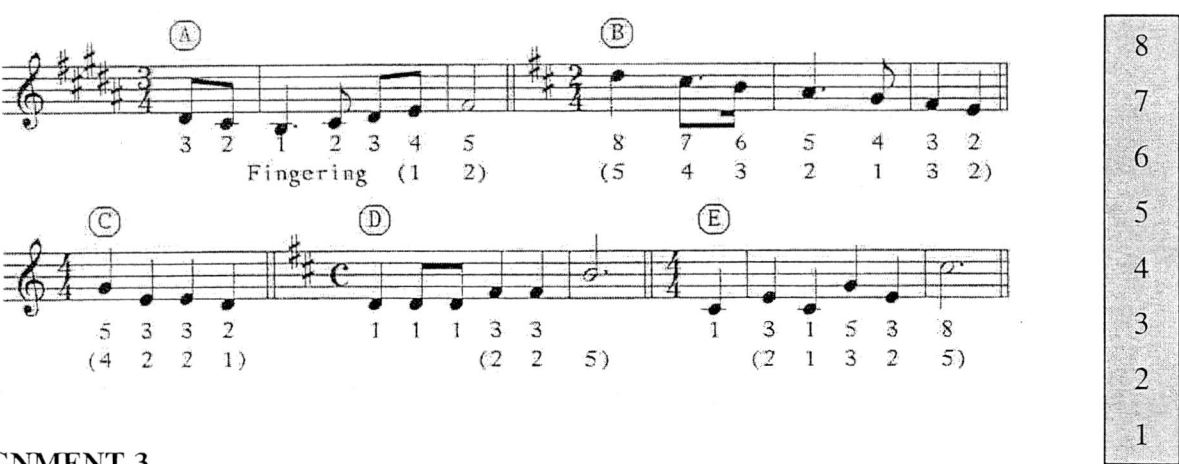

Example 4 - Melodies with a Range of One Octave

[Musical notation with labeled sections A, B, C, D, E showing melodies with fingering numbers:
A: 3 2 1 2 3 4 5   Fingering (1 2)
B: 8 7 6 5 4 3 2   (5 4 3 2 1 3 2)
C: 5 3 3 2   (4 2 2 1)
D: 1 1 1 3 3   (2 2 5)
E: 1 3 1 5 3 8   (2 1 3 2 5)]

[Side scale: 8 7 6 5 4 3 2 1]

ASSIGNMENT 3

1. Write the scale numbers for at least two of the songs in Example 4, then check your work by using the keyboard. Begin to train your ear to recognize the various skips and leaps in the melody.
2. Complete each of the following melodies by ear, then transpose it to another key.

> - The First Noel (TWC 162 in B and C) - **06.mid** or **CD 6**
> - Joy to the World (TWC 146 in C and D) – **07.mid** or **CD 7**
> - Jesus Loves Me (TWC 470 in D and Db)
> - Jesus Shall Reign (TWC 745 in Db and Eb)
> - Crown Him with Many Crowns (TWC 92 in Eb and E)
> - Rejoice, the Lord is King (TWC 262 in D)

Melodies within a Range of One Octave (5-5)

The tunes that follow include pitches from the lower octave (pitches below 1 or Do). To show the use of pitches from the lower octave, a line is drawn above the scale number. For example, the scale numbers for "Amazing Grace" would be written as follows:

$$\bar{5} \quad 1 \quad 3 \quad 1 \quad 3 \quad 2 \quad 1 \quad \bar{6} \quad \bar{5}$$

A knowledge of chords and their inversions is useful in picking out tunes by ear. For example, the first line of "Amazing Grace" lies within the hand position used for a second inversion chord (see Example 5).

Chapter 1 – Getting Started

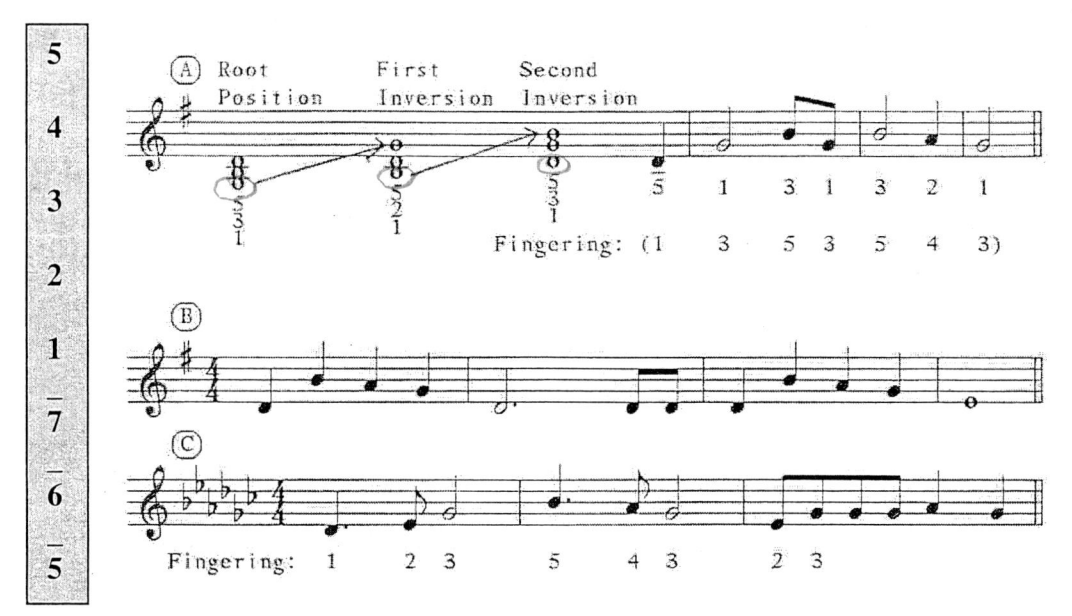

Example 5 - Melodic Patterns That Outline a Second Inversion Chord

Example 6 - Additional Melodies That Outline a Second Inversion Chord

ASSIGNMENT 4

1. Complete selected songs from Examples 5 and 6, and transpose each melody to the keys indicated.

   - Amazing Grace (TWC 502 in F and Gb)
   - Jingle Bells (F) – **08** and **09.mid** or **CD 8** and **9**
   - Praise Him in the Morning (F and G) w/Glenn Jones at the keyboard **10.mid** or **CD 10**
   - Leaning on the Everlasting Arms (TWC 609 in F and A)
   - O Come, All Ye Faithful (TWC 173 in Gb and Ab)
   - How Firm a Foundation (TWC 612 in Ab)

2. Starting with scale tone 5 (So) of the lower octave, sing, then write the scale numbers in the boxes for two of the following songs:

- Amazing Grace   Example $\bar{5}$ 1 3 1 3
- Happy Birthday
- Home on the Range
- How Firm a Foundation
- Red River Valley

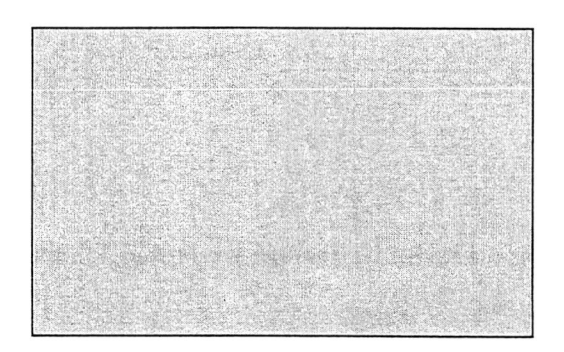

3. Continue to pick out tunes for the sheer joy of exploring. Give yourself an on-going assignment of playing all kinds of melodies: jingles, pop tunes, TV theme songs, folk songs, symphonic themes, hymns and choruses.

Note: In using the MIDI files one can delete, or mute, a given part (melody, bass, chords), then play that part on the keyboard, or other instrument. The CD recording provides a similar opportunity for practice, for the full complement of parts is heard only on the first track. On each succeeding recording of the same song, a different part is missing. MIDI technology allows not only the deletion of parts, but also the options of transposition of each example to other keys, and the variation of tempo.

Work Space

Notes on Chapter One

Chapter Two

DARE TO BE SIMPLE

A keyboard musician who knows how to use three basic chords can accompany hundreds of songs and is well on the way to playing by ear. A person who has a command of these chords can take a melody such as the following and provide an adequate accompaniment (see Ex. 8). The basic chords (I, IV and V) will be used and explained in the course of this chapter.

Example 7 - A Melody to Harmonize

Example 8 - Accompaniment Using Basic Chords

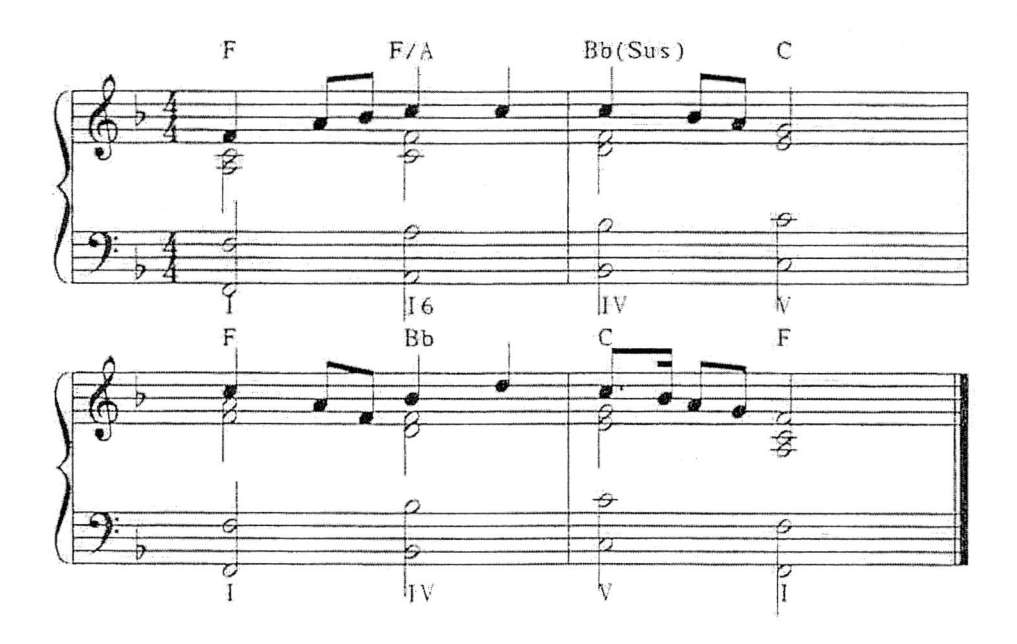

Although my purpose in writing is to help keyboard musicians develop an ear for varied harmonies and accompaniment styles, it is important to begin simply. The use of basic chords allows a keyboard musician with minimal experience and skill to play with a sense of musical flow. When accompanying group singing, it is extremely important to keep the song moving. More complex chords are not effective if the accompanist must slow the tempo in order to find the "right one."

Chapter 2 – Dare to Be Simple

Since the focus of this chapter is on basic chords, a student who is more advanced may want to skip to **Independent Accompaniment Styles** (p. 19) or to succeeding chapters. The material that immediately follows has been prepared for those who need help in selecting and mastering the use of basic chords.

Guidelines for Selecting Basic Chords

When the pitches of a melody outline the tonic chord (1 3 5), or when any of these pitches are repeated or used in various combinations, the tonic chord (I) is used. Clear indications for the use of the tonic chord (I) can be seen in some of the songs in Examples 2 and 3.

ASSIGNMENT 5

1. Write the scale numbers (or syllables) for the melody that follows, and circle groups of notes that are a part of the tonic chord (C major).

Example 9 - Kum Ba Yah

2. Sing and/or play several of the melodies in the box on the next page, and listen for tonic chord outlines.

- Amazing Grace (TWC 502)
- Immortal, Invisible (TWC 62)
- In Moments Like These (SPW 97)
- Jesus Loves Me (TWC 470)
- Just As I Am (TWC 445)
- Lamb of God (SPW 112)
- Leaning on the Everlasting Arms (TWC 609)
- Let All Things Now Living (Example 114)
- Lightly Row
- Nothing But the Blood of Jesus (TWC 471)
- O Come, Little Children (Example 20)
- Praise Him, Praise Him, All Ye Little Children
- Silent Night, Holy Night (TWC 164)
- Take the Name of Jesus with You (TH 116)
- The Joy of the Lord (SPW 229)
- What a Friend We Have in Jesus (TWC 622)

ASSIGNMENT 6

Play the melody of "Kum Ba Yah" with the right hand, and play a sustained C in the bass as accompaniment for each phrase (Example 10). This type of bass is called a pedal point. Change the bass to G at the end of the second phrase, also near the end of the song when the second note of the scale (Re, or 2) is heard again. Note that each of the first three phrases could end with the dominant chord, because the final pitches are all part of the dominant chord (G). However, this would result in three consecutive phrases that progress to V. By harmonizing the first and third phrases as circular progressions (progressions that begin and end with I), the effectiveness of ending the second phrase with the dominant is greater. The close of a musical phrase is called a cadence. When a phrase ends with a dominant chord (V), it is called an unfinished cadence, or half cadence.

Chapter 2 – Dare to Be Simple

Example 10 - Tonic Pedal Point with Shift to Dominant for Half Cadence

The subdominant chord (IV) is used when a melody outlines the scale tones - 4 6 8, or when one of these pitches, such as 6, is emphasized. The subdominant chord (IV) is built on the fourth note of the scale, which is F in the key of C. Where do the pitches of "Kum Ba Yah" suggest the use of the subdominant chord?

ASSIGNMENT 7

1. Play "Kum Ba Yah" as in ASSIGNMENT 6, but change the bass to F (IV) to support the pitches of the melody that suggest the use of IV (Example 11).
2. Select two of the following melodies and provide a tonic pedal point accompaniment as in Example 10, shifting to the dominant and subdominant chord root as needed:

> - Bind Us Together (TWC 690 or SPW 140 in F)
> - Clementine (F)
> - Michael Row the Boat Ashore (D)
> - Skip to My Lou (F)
> - What Can Wash Away My Sins? (TH 195 in F and Eb)

Chapter 2 – Dare to Be Simple

Example 11 – Kum Ba Yah (with Addition of Subdominant Harmony)

Building Basic Chords (I, IV and V) from the Tones of the Scale

The following example shows each of the primary (basic) chords derived from the C major scale. The scale tones in parentheses are the ones from which the chord is built (e.g. different combinations of C, E and G that form the tonic chord and its inversions).

Example 12 - Primary Chords and Their Related Scale Tones

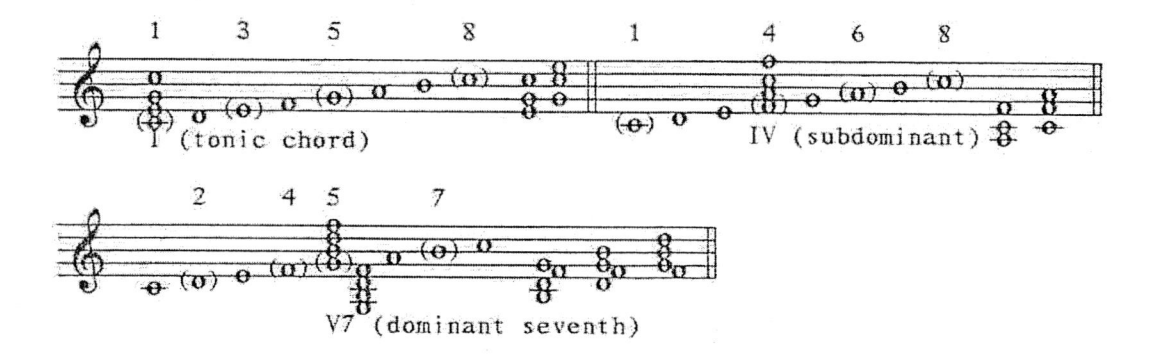

Note: An enjoyable way to develop an understanding and tactile sense of these chords is to play a "boogie woogie" bass line with a twelve-bar blues progression (**15** and **17.mid, CD 15** and **17**).

Chapter 2 – Dare to Be Simple

ASSIGNMENT 8

1. Play the D major scale, then play the primary chords as in Example 12.
2. Transpose the melody of "Kum Ba Yah" to D, then add primary chord roots with the left hand.
3. Provide an accompaniment consisting of left hand chord roots in octaves for: "Michael Row the Boat Ashore," "Lamb of God" and "What a Friend We Have in Jesus."
4. Play the following major scales and the primary chords based on each scale: Db, Eb, F and G.

Tonic and Dominant Drone Accompaniments

A tonic drone is the interval of a perfect 5th (P5) built on the first tone of the scale (Do, or 1). A dominant drone is the same interval built on the 5th tone of the scale. The following accompaniment uses the tonic (I) and the dominant (V) drone:

Example 13 - Tonic and Dominant Drone Accompaniment

ASSIGNMENT 9

1. Transpose the above melody with tonic drone accompaniment to the keys of E, F and F# (**04.mid** or **CD 4**). Then use the shift from tonic to dominant as in Example 15.
2. Provide a tonic drone accompaniment for the "Sussex Carol" (Example 14), shifting to a dominant drone for the contrasting section.

Chapter 2 – Dare to Be Simple

Example 14 - Sussex Carol

[musical notation]

The tunes in Examples 13 and 14 could be accompanied by more frequent shifts from tonic to dominant. For the Sussex Carol two chord changes per measure may be used.

Example 15 - Ode to Joy (Shift from Tonic to Dominant Drone)

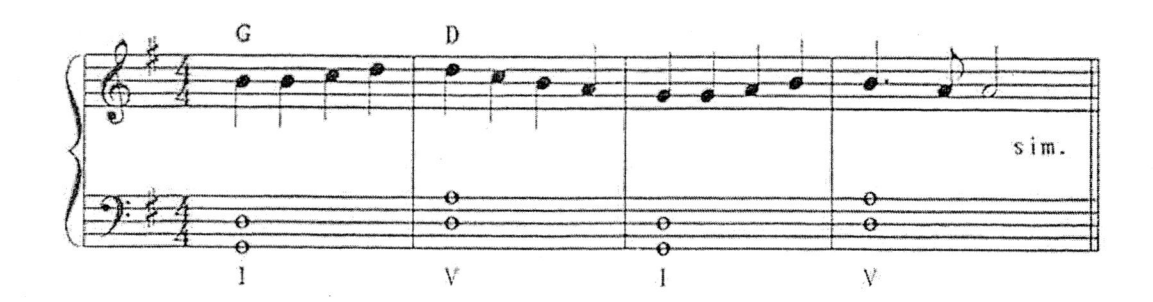

[musical notation]

ASSIGNMENT 10

1. Provide a drone accompaniment for the SUSSEX CAROL, shifting from tonic to dominant. For the contrasting section, begin with a sustained dominant drone, then change to a tonic drone.
2. Provide a tonic drone accompaniment for "Pat-a-Pan" in A minor. If this tune is not familiar, improvise a minor melody over a tonic drone.
3. Provide an accompaniment for "The Little Drummer Boy" by ear, using tonic (I), dominant (V) and subdominant (IV) drones.

Tonic and Dominant Chords Linked by a Common Tone

The pitch that is a part of two different chords is called a common tone. In the shift from the tonic to the dominant drone (Example 15), the top pitch of the tonic drone is the same as the bottom pitch of the dominant drone. In the accompaniment that follows, the common tone remains in the same part of the chord (top). See the assignment for common-tone chording on page 16 and also Appendix A.

Chapter 2 – Dare to Be Simple

Example 16 - Joyful, Joyful, We Adore Thee (I and V6)

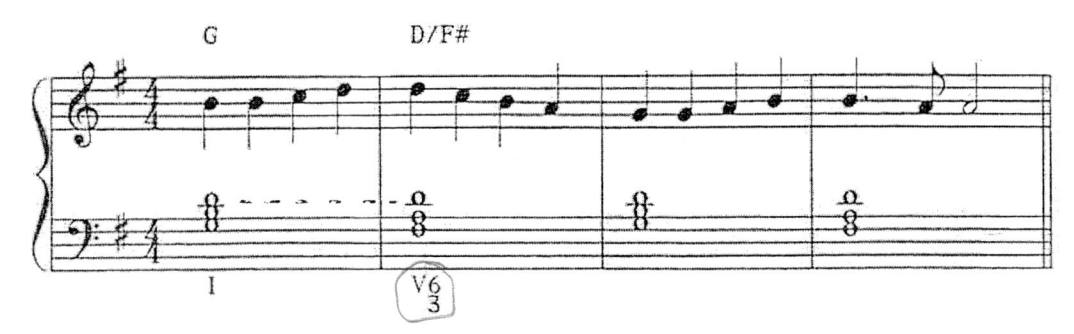

[Musical notation: 4/4 time in G major, four measures with chord symbols G and D/F#, labeled I and V⁶₃ below the bass staff]

Figured Bass

The above example needs a word of explanation. The Roman numerals and the small Arabic numbers (6 and 3) are part of a system of "musical short-hand" used in the time of J.S. Bach and still considered to be an integral part of music study. The Arabic numbers indicate the use of a first inversion chord (D/F#). More specifically, the number 6 indicates that the chord includes a pitch that is a 6th above the bass note (see the top pitch of the left hand chord), and the other number (3) refers to the middle pitch of the left hand chord, which is a 3rd above the bass. Chapter Ten is an explanation of this system of musical shorthand called figured bass.

ASSIGNMENT 11

1. Transpose "Joyful, Joyful, We Adore Thee" to F, with an accompaniment consisting of tonic (I) and dominant (V6) chords as in Example 16.
2. Play Example 17 in F, Eb and D. Try the key of Gb, too!
3. Play "God Is So Good" and "Lord Be Glorified" (see p. 2), using the basic chords notated in Appendix A, even though the ear may want a more interesting harmony.
4. Practice and memorize the common-tone chord progression of basic chords (Appendix A) in all keys.

A Brief Explanation of Non-Harmonic Tones

The following example, which includes both common tone chording and the use of figured bass, also includes abbreviations which may not be familiar (P.T. and Sus.). At the beginning of measure 4 (Example 17), there is a slight clash of harmony, which is known as dissonance. This is caused by the conflict between the melody pitch (B) and the left hand chord tones (D, F# and C). In measure 6 a similar clash occurs. This type of dissonance is called a suspension. In both instances the tone that clashes has been carried over (suspended) from the previous measure where it had been consonant (part of the left hand chord). Its effectiveness lies in the momentary clash, followed by the resolution to a tone that, once again, fits the underlying chord. In the explanation regarding the use of Arabic numbers to indicate chord inversions, both 6 and 3 were used to indicate a first inversion chord. In succeeding examples, you'll find that the number 3 is not included (V6 = V6).

Chapter 2 – Dare to Be Simple

Example 17 - Suspensions and Passing Tones

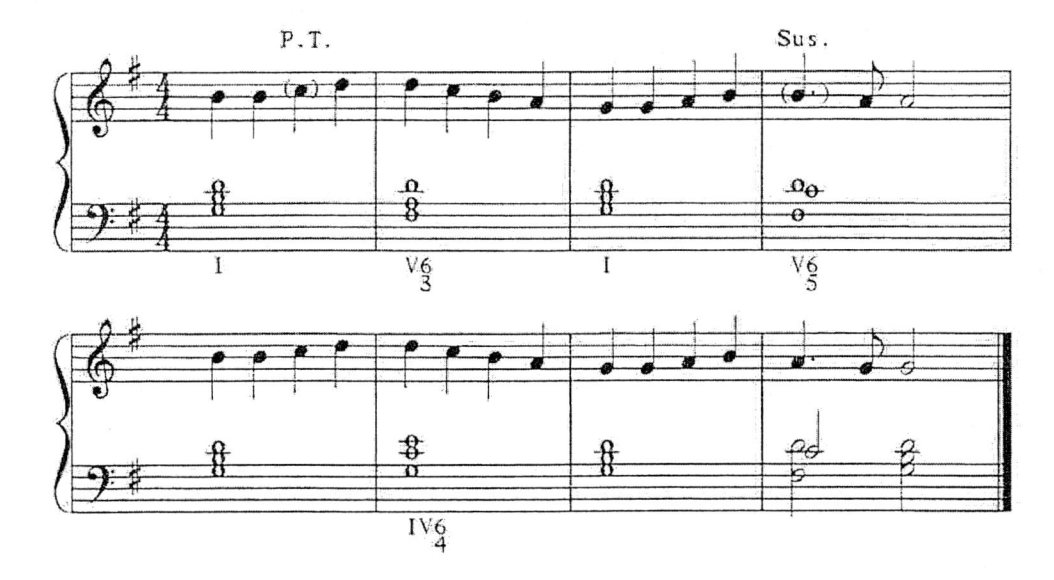

In the above analysis the initials P.T. indicate a dissonance called a passing tone. A passing tone is a non-chord tone that fills in the gap between two chord tones. Passing tones usually fall on a weak beat, and DO NOT REQUIRE A CHANGE OF CHORD. These tones, which are now dissonant, may also be harmonized as chord tones (see hymnal version of the above tune).

ASSIGNMENT 12

1. Circle the suspensions and passing tones in Example 17 and write Sus. or P.T. above the pitch that is dissonant.
2. Transpose Ex. 17 to F and Eb.
3. Select three of the following songs and provide a left hand chordal accompaniment using I, IV and V as in Example 17. After the basic chords are selected, suspensions may be added for enrichment. See notations in Appendix F (**55.mid** or **CD 55**).

    - Kum Ba Yah (TWC 630 in Db and D)
    - Jesus Paid It All (above MIDI file and CD)
    - Children of the Heavenly Father (TWC 84 in D and Eb)
    - I Surrender All (TWC 579 in C and Db)
    - O Come, Little Children (Example 20)
    - Michael, Row the Boat Ashore (Eb)
    - My Hope is Built (TWC 517 in F)
    - What a Friend We have in Jesus (TWC 622 in F)
    - What Can Wash Away My Sins? (TWC 471 in Eb and F)

Another kind of dissonance (non-chord tone) that is sometimes used is called neighboring motion. It involves movement, by step, away from a chord tone and back again without a change of harmony, as in Examples 18A and B. The dissonant pitch is called a neighbor tone. In the traditional harmonization of these songs, these same pitches are not neighbor tones, for there is a change of chord.

Example 18 - Neighbor Tones and the Appoggiatura

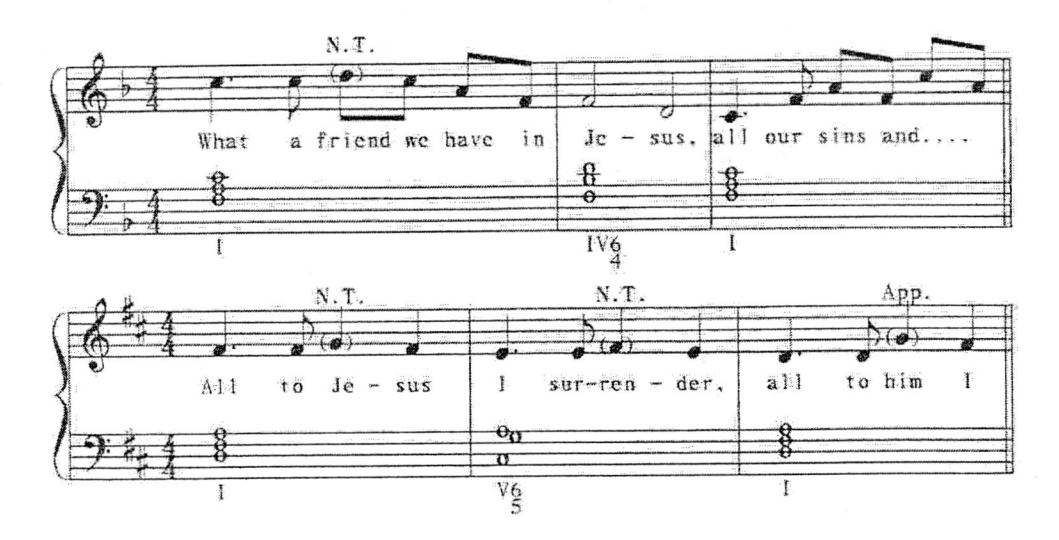

The Italian term *appoggiatura* describes a dissonant tone that is approached by a leap upward and followed by a step downward to a chord tone. In the Baroque Era, the soloist added the appoggiatura freely in the singing of recitatives (e.g. "And There Were Shepherds" from Handel's *Messiah*). Henry Mancini used this dissonance effectively in the first phrase of "Moon River."

An *appoggiatura* is shown in Example 18B. In Example 19, the same melodic pattern is harmonized without the appoggiatura. In this case the pitch that had been dissonant is now consonant.

Another type of dissonance occurs in the next measure. The escape tone, *échappée*, is a dissonance created by movement away from the direction of the melody. In Example 19 the escape tone (E.T.) is the only tone that does not continue the downward movement of the line.

Example 19 - The Escape Tone (échappée)

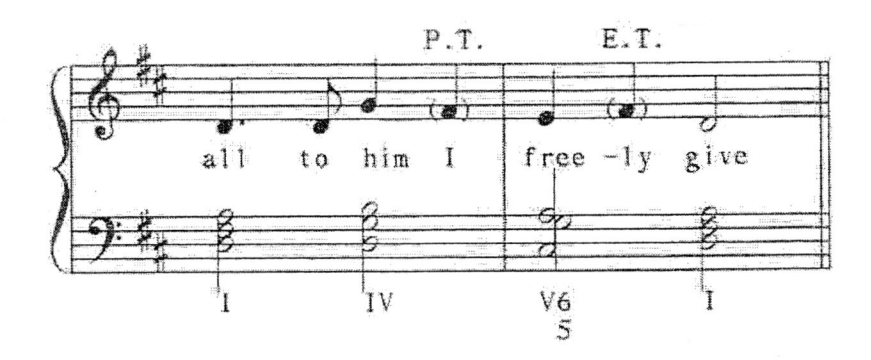

Chapter 2 – Dare to Be Simple

Independent Accompaniment Styles

There are several reasons why all accompanists should develop the ability to improvise simple, independent accompaniments like the ones illustrated in the examples that follow:

1. Children and adults must learn to sing without hearing the melody from the keyboard. Otherwise, they may never develop the independence needed in choral music.
2. Complex accompaniments can be distracting when the listener is trying to focus attention on the melody that is being learned.
3. Simple accompaniment styles allow the teacher/accompanist to maintain eye contact with the class or choir.
4. Simplicity of style allows the accompanist to transpose the song to accommodate the various ranges of singers as well as the various transposing instruments. (Note: The effectiveness of these accompaniments is increased when variations in touch and dynamics are used. They may also be enhanced by the use of dissonances, substitute chords and altered harmonies, all of which will be discussed in subsequent chapters.)

Suggested Preliminary steps

Each student should approach the following exercises in a manner that is appropriate to his/her level of experience. The student with a strong background in theory may want to skip the preliminary steps outlined below. However, there are experienced pianists who may need to simplify the accompaniments in order to sing *and* play at the same time, a skill which is enjoyable and often expected of keyboard musicians.

Basic Preliminary Steps to the Playing of Independent Accompaniments:

1. Write the scale numbers or syllable names above the notes of a melody.
2. Write a Roman numeral analysis below the bass line and/or a chord symbol analysis above the melody.
3. Circle the non-chord tones of the melody and identify them. Now play chords in block form in the right hand, while singing the melody.
4. Sing the bass pitches with numeral and letter names while playing the right hand chords.
5. Sing the melody with numbers or syllables while playing chords in block form.

ASSIGNMENT 13

1. Follow the preliminary steps in preparation for singing and playing Example 20 (**11.mid** or **CD 11**). Sing while playing the written accompaniment, then transpose it to Db and Eb.
2. Use same style of chording for "Children of the Heavenly Father" (TWC 84).

Example 20 - O Come, Little Children (Broken Chord Accompaniment)

Chapter 2 – Dare to Be Simple

Variations of the Bass Line

Tuba Bass

Having played the tuba in junior and senior high school, I realize how unfair it is to stereotype music for tuba. With apology to those who spin out beautiful music on this instrument, we'll use the term "tuba bass" when referring to the style of accompaniment shown in Example 21A.

Example 21 - Rejoice in the Lord (Tuba Bass and Walking Bass)

ASSIGNMENT 14

1. Listen to the recording of "Rejoice in the Lord" (**12.mid** or **CD 12**).
2. Learn the tuba bass accompaniment style shown in Example 21 by focusing on the bass line while playing sustained block chords with the right hand.
3. Vary the bass line of Example 20 by playing a walking bass (Example 21B).
4. Apply this style in accompanying the following songs:

    - The Joy of the Lord (SPW 229 in D and Eb)
    - King of Kings (SPW 94 in Em and Fm)

Walking Bass

Another effective means of creating a moving bass line is to use a "walking bass" (Example 21B). "Jingle Bells" (**08.mid** or **CD 8**) is another example of a walking bass.

ASSIGNMENT 15

1. Delete (mute) the chords of "Jingle Bells," and listen to the walking bass line (**13.mid** or **CD 13**) while playing the chords. Name the chords by letter name and by Roman numeral. **Note:** Thinking about the function of each chord (the Roman numeral name) is vitally important, if the accompaniment is to be transposed to other keys.
2. Delete the bass line and improvise a walking bass (**014.mid** or **CD 14**).
3. Provide a walking bass for "When the Saints," using Example 21B for reference.

Example 22 - Jingle Bells (With Walking Bass)

Claves Pattern

Chord Chart for Jingle Bells:

GM7	GM7	G7	C	Am7	D7	D7	G
GM7	GM7	G7	C	Am7	D	D7	G
GM7	GM7	GM7	G7	C	G	*A7	D
GM7	GM7	GM7	G7	C	G	D7	G

In the above chart, the tonic chord used at the beginning of each line has a major 7th (F#) added. The Am7 chord is the ii chord in G with a 7th added.

*A7 is not a basic chord in the Key of G. See Appendix C for the basic chord progression (I, IV, V7, I) with the addition of a dominant 7th chord built on the second tone of the scale (II7, or V7 of V).

Chapter 2 – Dare to Be Simple

Thus far in the accompaniments, the common tone between chords has stayed in the same part of the chord (top, middle or bottom). The following assignment is intended to reinforce your understanding of this concept.

ASSIGNMENT 16

1. Review Examples 16-21 and mark the common tones by connecting them with a line or highlighter pen.
2. Select three of the songs listed below and play a left hand block-chord accompaniment while singing and/or playing the melody (see Example 17).
3. Select an appropriate independent accompaniment style for selected songs below (see Examples 20-22):

- Arise and Sing (SPW 225)
- He Is Jehovah (SPW 227)
- I Love You with the Love of the Lord (SPW 138)
- I Will Enter His Gates (SPW 168)
- Stand Up (SPW 31)
- The Joy of the Lord (SPW 229)
- This Is the Day (SPW 236 or TWC 801)
- What a Mighty God We Serve (SPW 3)

Twelve-Bar Blues with a Boogie Woogie Bass

A chord pattern not often heard in worship is the classic twelve-bar blues progression. Playing this progression in several different keys is an enjoyable way to acquire an understanding of basic chords (**015.mid** or **CD 15**). Several years ago I heard the choir from The House of Prayer in Detroit, where Alice Lloyd is Director of Music. In addition to wonderful renditions of classic choral repertory, they sang a catchy melody to a twelve-bar blues progression with a marvelous keyboard improvisation provided by Mrs. Lloyd. Their words proclaimed the "Lordship of Christ" in our lives throughout the week and the whole year:

Sunday, Monday, Tuesday, Wednesday, Thursday, Friday, Saturday, He's Lord; (repeat)
He's Lord, everybody! Tell everybody He's Lord! Note: Create your own melody!

January, February, March, April, May, He's Lord!
June, July, August, September, October, November, December, He's Lord!
He's Lord, everybody! Tell everybody He's Lord!

Another possibility: Sing the names of the children in your class or choir.

Chapter 2 – Dare to Be Simple

Example 23 - Twelve-Bar Blues Progression

Note: The above progression could serve as a starting point for improvisation, including:
- Keyboard patterns
- Instrumental fills
- Vocal improvisations
- Additional lyrics

Chapter 2 – Dare to Be Simple

In Example 24 syncopation is used with basic chords to create a calypso style accompaniment.

Example 24 - Common-Tone Chording in Calypso Style

ASSIGNMENT 17

1. Play Example 23 as written and memorize it (**15.mid** and **CD 15**).
2. Delete the chords and play them (**16.mid** or **CD 16**).
3. Delete the "boogie woogie" bass and play it. (**17.mid** or **CD 17**).
4. Improvise a calypso style melody vocally while playing the accompaniment pattern notated above. Notate your melody in the space provided, if you like.

Arpeggiated (Broken Chord) Patterns

An accompaniment style that is very effective with flowing melodies is the broken chord pattern shown in Examples 25 and 27. The first example includes some slight variations. First, the bass note is not always the root of the chord (see measures 2,7,10, and 15). Second, there is a shift from C major to A minor, or from IV to ii7, the related minor chord (compare measures 3-4 with measures 11-12). Third, a key change is made by means of a basic half step modulation (ms. 16-17). Even in their simplest form, these accompaniments can be very effective if played musically. In preparation for the assignments that follow, continue to review the common-tone chord progression, starting with different positions of the tonic chord (see Appendix A and C).

Chapter 2 – Dare to Be Simple

Example 25 - Set My Spirit Free (Arpeggiated Chord Pattern)

ASSIGNMENT 18

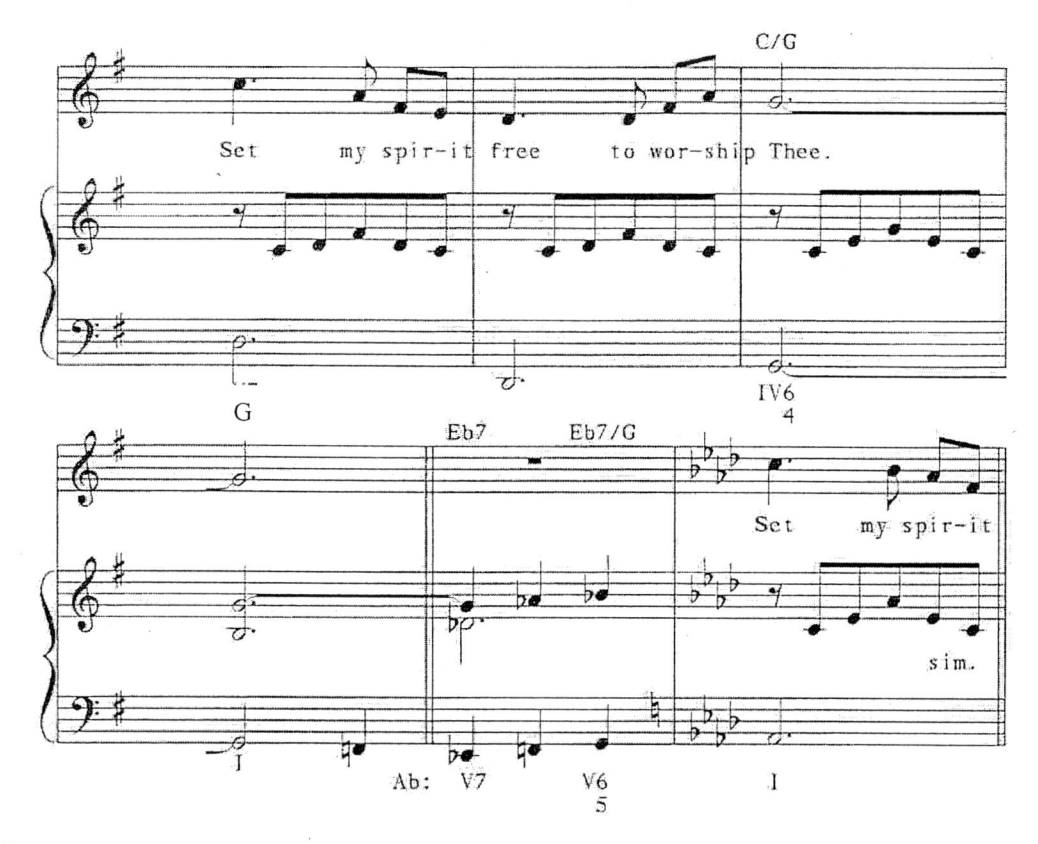

1. Sing and play "Set My Spirit Free" several times, then transpose it to Ab.
2. Sing "Silent Night" with block chords, then with broken chords (**18.mid** or **CD 18**). Transpose "Silent Night" to Bb, a better key for congregational worship.

When accompanying children's singing, it is best to play the right-hand pattern an octave lower than the range of their voices. Otherwise, the sound of the piano could easily upstage them. As one becomes accustomed to playing the chords in different positions, a shift of register within a song can be very effective. In the example that follows, such changes create parallel thirds and other consonances between the melody and the accompaniment (compare Example 26 with Example 20, measures 5-8).

Example 26 - Basic Chord Pattern with a Change of Position

Chapter 2 – Dare to Be Simple

Example 27 - Silent Night

Joseph Mohr, 1818 — Franz Gruber, 1818

Si - lent night! ho - ly night!

All is calm, all is bright

'round yon vir - gin moth - er and Child,

Chapter 2 – Dare to Be Simple

    Following the modulation to Bb at the close of Example 27, the flowing accompaniment style is varied in a way that reinforces the alto part. This is an effective way to help singers who are not yet confident in singing a harmony part. This, like the change of chord position in Example 26, will result in the breaking of the common tone principle. In the chapters that follow, this principle will no longer be strictly observed where "keyboard style" is used.
This term, "keyboard style," is used to denote the playing of three-note chords in the right hand with the melody on top.

Chapter 2 – Dare to Be Simple

If we were to explore the earliest forms of harmony, we would discover that they were quite primitive. Early attempts at harmonizing included parallel harmonies and melodies with drone-like accompaniment. This style, dating from the Renaissance Period (1450-1600) and still used today, serves as an effective accompaniment for "What Child Is This?" (**19.mid** or **CD 19**). The "Romanesque bass" consists of a descending step-wise succession of parallel chords (or open fifths) as notated in Example 28.

Example 28 - What Child Is This

ASSIGNMENT 19

1. Listen to the recording of "What Child Is This?" (**19.mid** or **CD 19**).
2. Play the chord chart for "What Child is This," changing chords on the downbeat of each measure except where there are two chords per measure (see m. 7 of Ex. 28).

Em	D	C	B
Em	D	C B	Em
G	D	Em	B
G	D	C B	Em

3. Play the above progression while singing, beginning with an accompaniment pattern appropriate to your level of keyboard skill (see Ex. 29 A, B and C).
4. Transpose the song to D minor, writing a chord chart only if necessary.

Chapter 2 – Dare to Be Simple

Example 29 - What Child Is This? (Different Accompaniment Styles)

Summary

For many who are using this text, this has been a review of basic information learned in previous study. For others it may be their first introduction. Those who are teachers are encouraged to use some of the ideas and materials in either private or classroom settings. Although the succeeding chapters will move on to more advanced concepts, there may be a need to review this and the preceding chapter occasionally. The playing of five-finger patterns and common-tone chording in all keys and in a variety of styles is foundational and can be used as warm-up material for the keyboard musician. Favorite tunes with basic chords can be transposed to other keys until you feel "at home" in all twelve keys – the ultimate challenge!

Work Space

Chapter 2 – Dare to Be Simple

Chapter Three

HARMONIZING SCALE FRAGMENTS

In the preceding chapter, melodies were accompanied on the basis of chord outlines and, to some extent, on the basis of what scale tone is in the melody. Now we turn to further study of chord selection based on the scale. Some melodies, like those in Example 30, progress in a scale-like manner. Such melodies are very singable and easily learned.

Example 30 - Melodies That Include Scale Passages

Other melodies are easily learned because of scale-like movement, but that movement may not be as obvious. In Example 31 below, the scale is spread out over several measures, with only one or two scale tones per measure. These scale tones serve as an underpinning, or basic structure for the melody.

Example 31 - Scale Lines That Serve as Basic Structure

ASSIGNMENT 20

1. Circle the notes that serve as the basic structure in Examples 32A and 32B, and write the scale number above the notes.
2. Transpose the descending scale progression (circled tones) of Example 32A to the key of Ab, then play the melody in Ab.
3. Transpose the scale progression that undergirds Example 32B to Eb, then play the tune. Transpose the tune to other keys.

Example 32 - Melodies Based on Scale Progression

[Musical notation: Melodies A and B based on scale progression]

To play the above melodies with supporting right hand chords, as in Examples 33-34, a knowledge of chord inversions is essential (see Appendix B). The playing of the Chord Inversion Drill (Appendix B) will serve to expand our palette of chord colors, moving beyond the primary chords (I, IV and V) to include the minor chords (ii, iii and vi) and the diminished chord (vii°). Although the use of minor chords as enrichment of basic harmonies is the topic of Chapter Five, there is occasional use of minor chords in this chapter.

Harmonizing Scale Fragments

The examples that follow could be thought of as a series of "musical push-ups" that move progressively higher (1 2 1, then 1 2 3 2 1, etc.). In Example 33 the opening phrase of "He Is Lord" is harmonized with the two most basic chords - I and V (**20.mid** or **CD 20**). The syllable names in parenthesis denote the scale tones on which the other pitches of the melody hinge. Although our ears are conditioned to hearing additional chords with this melody, at first we'll limit ourselves to these two primary chords.

Example 33 - Harmonizing Do and Re (1 and 2) with I and V

[Musical notation with chord symbols F, C, F, C, F and syllables 1(Do), 2(Re), 1(Do), 2(Re), 1(Do); lyrics: "He is Lord, He is Lord!"]

In Example 34, measures 5 and 7, the pitch G of the melody is enriched by the use of a ii chord (G minor) as preparation for the V chord (C). In measure 11 the IV chord (Bb) is used to delay the final I chord (F). As these chord changes occur, the **soprano pitch remains the same**. More specifically, on the down beat of measure 5, the melody is harmonized as the root of the G minor chord. Its function changes as it becomes the fifth of a C chord. In measure 11 the pitch F of the melody is harmonized, first, as the fifth of IV (Bb), then as the root of I (F). Playing by ear is facilitated by the development of a keen awareness of such changes in the function of repeated and sustained soprano pitches.

Chapter 3 – Harmonizing Scale Fragments

Example 34 - Harmonizing Re - Do (2 - 1) with ii - V, IV – I

ASSIGNMENT 21

1. Listen to the previous progressions, then delete the keyboard part of the MIDI file and play the keyboard part as notated in Example 34 (**20.mid** or **CD 20).**
2. Apply the same progression to the opening phrase of "In His Time" (SPW 39).
   Note: Even though we're conditioned to want more complex chords, the basic chords (I, IV and V) and the ii chord will suffice for now.

Chapter 3 – Harmonizing Scale Fragments

Harmonizing Do – Re – Mi (1 – 2 – 3)

The next scale fragment to be harmonized is Do Re Mi (1 2 3). Only primary chords are used first, then vi, the substitute for I, and ii are used (**21.mid** or **CD 21**).

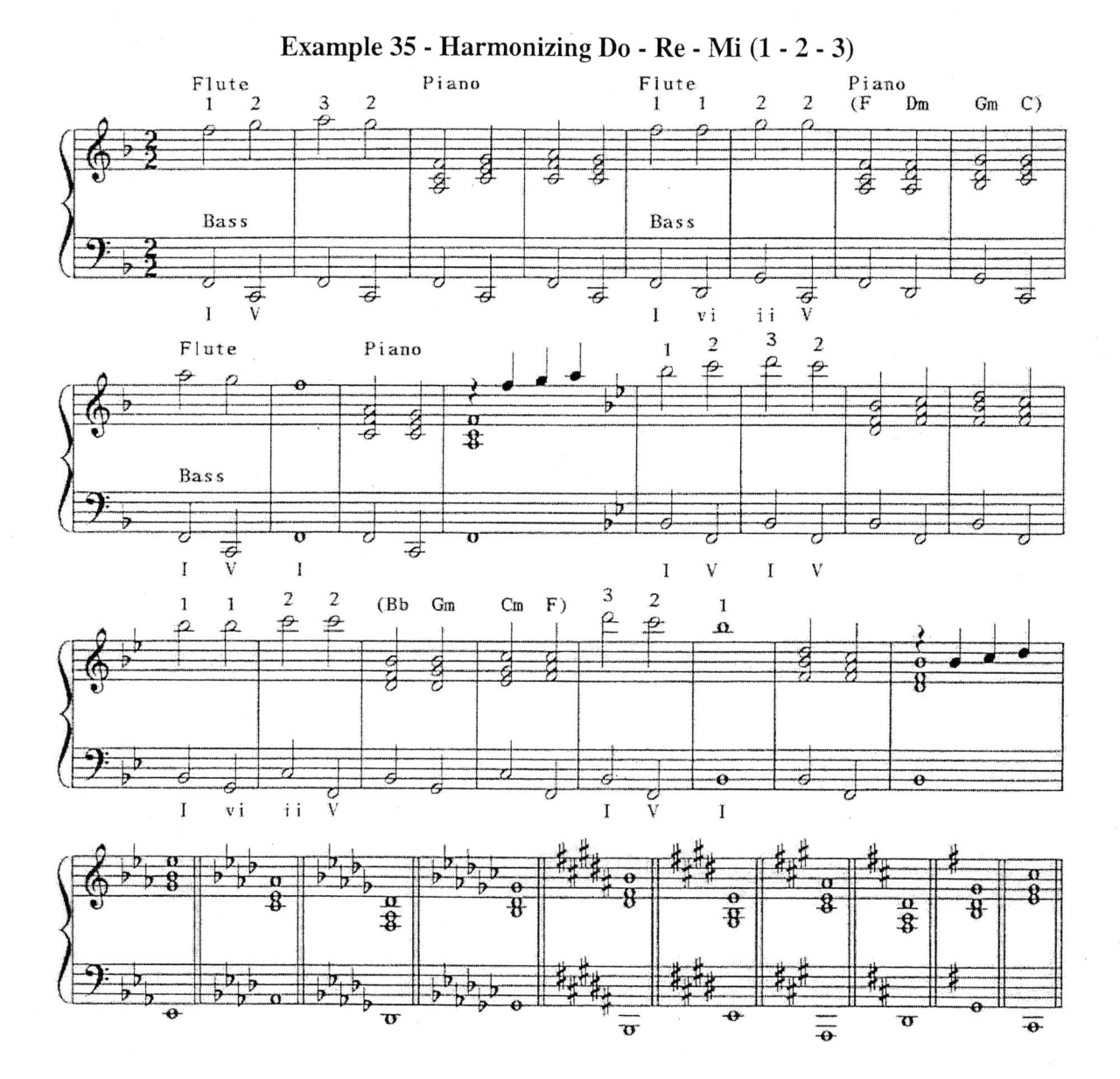

Example 35 - Harmonizing Do - Re - Mi (1 - 2 - 3)

ASSIGNMENT 22

1. Transpose the scale fragment in Example 35 to all keys. Note: Writing the progression in several keys would also be helpful. (Use the **Work Space**.)
2. Harmonize the following melodic fragment with I and V, then with the addition of substitute chords. Check the hymnal version, but explore other chords, too.

Chapter 3 – Harmonizing Scale Fragments

Example 36 - Like a River Glorious (Harmonizing Do - Re - Mi)

Be creative here.

For the next scale fragment, Example 37, only primary chords (I, IV and V) are used.

Example 37 - Do - Re - Mi - Fa (1 - 2 - 3 - 4)

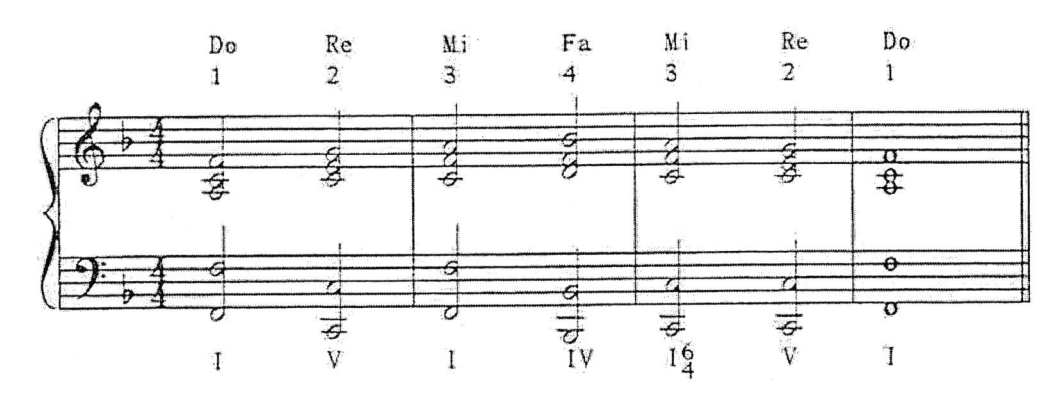

The familiar melody "God Is So Good" hinges on the above progression (see circled pitches of Example 38). The alternative ending (Example 38B) can be used for the concluding phrase of many songs. Because of its frequent use, learning it in all keys is a worthwhile effort.

Example 38 - God Is So Good

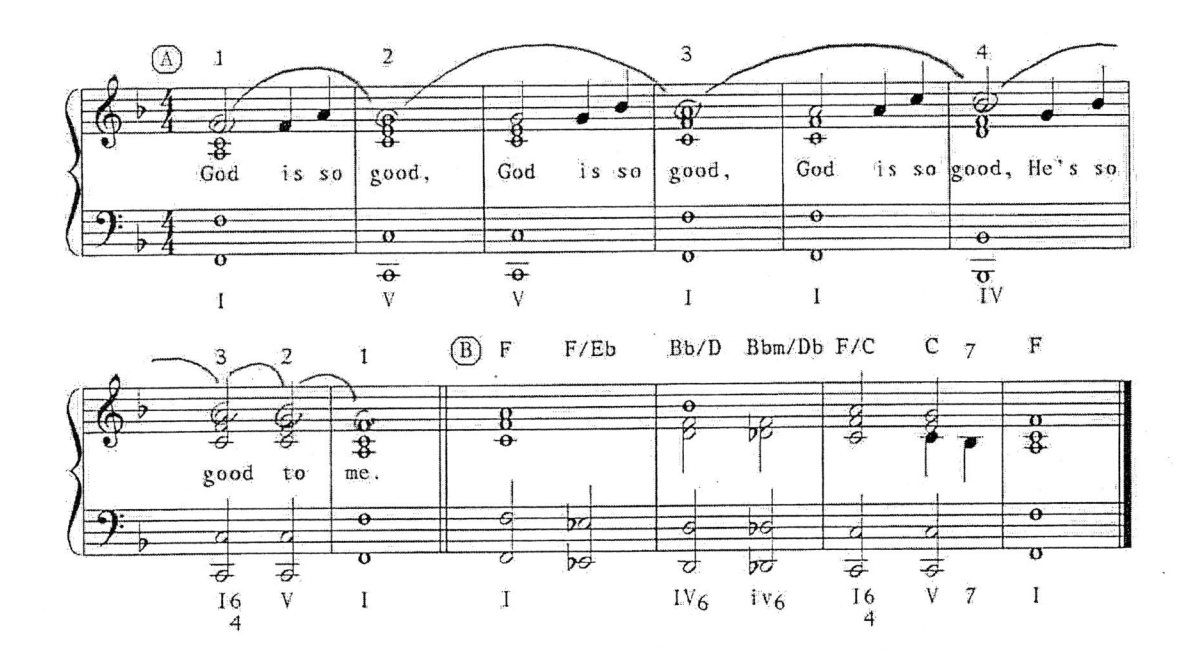

ASSIGNMENT 23

1. Play Examples 37 and 38 several times, then transpose them to C and the other keys notated in Example 39 (**22.mid** or **CD 22**).
2. Use the chords of Example 37 to harmonize "I Love You, Lord" by ear (SPW 72).
3. Adapt the descending bass progression (Example 38B) for the last phrase of several of the songs listed in the box below. The underlined word in each of the first three songs indicates where the progression begins.

> - Goodnight Ladies ("Goodnight, ladies, we're going to leave you now.")
> - He Is Lord ("Every knee shall bow, every tongue confess that Jesus Christ is Lord."
> - Home on the Range ("Where seldom is heard a discouraging word and the skies are not cloudy....."
> - Edelweiss (last two phrases)
>
>   Also, the last phrase of each of the following songs:
>
>   - Joyful, Joyful, We Adore Thee
>   - Over the Rainbow (with variation)
>   - Praise the Name of Jesus (TWC 128 or SPW 87)
>   - To Thee We Ascribe Glory (SPW 15 with variation)
>   - When the Saints Go Marching In
>
> Note: Where the progression is varied, use your ear to find the right chords!

4. Can you think of other songs that end with this same chord progression (Example 38B)?
   -
   -
   -

Work Space

Chapter 3 – Harmonizing Scale Fragments

Example 39 - Do - Re - Mi - Fa (1 - 2 - 3 - 4)

Note: It would be helpful to write the above progression in several keys to reinforce understanding. Additional work space is provided at the end of this chapter.

The harmonization of the next fragment (1 2 3 4 5 4 3 2 1) includes bass notes that are not the root of the chord, resulting in a smoother bass line. Please note that the fourth scale tone (Fa) is harmonized as a seventh of the dominant chord, then as the root of the subdominant chord, as in Examples 37-39. Each line concludes with a half-step modulation to the next key. This, along with other modulations, will be studied in Chapter Eight.

Chapter 3 – Harmonizing Scale Fragments

Example 40 - Do - Re - Mi - Fa - So (1 - 2 - 3 - 4 - 5) with Half-Step Modulation

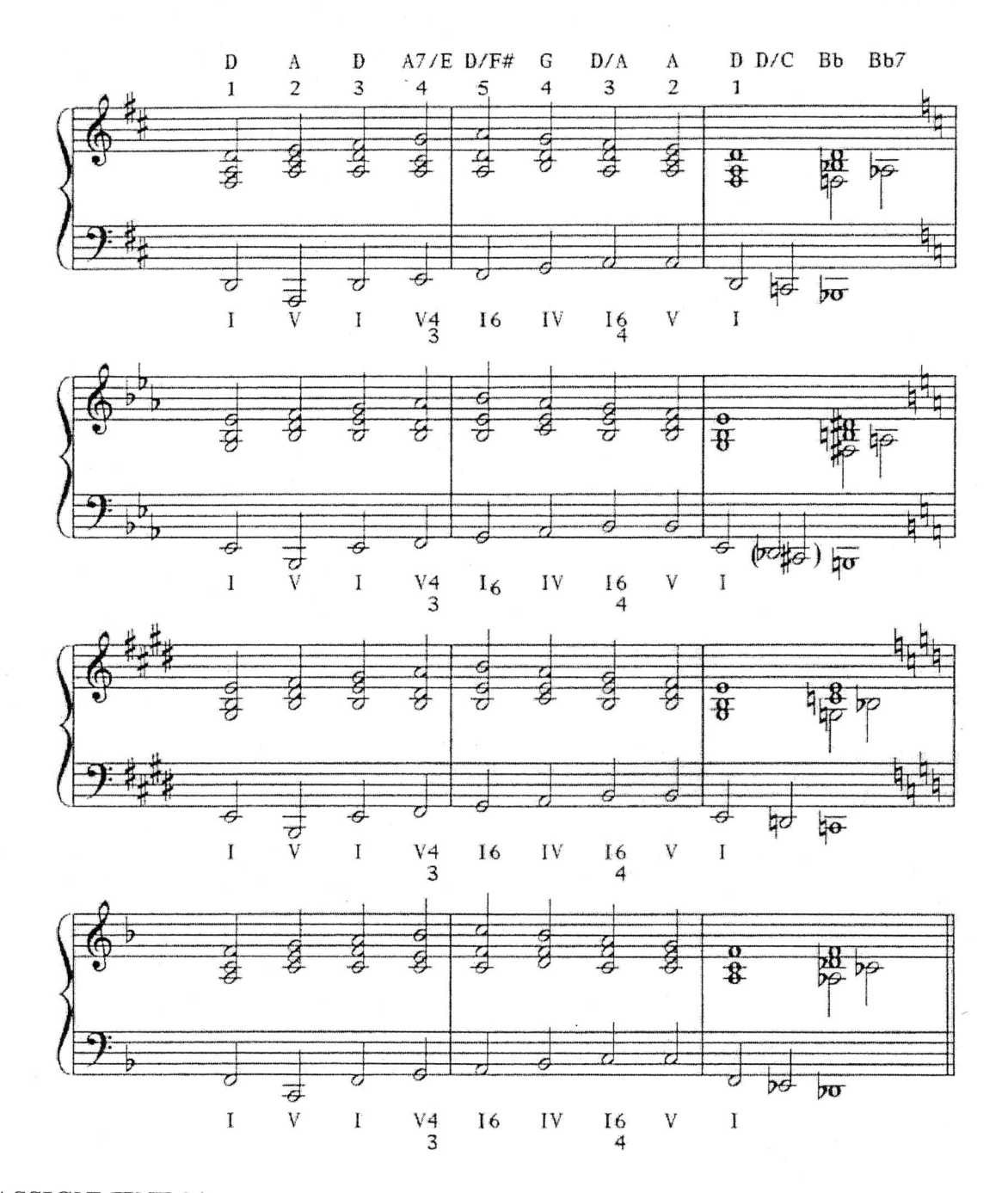

ASSIGNMENT 24

1. **Sing the bass** of Example 40 **with letter names, then with Roman numeral names while playing the right hand chords.** This is excellent ear training! (**01mid** or **CD 1**)
2. While playing the above progression, sing a vocalise (vocal warm-up exercise) such as the following on a neutral syllable like "loo" or "lah":

   1̱ 3 2̱ 4 3̱ 5 4̱ 6 5̱ 3 4̱ 2 3̱ 1 2̱ 7̄ 1̱

Chapter 3 – Harmonizing Scale Fragments

Example 40 could be used by studio teachers of voice or by choral directors as a basis for various warm-up exercises. Some teachers prefer a vocalise that begins with the highest pitch, as in Example 41.

Example 41 - Descending Vocalise with Half-Step Modulation

A command of scale harmonization includes the ability to start on any tone of the scale. The following application is one of many that can be made when the keyboard musician is able to adapt a basic progression to support melodic leaps as well as stepwise movement (see Example 42).

Example 42 – Harmonizing Do - Re - Mi - Fa - So - La (1 - 2 - 3 - 4 - 5 - 6)
(Twinkle, Twinkle Little Star)

The following variation is included as enrichment for the advanced student and as a preview of material to be covered in subsequent chapters.

Chapter 3 – Harmonizing Scale Fragments

> Additional Applications of Example 42:
> - Father, Lead Me Day by Day (Example 102, measures 5-6)
> - Spirit Song (SPW 134) Use basic chords shown in Example 42, starting with the third note of the scale. For the descending scale line that begins with La, See Example 42B.

ASSIGNMENT 25

1. Listen to "Twinkle, Twinkle Little Star" (**05.mid**) delete the keyboard part and play it. If you use **CD 5**, play along with the recording an octave higher, using the chords notated as Example 42A. **Note**: Those who teach children's classes could delete the melody of the MIDI file, and let the children sing it or play it on resonator bells, xylophone or other classroom instruments.
2. Apply the progression in the harmonizing of "Frere Jacques." Keep the same harmonic rhythm throughout the song, allowing some of the eighth notes to function as neighbor tones (N.T.) and passing tones (P.T.). After mastering the basic scale harmonization, play the harmonization that includes suspensions and succession of 5ths (last two systems on previous page). In a later chapter a mastery of harmonic progression by successive fifths will be acquired through practical applications in different keys and musical contexts.

ASSIGNMENT 26

Harmonize Fa - Mi (4 - 3) in all keys, using IV-I, then V7-I (Example 43).

Example 43 - Scale Fragments - Fa - Mi (4 - 3) with IV-I, then V7 I

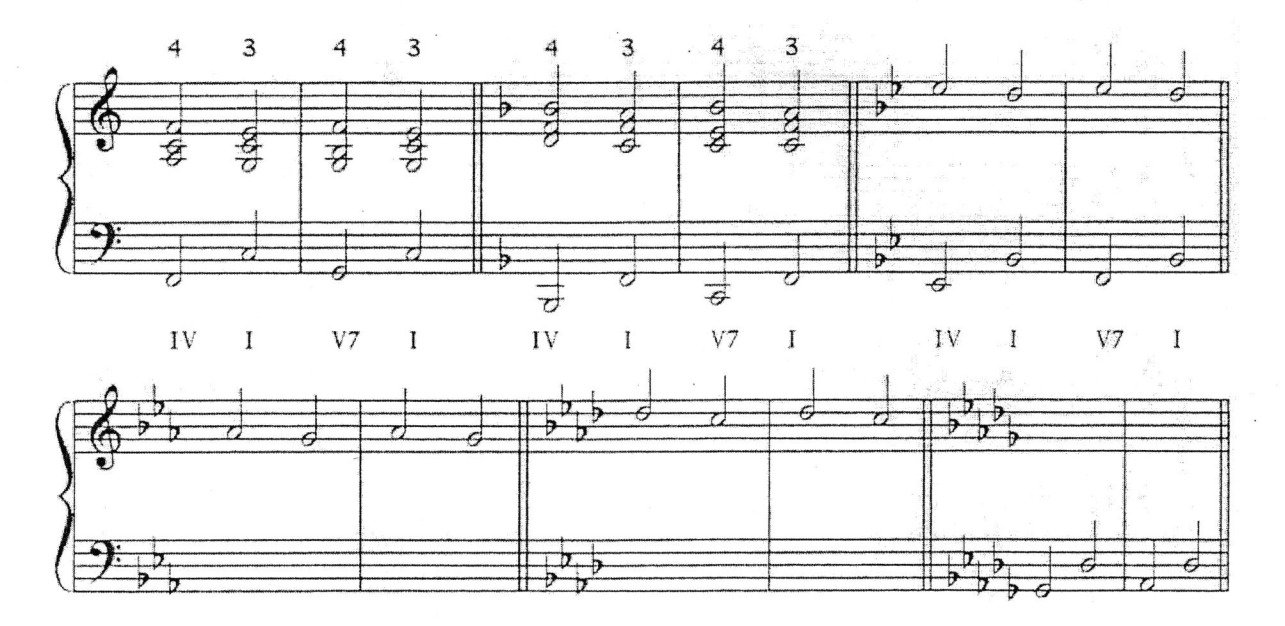

Chapter 3 – Harmonizing Scale Fragments

The ability to begin with any of the scale tones and move either up or down is a prerequisite for the effective use of scale harmonization as a basis for playing by ear. The following exercise in playing scale fragments in sequence is designed to develop the ability to start on different scale degrees (see Example 44). **Note**: When the third of the chord is in the bass, as in the case of V6 or I6, the third is usually omitted from the right hand chord.

ASSIGNMENT 27

1. Review the following examples, observing the principle of omitting the third of the chord in the right hand when the third is in the bass: Examples 8, 40-42. Other examples:

    - "Adagio" from Pathetique Sonata by Beethoven
    - "God So Loved the World" by Sir. John Stainer. (TH 207)

2. Play Example 44, then transpose it to other keys.

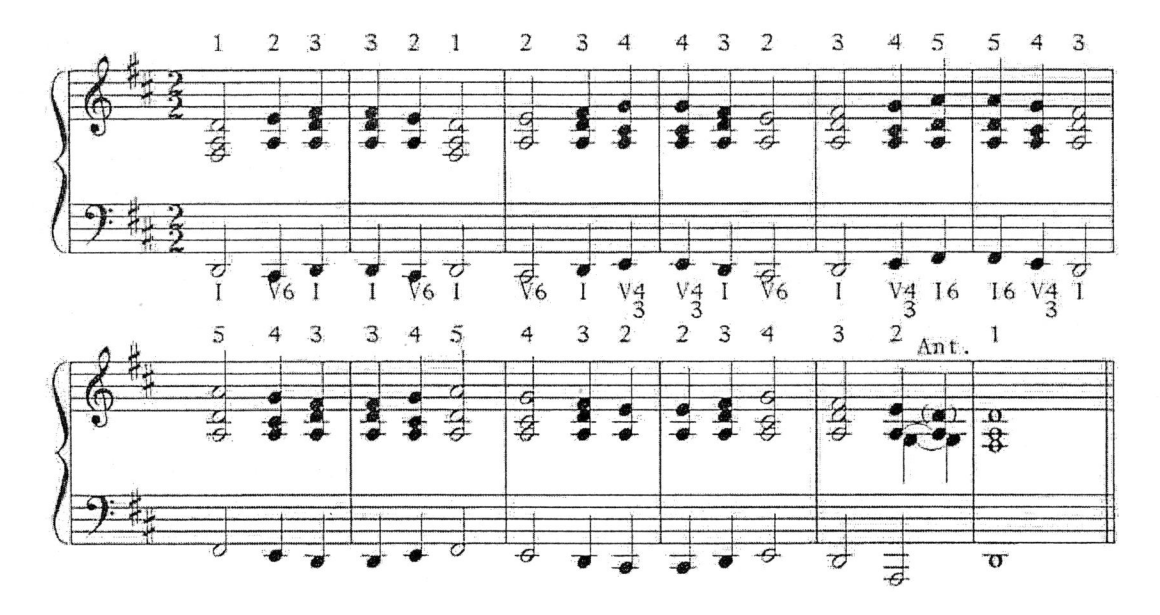

Example 44 - Scale Fragments in Sequence

Note: The pitch in parenthesis anticipates the chord tone that follows, and is called an anticipation.

Chapter 3 – Harmonizing Scale Fragments

Example 44 (continued)

A musician who plays intuitively could possibly play the previous exercises in different keys without giving much thought to chord structure. However, the same person might find it difficult to apply these progressions in a consistent manner. When playing with other musicians in a praise and worship band or other ensemble, one is expected to be in agreement in the use of chords. Two different chords played at the same time, or even two different bass notes, can cause problems.

The disciplined use of a scale fragment such as the following, with several songs and in different keys, will lead to both understanding and skill. The same progression in reverse can be used for the descending pattern (So Fa Mi). Suspensions may be added for enrichment (see Example 45B).

Chapter 3 – Harmonizing Scale Fragments

Example 45 – Harmonizing Mi – Fa – So (3 – 4 – 5)

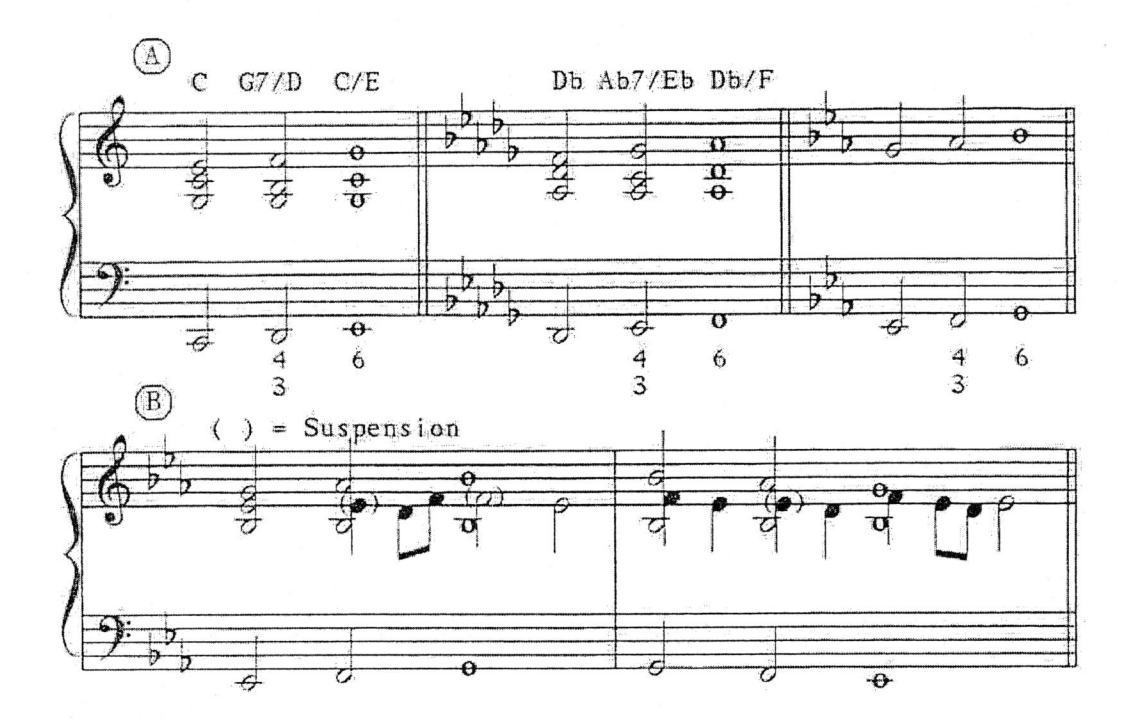

ASSIGNMENT 28

1. Apply Example 45A in harmonizing the first phrase of "Open Our Eyes" (TWC 536) in D and Eb, and "When Morning Gilds the Skies" (TWC 99) in C major. Check the hymnal to see if this progression was used by the composer. For additional applications see the box below.
2. Play Example 45 in all keys. For those who enjoy a challenge, the above scale fragment, as it occurs in the songs listed in the box below, could be transposed to other keys.

> Songs that begin with or include the progression notated as Example 45:
>
> - Open Our Eyes, Lord (SPW 199 or TWC 536)
> - Our God Reigns (first phrase) SPW 64
> - Sing Praise to God (TWC 50, first phrase)
> - Spirit Song (SPW 134, first phrase) Suggestion: Continue melody to the end, adapting the descending scale progression notated in Example 42B).
> - The Church's One Foundation (TWC 689, third phrase)
> - When Morning Gilds the Skies (TWC 99, first phrase)

Chapter 3 – Harmonizing Scale Fragments

A Rationale for the Mastery of Scale Progression

At this point you may be asking, "But what about songs that don't proceed by scale-wise movement?" My answer would be to learn scale harmonization so well that isolated scale tones and two-note fragments can be harmonized in two or three ways, using chords that have been learned. The continuing review of this chapter will help to develop this ability. Chord progressions that have been played in various keys and styles become part of a "memory bank" from which they can be instantly retrieved in a spontaneous manner during improvisation.

The Complete Scale

As a culmination of our study of progressively longer scale fragments (Examples 33-42), we will add the seventh scale tone to complete the ascending scale, harmonizing it with the diminished chord (vii^0). To harmonize the descending scale (Example 46B), the mediant chord (iii) is used for the seventh scale tone.

Example 46C is an application similar to that shown in Example 42 ("Twinkle, Twinkle Little Star"). The first phrase of the hymn ("Jesus Shall Reign") is an ascending scale line that ends with a descending scale fragment (8-7-6-5). Because of the accidental (F#), this fragment could be thought of as 4-3-2-1 in the key of G. Although this momentary shift to G is not a modulation, treating it as a cadence in G shows how a previously-learned scale progression can be used (see Examples 37-39).

The chapter that follows will provide opportunities to use the ascending and descending scale harmonizations in all keys.

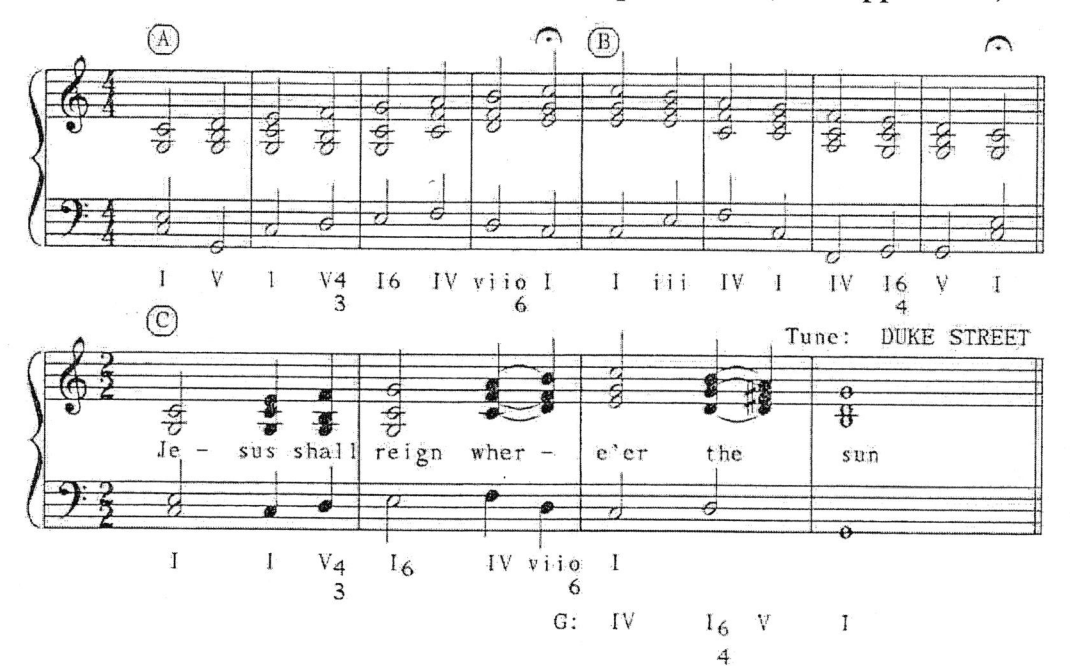

Example 46 - Harmonization of the Complete Scale (with Application)

The above study of scale harmonization is not intended to be an exhaustive treatment of the subject. Additional variations will be explored in subsequent chapters as sequential harmonies, substitute chords, altered chords and modal harmonies are considered. The student who wants to continue the pursuit of variant harmonizations of the scale should also explore the harmonies used in jazz and other genres of music. The ultimate goal is to have a command of a rich palette of chords.

Chapter 3 – Harmonizing Scale Fragments

Work Space

Chapter Four

HARMONIZING THE COMPLETE SCALE

The value of scale harmonization may not be apparent to the first-year theory student who struggles to play a basic chord progression for the ascending and descending scale in all keys. The degree of difficulty may be increased by the added requirement of singing the bass line with Roman numeral names while playing. It is this added challenge, however, that facilitates the learning of chord function. Without mental involvement, one could play the progression until muscle memory takes over, allowing the accurate playing of the chords. Hopefully, the value of disciplined study of scale harmonization will be apparent from the applications in both the preceding and subsequent chapters.

One of the first applications that can be made is the use of scale progressions to support vocal warm-ups. Malcolm Johns, a professor at Wayne State University, used the exercise shown as Example 47. His variation of the progression through the use of jazz chords and a "swing feel" gave it vitality and buoyancy. After mastering the basic progression, other harmonies may be explored (see Example 47B).

Another application that may serve as motivation for learning is the use of the descending scale progression with songs such as "Over the Rainbow," "Ring the Bells" and "Puff the Magic Dragon." Playing and singing the beginning of these melodies in different keys can add enjoyment to the task of learning the basic descending scale progression.

Example 47 - Vocalise Based on Descending Scale

Chapter 4 – Harmonizing the Complete Scale

> Songs that include a descending scale line:
>
> - A Mighty Fortress (TWC 43, last phrase)
> - From Heaven above to Earth I Come (see Lutheran hymnal)
> - Over the Rainbow (from *The Wizard of Oz*)
> - Puff the Magic Dragon (Recorded by Peter, Paul and Mary)
> - Ring the Bells by Harry Bollbach
> - The First Noel (last phrase)

ASSIGNMENT 29

1. Sing and accompany the warm-up notated in Example 47. Memorize the bass line by singing it with Roman numeral names while playing the right hand chords.
2. Transpose Example 47 to the keys notated in Example 48:
   - Listen to the progression (**23.mid** or **CD 23**).
   - Practice as two separate scale fragments (8765, 4321) in the keys notated.
3. Sing the first two phrases of "Somewhere over the Rainbow" and/or "Ring the Bells" by Harry Bollbach *(One Hundred Sacred Favorites,* Singspiration 1973) while playing the descending scale progression.
4. Adapt the progression in Example 47 for the beginning of "Puff the Magic Dragon." The phrase ends with a half cadence, which requires the use of either Dm G or D7 G.

Work Space

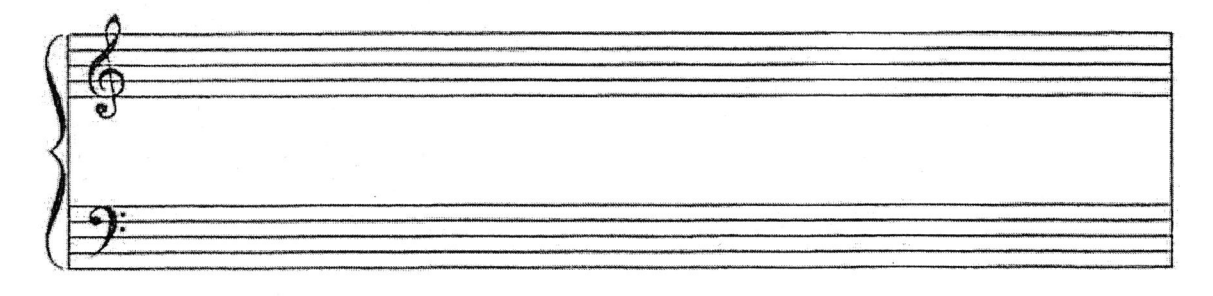

Chapter 4 – Harmonizing the Complete Scale

Example 48 - Descending Scale Progression

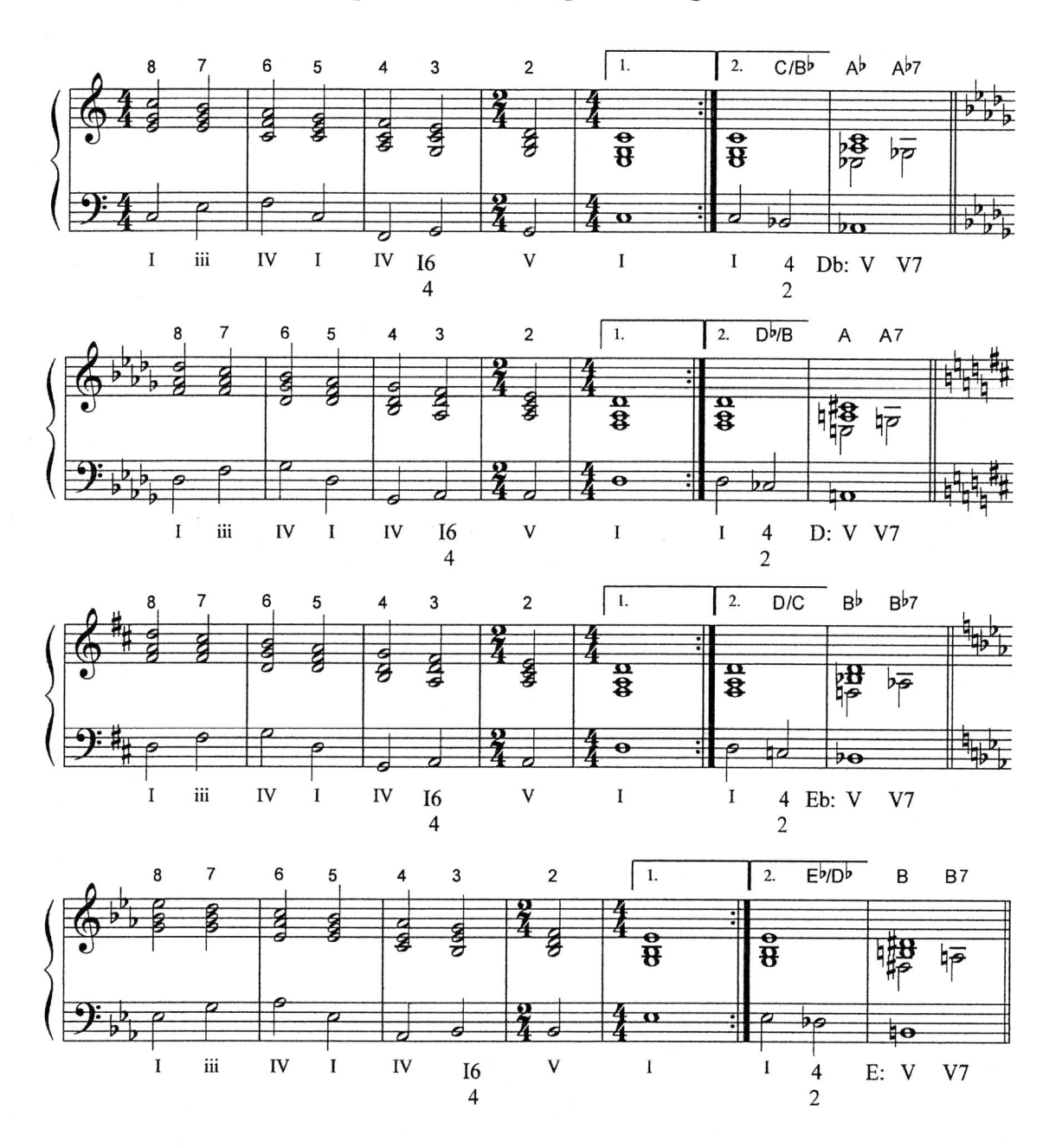

By changing the first chord of the above progression to Roman numeral vi, it can be used effectively to support a vocal warm-up consisting of a scale of descending thirds (Example 49).

Chapter 4 – Harmonizing the Complete Scale

Example 49 - Descending Scale of Thirds

Chapter 4 – Harmonizing the Complete Scale

Knowledge of Scale Progression as the Key to Transposition

At this point let me share a personal experience that helped me to see the value of scale harmonization. Early in my teaching career a colleague asked me, as rehearsal accompanist, to transpose "Adoramus Te" by Dubois to the key of D major. Rather than panic (which was my first impulse!), I decided to analyze the harmony. When I discovered that it begins with the familiar progression - I iii IV, the task was approached with some degree of confidence (Example 50).

Example 50 - Christ, We Do All Adore Thee

Chapter 4 – Harmonizing the Complete Scale

In transposing pieces at the keyboard, it helps to have more than one tool in your "kit." A knowledge of scale progression is one of several tools that can be used. There are times when I find it helpful to write in the chords for the new key. The chord symbols below are for "Christ We Do All Adore Thee." I'm more secure if I also think scale numbers (see numbers in parentheses).

(8)	(7)	(6)	(5)
D	F#m	G	A

(6)	(8)	(8)	(7)	(8)
G	D/F#	Em7	C#dim/E	D

A Roman numeral analysis is the best approach if one is expected to be able to play it in a variety of keys. Sometimes a figured bass line will suffice.

ASSIGNMENT 30

1. Continue Example 49 through all major keys.
2. Transpose Example 50 to Db and D. The following procedure is recommended:

   - Sing the bass line with Roman numeral names while playing it in the original key.
   - Transpose the bass line while playing or singing the soprano part.
   - Play it in keyboard style (Example 51A), then in four-part choral style (51B).

Example 51 - Keyboard Style and Choral Style Compared

The ascending and descending scale is a staple of a choral director's repertory of warm-up exercises. It is useful in tuning repeated pitches, major and minor thirds, and also for the review of basic rhythm patterns (see Example 52).

Example 52 - Ascending and Descending Scale Warm-ups

ASSIGNMENT 31

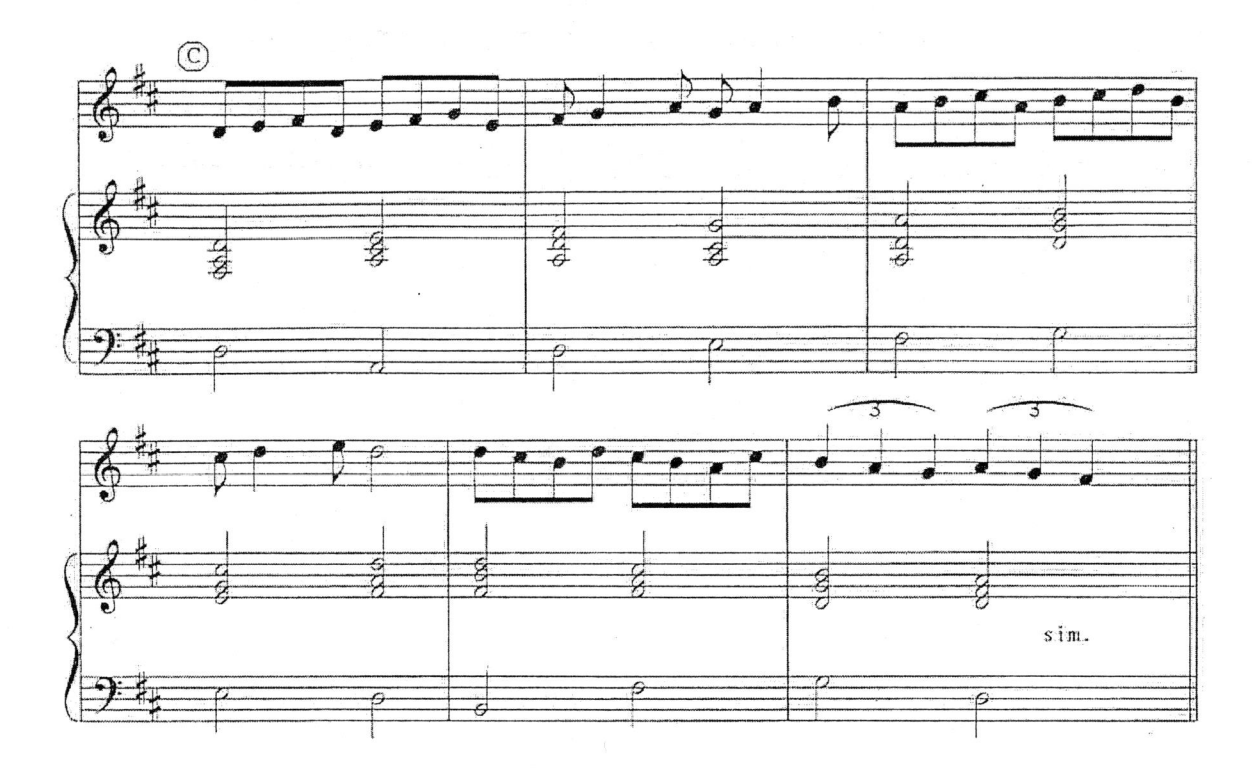

1. Sing the bass line of the preceding progression while playing the right hand chords (Examples 52A-C).
2. Sing the vocal warm-ups on a neutral syllable, or use the suggested sounds. Transpose the warm-ups to lower and higher keys (**24.mid** or **CD 24**). The flute part could be deleted, and other patterns could be inserted.

The following scale harmonization can be used to rehearse ternary rhythms (Example 53) and also shifts from ternary to binary and vice versa (Example 54). The patterns to be sung can be selected from an anthem that is to be rehearsed. The use of scale progressions for vocal warm-ups serves as a means of continuing review of scale harmonization.

Chapter 4 – Harmonizing the Complete Scale

Example 53 - Scale Warm-up for Review of Ternary Patterns

Work Space

Chapter 4 – Harmonizing the Complete Scale

Example 54 - Scale Warm-up with Shift of Meter

As the material in succeeding chapters is studied, new possibilities for scale harmonization will be discovered. As these new chords, along with those studied in previous chapters, are applied in different keys and with different styles of music, a foundation will be laid that will enable you to hear and use a rich variety of chords in playing by ear. It is important to remember that **"time and patience"** are needed for the disciplined efforts that eventually lead to freedom. It is also important to nurture creativity along the way, delighting in new sounds as they are discovered. The practical use of these chords to enhance the harmonies of familiar songs will serve as motivation for continuing musical growth. In language development, students are encouraged to use a new word in a sentence. This is equally valuable as a means of mastering the use of new chords.

The chapter that follows is a continuation of the study of scale harmonization. Special emphasis will be placed on changes of harmony that occur during the sustaining or repeating of a tone in the melody.

Chapter 4 – Harmonizing the Complete Scale

Work Space

Chapter 4 – Harmonizing the Complete Scale

Work Space

Chapter Five

SUBSTITUTE CHORDS: THE CHANGING FUNCTION OF A TONE

When our study of harmony moves beyond the basic chords (I, IV and V), the chords that immediately come into play are the minor chords (ii, iii and vi). In this chapter we'll explore, in greater depth, the use of minor chords as a means of enriching basic harmonies. The minor chords serve as substitutes for the basic chords. For example, a shift from a C major chord to an A minor chord, or from F to Dm, is very common. The reason these changes are satisfying is explained in the following discussion of the various minor chords commonly used in conjunction with their related major chords.

The Submediant Chord (vi) as a Substitute for the Tonic Chord (I)

The submediant chord (vi) is often used in place of the tonic chord. To see and hear what they have in common, play a C major triad on the keyboard, then move down a third and play an A minor triad. Note that these two chords have two pitches that are the same (see Example 55A). The root and third of the C major triad are the same as the third and fifth of the A minor triad. An even smoother transition from C major to A minor can be made by keeping both common tones in the same part of the chord (Example 55B and C).

Example 55 - The Changing Function of the Soprano Pitch (from root to 3rd)

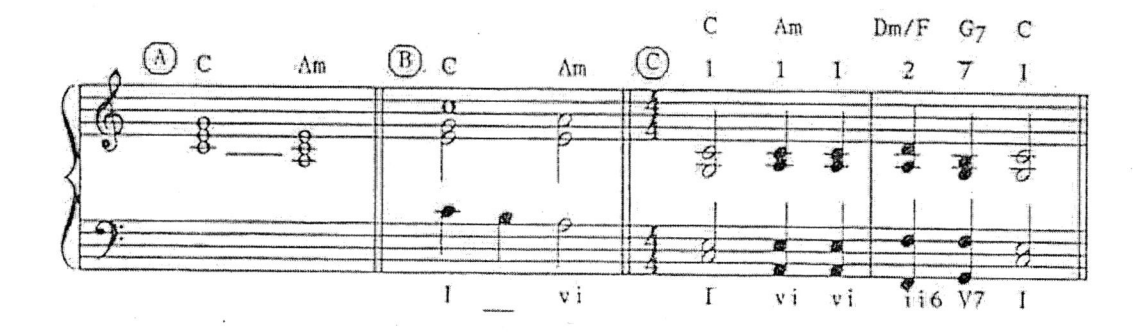

The same progression (I to vi) occurs in the second phrase of "Fairest Lord Jesus," but the repeated tone that changes function is the soprano pitch - E, which functions as the third of the C chord, then as the fifth of the A minor chord (Example 56). **Note**: As the passing tone in the bass part is played (Examples 55B, 56A and B, 57A and B), the right hand chord does not change.

Chapter 5 – Substitute Chords

Example 56 - The Changing Function of the Soprano Pitch (from 3rd to 5th)

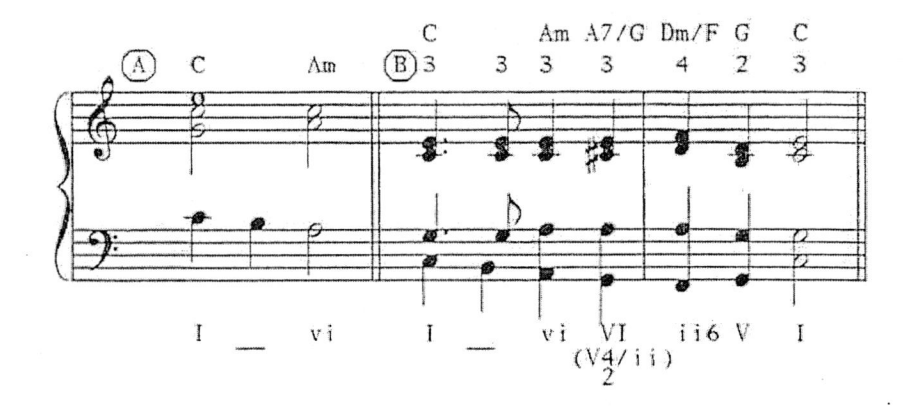

ASSIGNMENT 32

1. Play the first two phrases of "Fairest Lord Jesus" in four-part hymn style (Examples 55C and 56B), then in keyboard style with soprano, alto and tenor in the right hand, and bass in the left hand with octaves (see Example 57B).
2. Play the first two phrases of "Fairest Lord Jesus" in D major (Example 57A) as written, then in keyboard style (three-note chord in right hand).
3. Using Example 57B as a guide, transpose the progression to Eb.

Example 57 - Fairest Lord Jesus (First Two Phrases)

Chapter 5 – Substitute Chords

ASSIGNMENT 33

Play the first phrase of "If You're Happy and You Know It" with only I and V7, as notated in Example 58A, then with a shift from I to vi (Example 58B).

Example 58 - If You're Happy and You Know It

[Musical notation showing two versions, A and B, with chord symbols: V7 I vi ii V]

A Brief Review of Changing Function

One way of describing what happens in the previous progressions is to say that the soprano pitch changes function when the supporting harmony changes to the substitute chord (vi). In the first phrase of both songs, "Fairest Lord Jesus" and "If You're Happy," the soprano pitch functions, first, as the root of the tonic chord (I), then as the third of the vi chord. In Example 56B the soprano pitch functions, first, as the third of the I chord, then as the fifth of the vi chord. In the second measure of Example 58B, the soprano pitch (A) also changes function. It is first the root of the ii chord (A minor), then the fifth of the V chord (D major).

ASSIGNMENT 34

Enrich the harmony of the first phrase of "Joyful, Joyful, We Adore Thee" by using the submediant harmony (vi) in measure 3, instead of the I chord (Example 59). Transpose this phrase to F and Eb. (**Note**: Always remember to keep the melody in the top voice, with the rest of the chord underneath.)

> The following are just a few of the many songs for which a shift from tonic (I) to submediant (vi) is, or could be used for the opening phrase:
>
> - Heart and Soul
> - I Will Come and Bow Down (SPW 247)
> - I Worship You, Almighty God (SPW 28)
> - Jesus, Name above All Names (SPW 76)
> - Marching to Pretoria

Chapter 5 – Substitute Chords

Example 59 - Joyful, Joyful, We Adore Theee (with vi as Substitute for I)

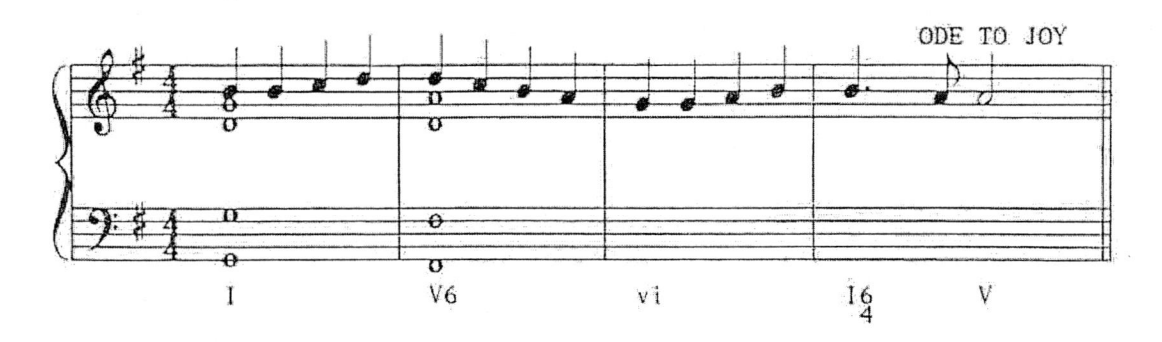

I   V6   vi   I⁶₄   V

The traditional harmonization of OLD HUNDREDTH is sometimes enriched by means of a deceptive cadence (vi) at the end of the third phrase - "Praise Him above, ye heavenly <u>hosts</u>" (Example 60, m. 6).

Example 60 - OLD HUNDREDTH

I V vi iii

6   ⁴₂ 6   6 vi 6   6   7

ASSIGNMENT 35

1. Complete Example 60, using the hymnal for reference only if necessary. Memorize the bass line, then memorize the full harmonization, and transpose it to F and Ab, or two other keys more relevant to your needs. These keys are all useable for congregational singing.
2. Harmonize "Lamb of God" by Twila Paris (SPW 112), using only I, IV and V, then enrich the harmony by substituting vi for I where appropriate.
3. Enrich these hymns by using vi: "He Leadeth Me" (measure 3) and "Blessed Assurance" (measure 3).

Chapter 5 – Substitute Chords

The Mediant (iii) As a Substitute for the Tonic Chord (I)

A less frequently used substitution for I is the mediant chord (iii). This chord is closely related to I in that the third and fifth of the tonic chord (I) are the same as the root and third of the iii chord (see Example 61).

Example 61 - The Mediant Chord as a Substitute for Tonic

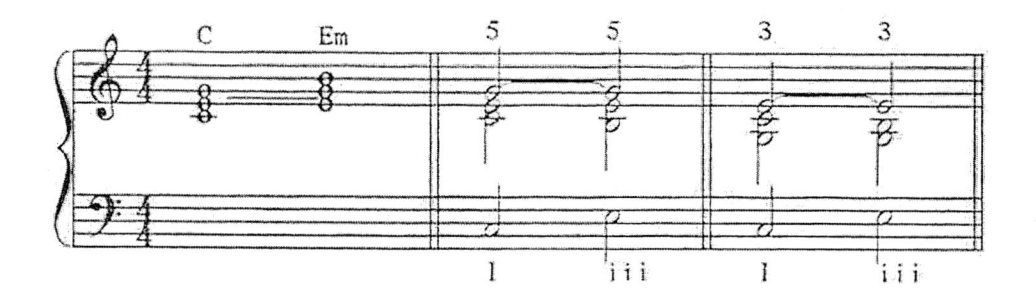

> Two well-known congregational songs that include a change from I to iii are:
> - Jesus, Name above All Names (TWC 106 or SPW 76)
> - Pass It On (TWC 739)

ASSIGNMENT 36

1. Play "Pass It On" (TWC 739), then do a Roman numeral analysis in preparation for transposing it to the key of Eb.
2. Play "Jesus, Name above All Names." For the sake of comparison, harmonize the second measure with vi instead of iii. Either chord is correct.
3. Play the modified harmony (iii instead of vi) for "Fairest Lord Jesus" (Example 62). The iii chord could be used for variety when accompanying this hymn.

Example 62 - Fairest Lord Jesus (Second Phrase with Mediant Chord iii)

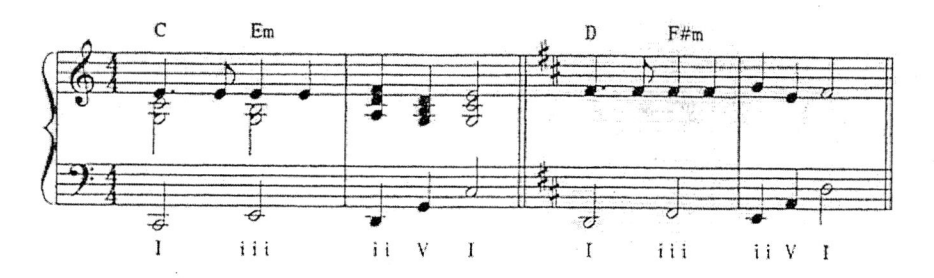

Another example of the mediant chord (iii) used as a substitute for the tonic chord (I) is illustrated in the following harmonization of a melodic sequence:

Example 63 - Melodic Sequence with iii Used as a Substitute for I

I   vi   ii   V   I   iii   IV V7 I

The Supertonic Triad (ii) as a Substitute for IV

There is another way of describing what happens when the harmony shifts from a major chord to its related minor. In the preceding musical example, the change was viewed from the perspective of the soprano pitch and its change of function. It could also be viewed as a slight change in chord color. Dr. Ben Husted, a theorist and personal friend, likens the change from subdominant (IV) to supertonic (ii) to a change from blue to a darker shade of blue. Just as there are different shades of a primary color, there are different shades of a primary (basic) chord.

A good illustration of this is Example 25 ("Set My Spirit Free") in which there a change from IV to ii in measures 11-12. This shift from C major to A minor is very smooth, for the downward movement of the bass by the interval of a third does not create a strong sense of harmonic movement. The result is the feeling that the preceding harmony has been extended, with a slight variation in color. However, in other uses of ii as a substitute for IV, the result is a strong sense of harmonic movement, as in Example 64, where the substitution of ii creates movement by succession of fifth in the bass (see Chapter Six for information on "succession of fifths," sometimes referred to as "circle of fifths").

Chapter 5 – Substitute Chords

Example 64 - Chord Substitution (ii for IV)

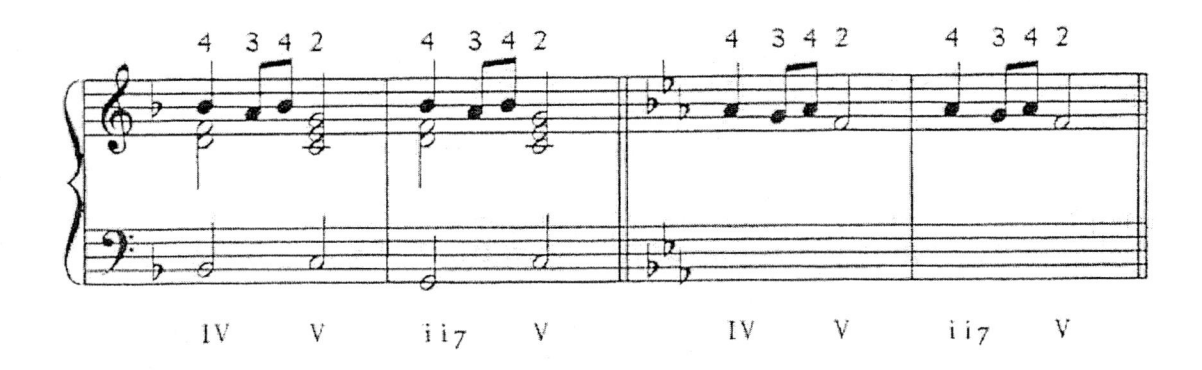

[musical notation]

IV   V   ii7   V   IV   V   ii7   V

The keyboard musician who has a command of harmony is able to use chord changes deliberately to create intensity in the musical line. To develop this ability, practice is needed in using different chords that can be used interchangeably, chords such as IV, ii, ii7 and ii6.

ASSIGNMENT 37

1. Play "Alleluia" (TWC 114) as written, then with shifts from IV to ii where appropriate.
2. Transpose the melodic/harmonic sequence in Example 63 to all keys.
3. Play Examples 64 and 65 in several keys in order to develop skill in hearing and using the different subdominant/supertonic chord colors (IV, ii7 and ii6).

Example 65 - Distinguishing between IV and ii6

[musical notation]

I   vi   IV V   I   I   vi   ii6 V   I

To see and hear how a repeated pitch can change function several times, see Example 66. After listening to (**25.mid** or **CD 25**) and playing this example in numerous keys, it is important to vary the order in which the chords are played. Examples follow:

- I to IV (see Example 66, 2nd system)
- vi to ii$_7$ (see Example 66, 3rd system)
- IV to V$_{4-3}$ (see Example 66, 4th system)

Varying the order, or sequence, of the chords is preparation for the practical application of this concept, as in Example 68 (**26.mid** or **CD 26**). As the soprano pitch is repeated, the circle of 5ths progression creates a change in function, or meaning, of the soprano pitch from 3rd to 7th. This same change of function occurs in the change from Gm to C$_7$ (Example 68).

Chapter 5 – Substitute Chords

Example 66 - Hearing Changes in the Function of a Given Pitch

> The chord with 5+ written above it is an augmented E chord. In jazz notation the top pitch is not written as B#, but rather as C which is a scale tone of the key.

Study and play the concluding phrases of the following hymns, listening to the different uses of the supertonic chord (ii). Note: All hymns listed here are found in *The Worshiping Church - TWC*.

- ii Our Great Savior (89) as harmonized by Rowland Pritchard
- ii$_6$ Joy to the World (146)
  Holy Night (160)
  Praise Him! Praise Him! (96)
  To God Be the Glory (72)
- ii$_7$ Great is the Lord (44)
  Sing Praise to God Who Reigns Above (50)
  The Church's One Foundation (689)
- ii$_6^5$ All Creatures of Our God and King (356)
  My Faith Looks Up to Thee (552)
  Sacred Head, Now Wounded (221)

Exploring Additional Changes of Function

Through the continuing analysis of soprano pitches in relation to chord roots, a keyboard musician can learn to hear the various functions of a given pitch. In my quest for knowledge regarding what happens when people play by ear, I have talked to numerous people who have this skill. Some of them play in an intuitive manner without processing what is happening. Others who have studied functional harmony are able to discuss what happens as they play. The common thread that seems to permeate the experiences of many who play by ear is an awareness of the relationship of the soprano pitch to the root of the chord. For some people the finding of the right chord is inextricably linked to the playing of the melody with the right hand. The following exercise is designed to develop an acute awareness of the various functions of a given pitch. In that music is sound, not dots on a page, it would be good to listen first (**25.mid** or **CD 25**). For those who would like to pursue this further, additional progressions are included as Appendix G^1, G^2, and G^3 (**57, 58** and **59.mid** or **CD 57, 58,** and **59**).

ASSIGNMENT 39

1. Transpose Example 66 to F, Eb and D, listening to the change of function of the repeated soprano pitch (**25.mid** or **CD 25**). **Note to Instructor:** This assignment, like others, may need to be modified to accommodate different levels of ability.
2. Play "Lord, Be Glorified" (TWC 537) and analyze each soprano pitch to determine its relationship to the chord root (e.g. root, 3rd, etc. as noted above the staff in Example 66).
3. For additional songs that illustrate the change of function of soprano pitches, see the box below. Select several titles in the box, and analyze the changing function of the repeated and sustained soprano pitches.
4. An additional challenge:
   Change the key signatures of Example 66 to 3 flats (C minor), 5 flats (Bb minor), and 1 sharp (E minor), then play the same progression.
   See Appendix G^1 if help is needed (**57.mid** or **CD 57**).

Chapter 5 – Substitute Chords

> Note: To review the concept of changing function, see Examples 57-66. Additional examples are listed below:
>
> - "Air" from *Suite in D* by J.S. Bach (first phrase)
> - "Be strong in the Lord and be...." (TWC 661, first phrase)
> - Great Is Thy Faithfulness (TWC 60, first phrase)
> - He Is Lord (SPW 122, also "He is risen from the dead....")
> - Heart and Soul
> - *I Will Come and Bow Down (SPW 247)
> - *I Worship You, Almighty God (SPW 28, first phrase)
> - *In His Time ("He makes all things beautiful in His time.")
> - In My Life, Lord (TWC 537)
> - Now the Day Is Over – Traditional hymn
> - The Lost Chord by Arthur Sullivan (first two phrases)
>
> *Printed music available in The Celebration Hymnal.
> Note: The underlined words or syllables denote pitches that are the same, but are harmonized with different chords.

All of the above examples show change of function within the context of a major tonality. Songs and instrumental selections in the minor mode could be studied from the perspective of changing function (e.g. "Moonlight Sonata" by Beethoven). In the musical examples assigned, the harmonic rhythm (rate of chord change) is relative slow, allowing time for the ear to hear the changes in function.

Understanding the function of soprano pitches is dependent upon a strong sense of bass progression. This is the reason for continuing emphasis on singing, playing and analyzing bass lines. Know also that there are bass lines that could like-wise be studied from the perspective of changing function (e.g. "Prelude in C" by Bach, Example 171).

A person whose playing by ear is totally dependent upon having the melody as the top voice in the right hand would likely benefit from the playing of independent accompaniments introduced in Chapter Two (see pages 19-31). This facilitates a shift of focus from the melody to the harmony and, more specifically, to the pitch that is repeated or sustained, as chords change.

Muscles Have Memory!

A cognitive awareness of the changing function of a pitch is not enough. Continuing practice is necessary. Fortunately, muscles have memory, and that which is processed by the ear and mind, and programmed into the fingers through repeated practice, will eventually be available for instant retrieval. In playing by ear, there isn't time to think about everything you play. Some responses must be automatic. It may take years for some musicians to develop such a command of keyboard harmony. However, a great desire, coupled with disciplined practice, can help to compensate for a lack of innate ability. Perhaps knowing that mastery comes through time and considerable practice will serve as encouragement to those who are apt to give up too soon.

The Importance of Transposition

Because transposition has been an integral part of my own development of an understanding of harmony, most of the assignments in this and preceding chapters have included the transferring of what is learned to other keys. Unless a song is transposed, the keyboard musician is likely to learn only the melody and the succession of chords that go with it. Transposition sharpens our awareness of such things as:

- the scale degree of the starting pitch
- bass line movement and chord function
- the relationship of the melody to the bass
- other structural elements such as chord outlines, intervals, and scale fragments.

The process of playing both melody and chords by ear is one that involves various kinds of musical perception, as well as a fine sense of ear-hand coordination. Each person is likely to approach this task in a way that is uniquely suited to his/her musical background. However, regardless of your approach, you will find that a working knowledge of standard chord progressions is helpful. In the chapter that follows, we will focus on the use of minor chords and how they are used in harmonizing a scale.

Chapter 5 – Substitute Chords

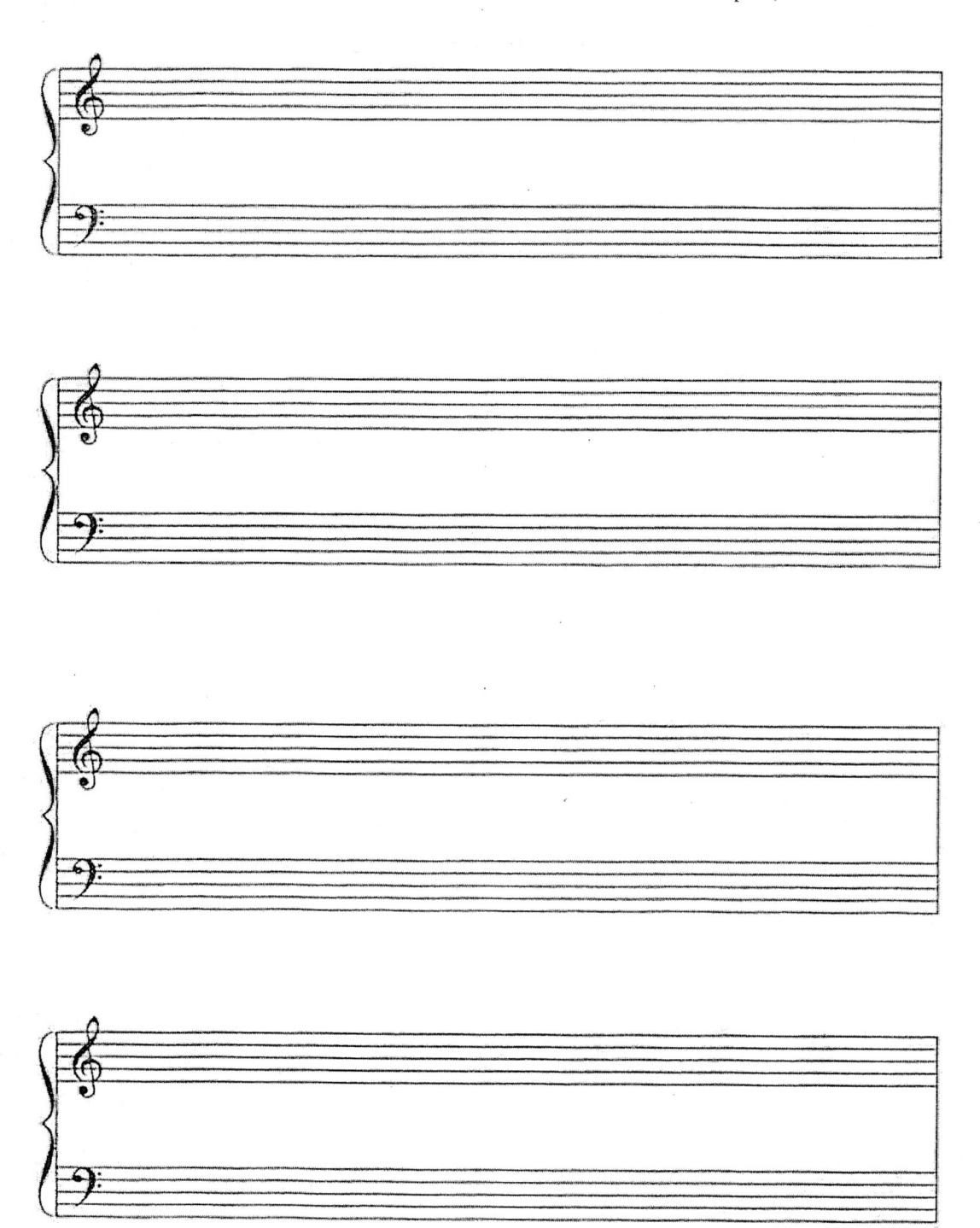

Chapter Six

SCALE HARMONIZATION: USING SEQUENCES

Descending Scale from So (5) with Succession of Fifths: iii vi ii V I

One of the strongest harmonic progressions is a pattern often referred to as the "circle of fifths," or succession of fifths. Although the following melody could be harmonized with primary chords as shown in Example 67A, the bass progression downward by fifths is much stronger (Example 67B). It is important to note that <u>sequential progressions are commonly used with a scale-like melody</u> (see Arabic numbers).

Example 67 - HYFRYDOL (with Primary Chords, then Succession of 5ths)

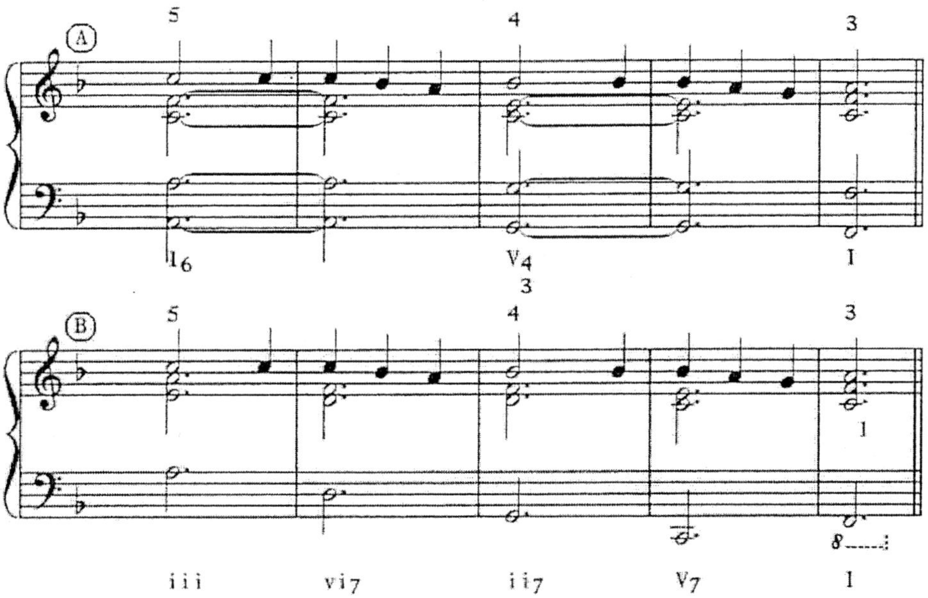

Greater harmonic strength can be achieved through movement downward by the interval of a perfect 5th (P5), then up a perfect 4th, which is the inversion of a perfect 5th (P5). By alternating between the intervals of P5 and P4, the bass line is kept within the range of the staff and the bass voice part (Example 68). Continuous movement downward by 5ths, as in Example 67B, would eventually lead beyond the bottom limits of the instrument or voice. In the example that follows, the bass moves down a 5th (Am to Dm7), up a 4th (Dm7 to Gm7), etc. (**26.mid** or **CD 26**)

Example 68 - HYFRYDOL (Alternation between the Interval of a 5th and 4th)

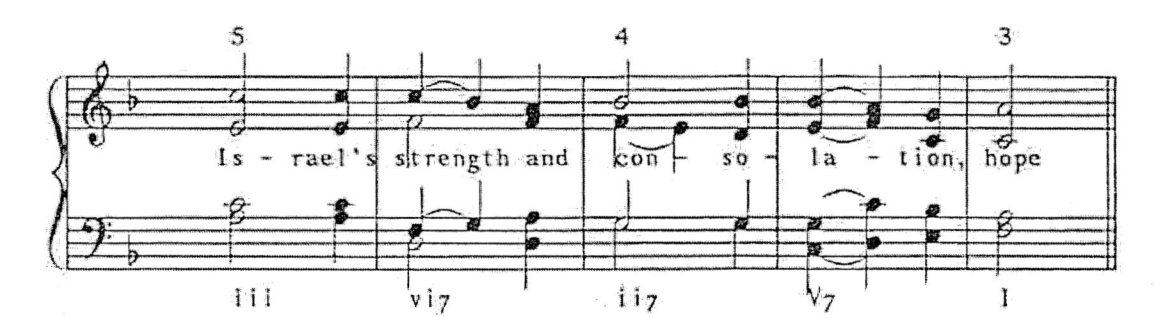

Chapter 6 - Sequences

In the example that follows, the succession of 5ths is delayed one measure (**27.mid** or **CD 27**).

Example 69 - Angels We Have Heard on High

> Songs for which a succession of fifths may be used to harmonize the descending scale line - 5 4 3 2 1
> - Give Thanks (Example 80, second half)
> - Let All Things Now Living (see Example 114)
>   (Listen for the phrase that descends from 5 to 1, **33.mid** or **CD 33**.)
> - Try to Remember (from *The Fantastiks*)
> - Twinkle, Twinkle, Little Star (Example 42B, middle section)

In measure seven of Example 69, the progression has been altered slightly by the use of an accidental. The upper case Roman numeral indicates this change from minor (vi) to major (VI). The analysis preferred by theorists is V of ii, which indicates that D major functions as the dominant of Gm. This is called a secondary dominant, as compared with C major, which is the primary dominant (V) in the key of F major. In working with musicians in a praise and worship band, this chord can be processed and played quickly if you think of it as a "tall VI." In like manner, V of V can be located quickly when you realize that it is a "tall II" and V of vi is a "tall III."

ASSIGNMENT 40

1. Change the bass line of Example 67B by alternating between 5ths and 4ths.
2. Listen to Example 69 and sing the bass part with Roman numerals (**27.mid** or **CD 27**)..
3. Transpose this same refrain to G and Eb. Refer to Example 70 if necessary.
4. Use the sequential progression - iii vi7 ii V7 I vi ii V for "Twinkle, Twinkle, Little Star" (see last two measures of Example 42B).

Work Space

(Harmonize 5 – 4 – 3 – 2 – 1 in an additional key.)

Chapter 6 - Sequences

Example 70 - Angels We Have Heard on High (Transposition to G and Eb)

(A)

I (or iii)   vi (or VI)   ii   V

I   IV   V

(B)

I (or iii)   vi (or VI)   ii   V

I   IV   V

Work Space

Notate the countermelody played by the oboe, or create your own (**27.mid** or **CD 27**).

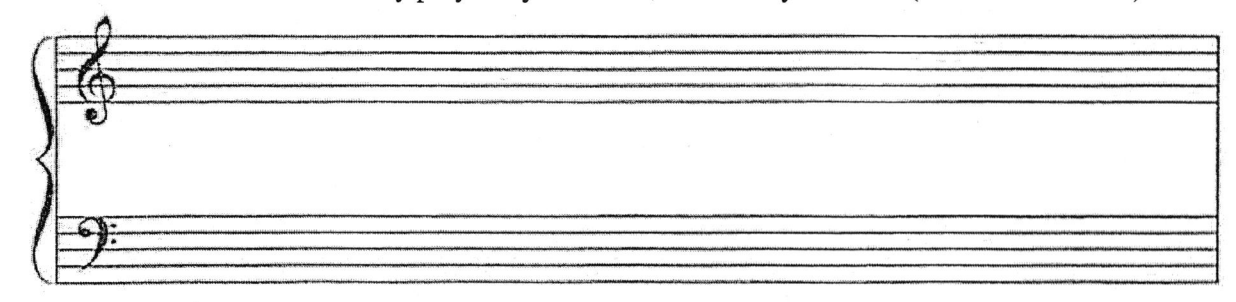

Chapter 6 - Sequences

Succession of Fifths in a Minor Key

In the preceding examples, the circle of fifths progression began with the fifth scale tone (5, or Do) with the mediant chord (iii). In the example that follows, the beginning chord of the circle of fifths progression is C minor, which is the tonic chord (i) in the key of C minor. **Note**: The chords derived from the tones of a minor scale differ from those derived from a major scale (see Example 71).

Example 71 - Diatonic Triads of the C Minor Scale (natural minor)

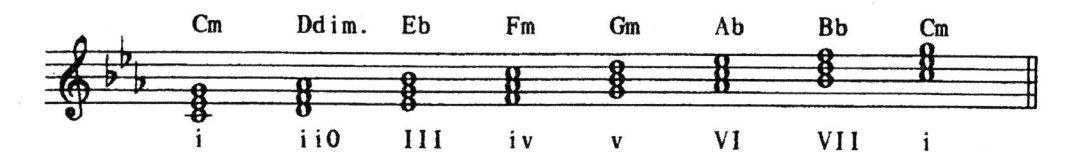

In the early Baroque Era, a composer would sometimes provide a basic melodic pattern like the one in Example 72, along with a figured bass line. The embellishing of the melodic line was the responsibility of the performer, who would improvise a slightly more elaborate melodic line for each phrase, gradually building the intensity (see Example 73). The chords and bass line were played on the harpsichord and the bass line was doubled by the viola da gamba, a precursor of the modern-day cello. This example, originally written for oboe, has been performed on many different solo instruments (**28.mid** or **CD 28**).

Example 72 - Sequential Melodic Pattern from "Adagio"

Marcello

Example 73 - Adagio (with Embellished Melodic Line)

Alessandro Marcello

Chapter 6 - Sequences

In Example 73 the dominant chord is changed from minor (v) to major (V). The natural sign under the bass note in measure seven indicates that the third of the chord (Bb) is to be raised (sharped). The progression V to i in a minor key provides a strong cadence, just as it does in a major key.

ASSIGNMENT 41

1. Listen to "Adagio" by Marcello (**28.mid** or **CD 28**), then delete the accompaniment and play the written progression as accompaniment.
2. Delete the melody and improvise an embellished version of the melody while listening to the accompaniment. (Note: Remember that for this, and other recorded examples, the deletion of a part on MIDI is accomplished by deleting or muting a track.)
3. Select pattern A or B in Example 75 and extend the melody in different ways by improvising as the progression is continued.

Example 74 - Sequential Melody Based on Succession of Fifths

Another way to experience a succession of fifths and fourths is to move through the major key signatures (Example 75). In planning an uninterrupted flow of hymns and choruses, the selection of songs according to this sequence of keys facilitates a continuous flow of worship[in song (**46.mid** or **CD 46**).

Example 75 - Key Signatures Listed by Succession of Fifths

Continue the succession by fifths.

79

Descending Scale from Mi (3) with Pachelbel Canon Sequence

Another sequential pattern that is used with scale-like melodies is the chord progression associated with the well-known "Canon in D" by Johann Pachelbel (**29.mid** or **CD 29**). As a rule this harmonic progression is used with melodies that begin with the third tone of the major scale (Example 76). One of the many songs that is harmonized, in part, with this basic progression is "God Himself is With Us" (Example 77). The use of the A major chord in measure four does not alter the basic sequential pattern of the bass.

Example 76 - Sequential Bass (Down a 4th, up a 2nd)

Example 77 - God Himself is With Us

Chapter 6 - Sequences

The sequential bass line shown in Example 76 is often altered to form a descending bass line, as in Example 78A and B (**30.mid** or **CD 30**). This is achieved by playing the second chord (C major) in first inversion (V6 instead of V). Two other chords are likewise played in first inversion: A minor and F (see measures 4 and 6 of Example 78A). Example 78B is an adaptation of this progression for use with the chorus, "Lord, Be Glorified" (see Example 83).

Example 78 - Pachelbel Progression Altered to Form Scale in Bass

(A) I V I V6 vi iii vi iii6 IV I IV I6 IV vii°6 I
    F C/E   Dm Am/C Bb C7 Bb/D C/E   Bb Edim/G F

(B) I V6 vi iii6 IV V7 IV6 V6 : I vii°6 I

Work Space

(Write and play Example 78B in two additional keys.)

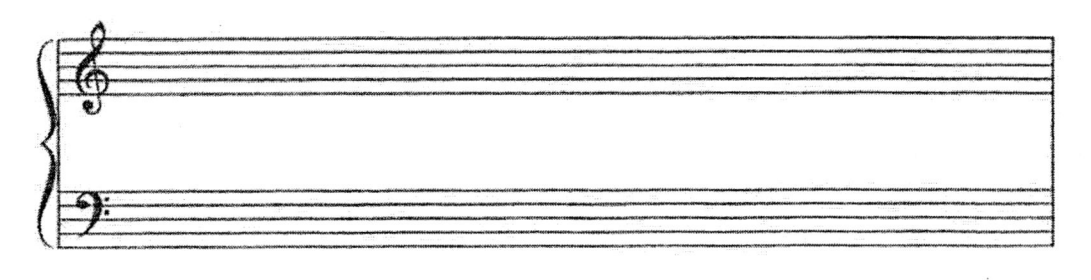

81

Chapter 6 - Sequences

ASSIGNMENT 42

1. Memorize the progression shown in Example 76, then embellish the melodic patterns introduced in measures 1-2 and 5-6, or improvise freely as on the recording (**29.mid** or **CD 29**).
2. Play Example 78A in several keys.
3. Play Example 78B as accompaniment for "Lord, Be Glorified." Transpose the song to keys often used in congregational worship (C, D and Eb).

Important Observations

It should be noted that a sequential chord progression is usually linked with a scale-like melody. Review Examples 67-70, 72-74 and 76-77, making the following observations:

1. In Examples 67-70 the melody of each musical excerpt begins on the fifth tone of the scale and moves downward by step.
2. In Examples 72-74 there is descending scale-wise movement in the melody, but the starting pitch is not always the fifth tone of the scale.
3. In Examples 76-78 there is melodic movement downward from the third tone of the scale.

A melody that demonstrates the connection between scale-wise melodic movement and sequential harmony is "Give Thanks" by Henry Smith (Example 80). The first half of the melody descends from the third tone of the scale, for which the Pachelbel progression with altered bass line is used (see chords in parentheses). The second half of the melody descends from the fifth tone of the scale, and the bass line is a succession of fifths and fourths.

The dominant chord at the half cadence is preceded by an Eb major chord (Example 80, m. 7-8). Example 79 shows several possible half cadences for this phrase. The alteration of the leading tone triad (vii°) to form the subtonic chord (VII) is shown in Example 79B. In Chapter Nine this will be discussed from the perspective of modal harmony.

Example 79 - The Use of the Subtonic Chord (VII) at a Half Cadence

Chapter 6 - Sequences

Example 80 - Give Thanks

Chapter 6 - Sequences

Words and Music: Henry Smith ©1978 Integrity's Hosanna! Music. %Integrity Music, Inc. P. O. Box 851622, Mobile, AL 36685. All rights reserved. International copyright secured. Used by permission.

84

Chapter 6 - Sequences

ASSIGNMENT 43

1. Play the block chords of Example 80 while singing the melody. As the first section is repeated, use a descending bass line (notes in parentheses).
2. Sing the bass line with Roman numeral names while playing the right hand chords.
3. Play the melody and chords with the right hand.
4. Transpose the melody, then the accompaniment to G and Eb.
5. Transpose the cadence, "what the Lord has done for us" to all keys.

Thus far the harmonic rhythm (rate of chord change) has been rather slow, with one or two chords per measure. In the German chorale "Praise to the Lord, the Almighty," the same sequential progression (I V vi iii IV 1) is used, but the chord changes occur at a faster rate (Example 81).

Example 81 - Sequential Bass with Fast Harmonic Rhythm

Praise to the Lord, the Almighty

ASSIGNMENT 44

1. Identify each chord of Example 81 by letter name and chord quality (major, minor or diminished).
2. Transpose the melody, then the bass to the key of G; then play both parts.
3. Fill in the chords, making selections on the basis of the figured bass (Ex. 82).

Example 82 - Figured Bass for "Praise to the Lord, the Almighty"

Improvisation

Although improvisation is the topic of a later chapter, it should be regarded as integral to all musical development. When you use scales, chords and other musical elements in creating your own music, there is a sense of understanding and ownership that is attainable in no other way. As soon as a basic chord progression is learned, it should be used as a basis for musical expression. If you've been making music for any length of time, your ears (and fingers) are full of musical ideas that could be used in new ways. Example 83 is provided as a starting point for continuing improvisations of melodic variations and accompaniment patterns. Don't be afraid to make mistakes. The more you launch out and create, the more confident you'll become!

Work Space

Chapter 6 - Sequences

Example 83 - Lord, Be Glorified

Words and Music by Bob Kilpatrick ©1978 Bob Kilpatrick. Adm. by The Lorenz Company. All rights reserved. Used by permission.

Chapter 6 - Sequences

ASSIGNMENT 45

1. Listen to the recording of Example 83 (**31.mid** or **CD 31**) that was used as accompaniment for the playing of the tune by ear (Chapter One). Delete the melody, and improvise melodic variations while listening to the bass line, or while playing the bass line (in the absence of MIDI).
2. Delete the chord progression, and improvise different accompaniment patterns. This could be used for group improvisations in a piano class.
3. Improvise on "Sarabande" by Johann Pezel (Example 84). After playing several melodic variations in the original key, explore other keys (e.g. Eb, Em, Gm). This sequential melody appears to move downward by thirds, rather than seconds. However, the scale line is continued by the inner voice part in measures 2, 4 and 6 (see notes in parentheses).

Example 84 - Sarabande

Note: For an explanation of N6 (first measure of last system above) see p. 132.

Chapter 6 - Sequences

> Melodies that are, or could be harmonized with the "Canon in D" progression:
>
> - All Is Well by Michael W. Smith
> - Give Thanks (first half)
> - God Himself Is With Us (Example 77)
> - Jolly Old St. Nicholas
> - Lord, Be Glorified (Example 83)
> - Praise to the Lord the Almighty (Example 81)
> - Sarabande (Example 84)
> - Seek Ye First (SPW 182)
> - You Are My All in All (SPW 220)

Work Space

Write the melody and sequential bass for two of the above melodies. Include key and time signature.

Chapter 6 - Sequences

The Alteration of Chords in Sequence

Another common sequential bass pattern is shown in Example 85. Unlike the previous patterns, this one ascends (up a 4th, down a 3rd) and the melody ascends by step. You'll find this progression in hymns, choruses, classical music, show tunes and other genres of music. In Example 85A and C the pattern begins with the tonic chord and moves up a 4th, then down a 3rd and up a 4th: I–IV–II (or "tall II") -V. Sometimes the pattern is extended one more step, as in "Do Re Mi" from *The Sound of Music* – I-IV-II-V-III (or "tall III") -vi. The same pattern may begin with the dominant chord, as in Example 85B and the beginning of the refrain of "Great is Thy Faithfulness."

Example 85 - Ascending Bass Pattern (Up a 4th, Down a 3rd)

ASSIGNMENT 46

1. Transpose Example 85A and C up a half step and down a whole step.
2. Sing the melody of Example 85C while playing the accompaniment.
3. Extend the above bass pattern one more step for the following songs:
    - There is Strength in the Name of the Lord (TWC 113)
    - Holy, Holy is the Lord of Hosts (SPW 35)
    - Do Re Mi
4. Play the beginning of the refrain of "Trust and Obey" (Ex. 86B) and transpose it to Eb.
5. Play the refrain of "Great is Thy Faithfulness" in Eb, D and Db.

Chapter 6 - Sequences

In each of the previous examples, the chord that has been altered (changed from minor to major) functions as the dominant of the chord to which it leads, hence the analysis - V of V and V of vi. As was noted previously, the altered chord is called a secondary dominant, because it doesn't lead to the tonic chord as the primary dominant (V) does. Sometimes the altered chord is inverted - (V6 of ii and V6 of vi) as in Example 86.

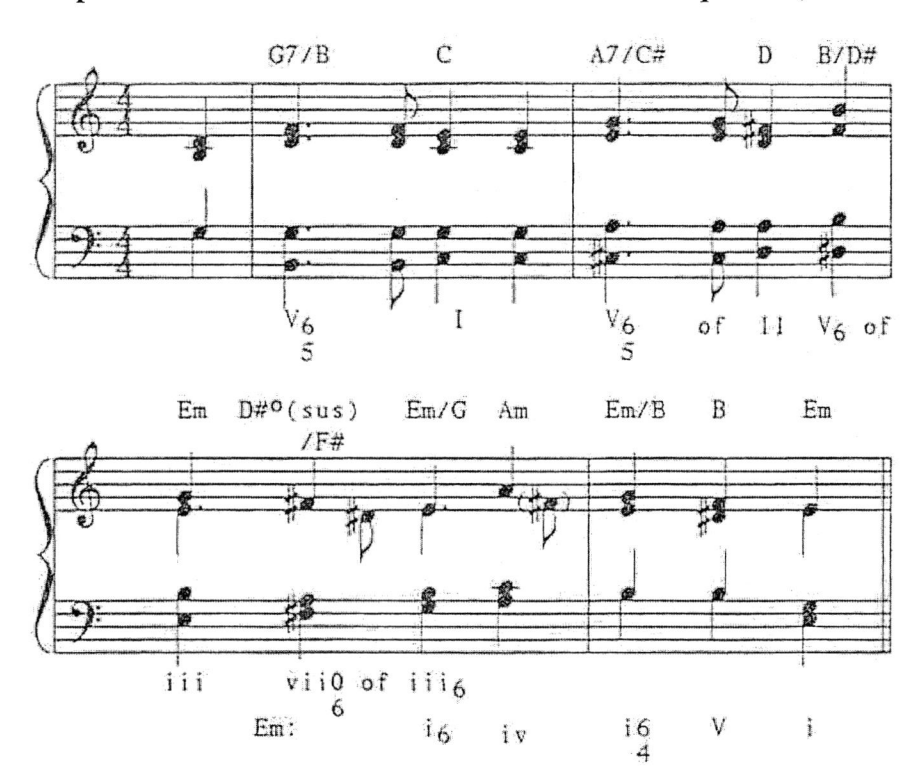

Example 86 - The Inversion of Altered Chords in Sequence (MELITA)

In the following excerpt from "March" by J.S. Bach, the two-part texture doesn't give the full sound of the secondary dominants, but the bass pitches clearly indicate the sequential nature of the harmony.

Example 87 - Sequential Harmony in a Keyboard Classic

Although the accidentals (G# and A#) in the bass line of the previous example may suggest the chords E7 and F#7, it would be more accurate to identify them as G# dim. and A# dim., since the roots of the secondary dominant chords are not included. Another example of diminished chords fulfilling a secondary dominant function can be seen in the following variations on a basic sequence (Example 88). For a review of diminished chords see Appendix D.

Chapter 6 - Sequences

Example 88 - Variations on a Sequential Harmony

Altered Chords at Cadences

The most frequent use of an altered chord is the change of the supertonic chord from minor (ii) to major (II) at a half cadence. The use of this chord in a succession of fifths leading to V serves to strengthen an otherwise weak cadence (compare Examples 89A and B). A half cadence is sometimes called an *incomplete* or *unfinished cadence*..

Example 89 - The Altered Supertonic Chord at a Half Cadence

Chapter 6 - Sequences

ASSIGNMENT 47

1. Play the following hymns from the hymnal, then strengthen the half cadence(s) through the use of the altered supertonic (II, the same as V of V):

   - Jesus Loves Me (TWC 470, m. 12)
   - He Leadeth Me (TWC 635, m. 4 and 12)
   - Leaning on the Everlasting Arms (TWC 609, measures 4 and 12)

2. Review the altered supertonic in all keys (Appendix C).

An altered chord may be used to establish tonal centers other than the key of the dominant. In Example 86 there is a strong sequential progression to the mediant harmony: G7 to C, A7 to D, B to Em. The B major chord suggests the new tonal center (E minor), then confirms it in the cadence that follows.

Cadences: Authentic and Plagal

A cadence that ends with a tonic chord (I) is called an *authentic cadence*. The tonic chord is preceded by the dominant chord (V). The term *plagal cadence* is used with reference to the progression IV-I used for "Amen" at the close of a hymn. Both *authentic* and *plagal* cadences are regarded as perfect cadences when the final pitch of the melody is 1, or Do.

The final phrase of "Away in a Manger" (Example 90) ends with a *perfect authentic cadence*. If we were to stop on the third chord (FM7) the cadence would still be authentic, but imperfect. The strong sequential progression by fifths (ii V7 I) is used twice, but a sense of completeness is not achieved until the second time when the melody comes to rest on 1, or Do. Other terms used to denote this sense of rest are *finished*, or *complete cadence*. (Note: A flatted 9th has been added to the dominant 7th chords, and a tri-tone substitute chord is used in measure three. These and other chords will be discussed in Chapter 9.)

Example 90 - AWAY IN A MANGER

Although this chapter has not been an exhaustive study of sequential harmonies, it will serve as a basis for understanding other sequences. In Chapter 7, which deals with the process of selecting appropriate chords for any given melody, the usefulness of sequential progressions will be apparent.

Chapter 6 - Sequences

Work Space

Chapter Seven

HARMONIZING A MELODY: THE PROCESS

There are several approaches to the harmonization of a melody. Chords may be selected on the basis of chord outline and scale degree analysis, as explained in Chapter Two. In Chapters Three and Four a strong basis for harmonizing melodies was established through the study of scale harmonization, with an emphasis on primary chords. In Chapters Five and Six the palette of chord colors was expanded to include minor chords, also the alteration of minor chords to from secondary dominants.

In an attempt to bring all of these approaches together, we will look at a systematic method offered by Dr. Allen Forte. He calls this "The Six Steps in Soprano Harmonization" (Forte 1979, 227- 233). Later in the chapter we'll see that Forte's "Six Steps" can be used in conjunction with other approaches, serving as a grid for their use. To illustrate Forte's procedure I have selected the first phrase of the German hymn tune FREU DICH SEHR. This tune is often associated with "Comfort, Comfort, Now My People" which is a metrical paraphrase of verses from Isaiah 40 (see TWC 132).

A Six-Step Approach to Harmonization

Step One: Analyze the melody for scale degree succession (scale numbers), embellishing tones (non-harmonic tones) and phrasing (type of cadence).

Example 91 - Melodic Analysis of FREU DICH SEHR

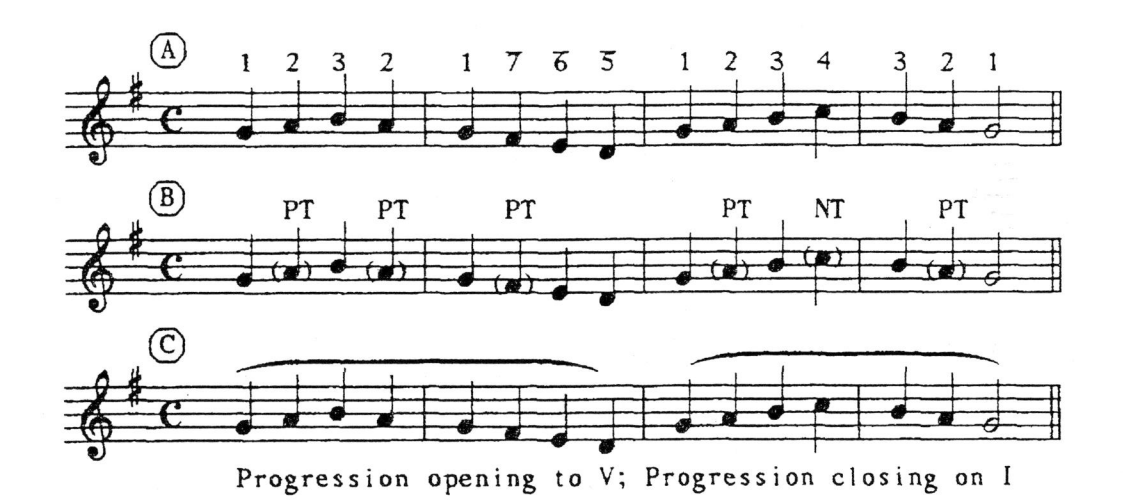

Step Two: Harmonize the melody with minimal harmonies (Forte's term for primary chords) in root position.
Note: Most of the pitches analyzed as non-harmonic tones in Ex. 91 are now regarded as chord tones.

Chapter 7 – Harmonizing a Melody

Example 92 - Primary Chords in Root Position

Step Three: To create a more interesting bass line, invert some of the basic chords, placing the third or fifth of the chord in the bass.

Example 93 - Primary Chords Inverted

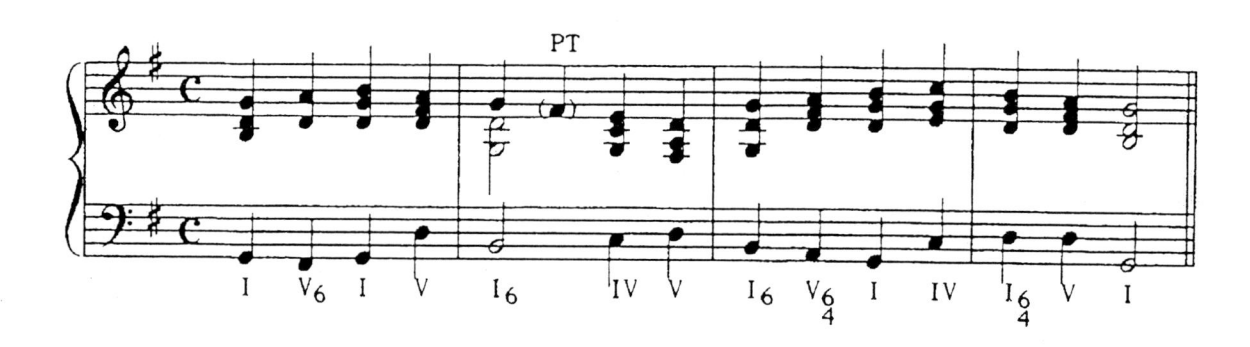

Step Four: Use substitute chords to enrich the basic harmony.

Example 94 - Substitute Chords for Enrichment

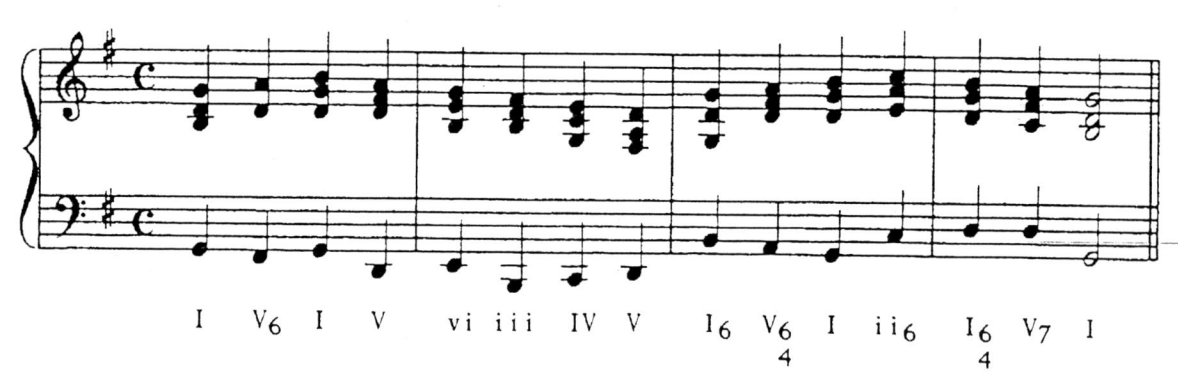

Chapter 7 – Harmonizing a Melody

Step Five: Add seventh chords and inverted seventh chords. **Note**: We are referring here to chords that have added sevenths (measures 1, 2 and 4), <u>not</u> to the leading tone triad (vii°), as in measure 3.

Example 95 - Seventh Chords and Inverted Seventh Chords

I V₆ I vii°7 vi iii IV V₄₂ I₆ vii°6 I ii₆ I₆₄ V 7 I
           of vi

Note: The above step has been fully notated, but Forte suggests this as Step Six (see comment in next paragraph).

Step Six: Notate in full.

   In Dr. Forte's procedure, only the soprano and bass parts are written, along with the figured bass symbol. The chords have been notated in the above examples in view of the fact that some who use this text will not have a working knowledge of figured bass. In Step Six, that which was played as Step Five would be written.

   The value of Step Two may not be apparent, particularly since it lacks the richness of the harmonic development that we're accustomed to hearing. Concerning the value of minimal harmonization, Forte writes, "The importance of the minimal harmonization cannot be overestimated. From this firm basic structure one can proceed in an orderly fashion to construct more elaborate settings (Forte 1979, 229).

Work Space

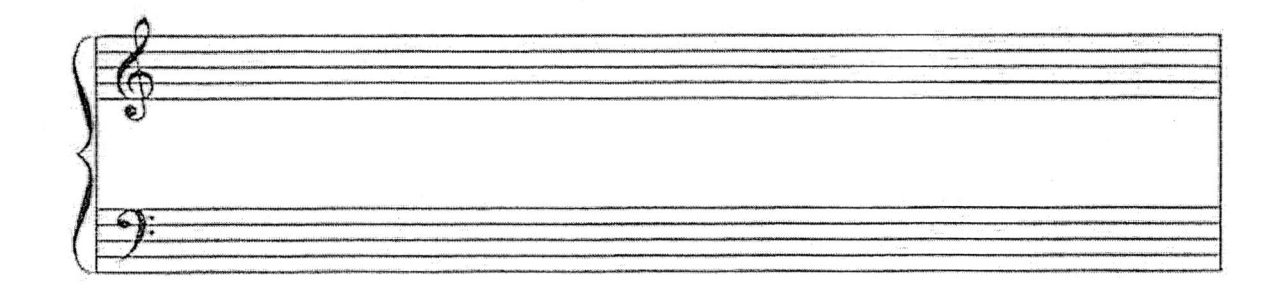

97

Chapter 7 – Harmonizing a Melody

Using the Six-Step Approach

Step One: In Example 96 a scale degree analysis is shown, and Roman numerals are included at the end of each phrase to indicate whether the harmonic progression ends on I (authentic cadence) or on V (half cadence). Several embellishing tones are included, but they are not marked.

Example 96 - Father, Lead Me (Scale Degree and Phrase Analysis)

Father, Lead Me Day by Day

1. Father, lead me day by day, ever in your own strong way;
   Teach me to be pure and true; show me what I ought to do.

2. When in danger, make me brave; make me know that you can save;
   Keep me safely by your side; let me in your love abide.

3. When I'm tempted to do wrong, make me steadfast, wise and strong;
   And when all alone I stand, shield me with your mighty hand.

4. May I do the good I know, serving gladly here below.
   Then in heaven I will be praising you eternally.

   Text: John Hopps, 1834-1911; altered by R.S., 1995

The above text is included because of its usefulness as spiritual nurture for young children. It is also excellent material for teaching note-reading.

Chapter 7 – Harmonizing a Melody

Step Two: Minimal harmonies in root position are used in Step Two, and they are notated in keyboard style. The bass may be played in octaves for a greater fullness of texture.

Example 97 - Primary Chords in Root Position

Step Three: Some of the primary chords are inverted to add interest to the bass line. This may also create intensity between the soprano and bass lines, as in Example 98, measure 2 (see contrary motion between soprano and bass). Contrary motion between the soprano and bass is also used in measures 5-6.

Example 98 - Minimal Harmonies Inverted

Chapter 7 – Harmonizing a Melody

Step Four: In this step substitute chords are used to enrich the harmony by creating a strong sense of movement via succession of fifths (measures 2 and 4).

Example 99 - Substitute Chords (ii and vi)

I   vi   ii   V₇   I   I₆   V⁶₄   I   V₆   vi   ii₇   V

I₆   IV   I₆   ii   V   I₆   ii₆   I₆   V⁶₄   I

Step Five: In this step seventh chords and their inversions are used, and the supertonic seventh chord is altered (see E7 chord in m. 4). The inner voice parts have been omitted as a challenge to students to work on reading figured bass.

Example 100 - Seventh Chords and Inverted Seventh Chords

P.T.   P.T.   6   7   6 6⁴   6   7♯   4 2

6   6   4 3   4 2   6   6   6 4   7

Step Six: Step Five is notated in full.

Example 101 - Notation of Completed Work

ASSIGNMENT 48

1. Sing Example 91, then play Examples 92-95, singing the bass line with Roman numeral names.
2. Play Examples 97-101, filling in the missing data of Example 100.
3. In the examples that follow, apply steps two to five of Forte's procedure. Work without referring to the previous harmonization of the same melody. Your work may differ from that of the tutorial (Examples 97-101).

Example 102 - Father, Lead Me (Primary Chords - Step Two)

Example 103 - Primary Chords Inverted (Step Three)

Example 104 - Substitute Chords (Step Four)

Chapter 7 – Harmonizing a Melody

Example 105 - Seventh Chords and Inverted Seventh Chords (Step Five)

Review

Selecting Chords on the Basis of Chord Outlines

The following procedure is intended to serve as a review of principles presented in Chapter Two (Dare to Be Simple) and Chapter Five (Substitute Chords). The procedure will facilitate the combining of several approaches, including the principles of harmonization outlined by Dr. Forte.

Step One: Sing the melody with scale numbers or syllables, and write them above the notes (see Example 107, m. 1). Circle the groups of notes that suggest basic chords. Also, indicate whether each phrase moves to a half cadence (V) or an authentic cadence (I).

Example 106 - Rock of Ages (Melody Only)

Chapter 7 – Harmonizing a Melody

Step Two: As in the procedure outlined by Dr. Forte, provide an accompaniment that consists of minimal harmonies (I, IV and V) in root position. Play the melody with the basic chords and listen for dissonances. Write the analysis above each dissonant (non-harmonic) tone: neighbor tones (N.T.) and passing tones (P.T.).

Example 107 - Rock of Ages (with Basic Chords)

Step Three: Use inversions of the basic chords to create a more interesting bass line.

Example 108 - Rock of Ages (with Inversions of Basic Chords)

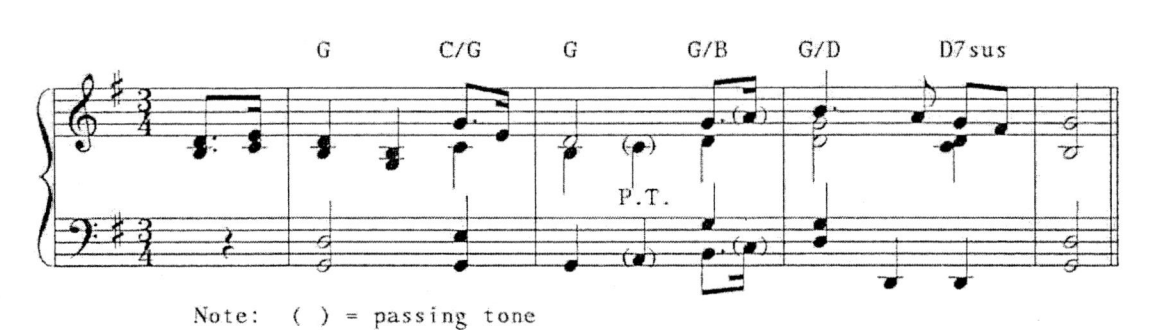

Note: ( ) = passing tone

Work Space

Chapter 7 – Harmonizing a Melody

Step Four: Enrich the harmony using substitute chords.

Example 109 - Rock of Ages (with Substitute Chords)

The above example is an illustration of how one might shift from keyboard style to choral style during the playing of an accompaniment by ear.

Step Five: Add seventh chords and other variations.

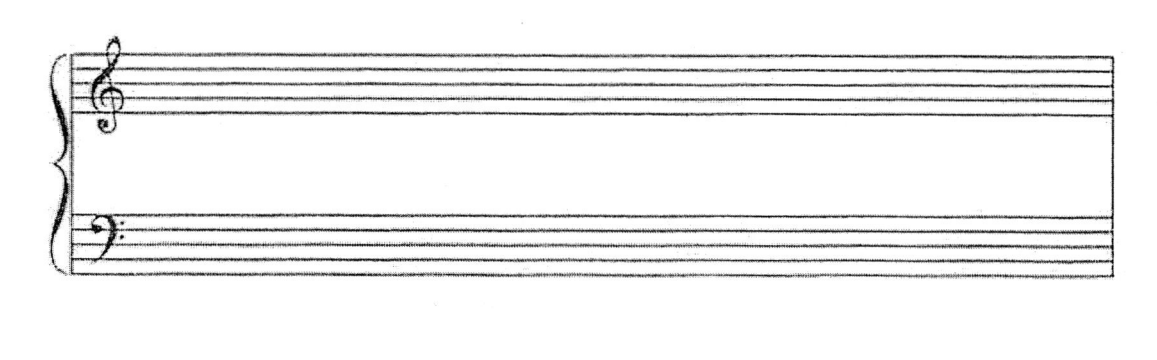

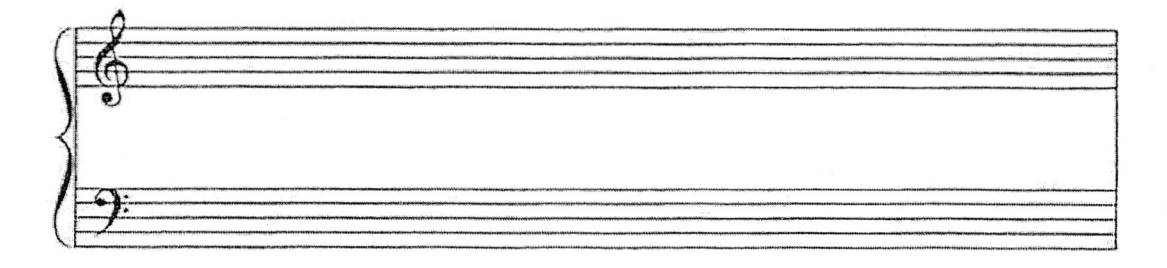

Although additional changes could be made, there is something to be said for simplicity. In the traditional harmonization of this melody, each phrase ends with the tonic chord, which creates a sense of rest. An altered supertonic chord (A9) could be used on the downbeat of measure 3, but this would

Chapter 7 – Harmonizing a Melody

possibly detract from the serenity that a simpler harmony affords. Another possible variation would be to embellish the progression from B minor to A minor with a passing diminished seventh chord (see Example 109, m. 6).

ASSIGNMENT 49

1. Play through each step of the above procedure (Examples 106-109) with, then without the notes.
2. Write out Step Five, using the work space provided.
3. Apply this procedure in the harmonizing of two or three of the following songs:

   - My Jesus, I Love Thee (TWC 101)
   - Precious Lord, Take My Hand (TWC 638)
   - There is a Balm in Gilead (TWC 611)
   - Turn Your Eyes upon Jesus, *Refrain* (TWC 452)
   - What a Friend We Have in Jesus (TWC 622)
     (Try one in the gray box, too.)

   - Immortal, Invisible (TWC 62)
   - In Moments Like These (SPW 97)
   - Jesus Loves Me (TWC 470)
   - Let All Things Now Living (Example 114)
   - Nothing But the Blood of Jesus (TWC 471)
   - The Joy of the Lord (SPW 229)

Selecting Chords on the Basis of Underlying Scale Lines

The concepts presented in Chapters Three through Six are foundational to the process of selecting chords. Continuing review of these concepts and their application is essential. The following assignment provides an opportunity to apply the understanding and skills acquired through the study of scale harmonization.

ASSIGNMENT 50

1. Look for scale lines that serve as underpinnings of DIADEMATA, "Crown Him with Many Crowns" (Example 110). Highlight the underlying scale fragments by using scale numbers and curved lines as in Example 80 (p. 84). You should find at least five phrases or partial phrases that can be reduced to a scale line.
2. Without referring to a hymnal, select chords that will serve as accompaniment.
3. Compare your work with the original harmonization (TWC 92).
4. Transpose each fragment to other keys (Example 111A-E).

Example 110 - DIADEMATA (Finding Underlying Scale Lines)

Chapter 7 – Harmonizing a Melody

Example 111 - Scale Fragments from DIADEMATA

107

Example 111 (continued)

Chapter 7 – Harmonizing a Melody

Scale-Like Melodies: Intuition or Intention?

When a melody progresses in a scale-like manner, one may question whether or not the composer was aware of it. However, when hearing a song like "Do Re Mi" from *The Sound of Music,* there seems to be no question at all. The two songs that follow were composed with a descending scale line in mind. The first half of "Venite Adoremus" (Example 112), like Pachelbel's "Canon in D," is based on a scale line that descends from the third tone of the scale (3). At the half cadence there is a transfer of register to the upper octave, and the scale continues with the pitch - D (5). The second half of the melody could be harmonized with a basic descending chord progression (see Example 42A, ms. 2-4). The middle staff of Example 112 shows the scale progression that moves at the rate of the quarter note. In Schenkerian analysis this is called the Middleground (Mittelgrund). This could be thought of as the skeletal structure of the melody. The complete melody, which is notated on the third staff, is called the Foreground (Fordergrund). The Fundamental Structure (Ursatz), which is shown on the top staff, is the reduction of the melody to its most basic form (3-2-1). For an introduction to Schenkerian analysis, see the text by Oswald Jonas (Reference List). (**32.mid** or **CD 32**)

Example 112 - Venite Adoremus (Melody Based on Scale Progression)

Chapter 7 – Harmonizing a Melody

Assignment 51

1. Sing "Venite Adoremus" with scale numbers, then harmonize the melody in keyboard style.
2. Transpose the melody to the key of F, then harmonize it.

The second example of a scale-like melody (Example 113) is based on the descending pattern 5-4-3-2-1. The first phrase moves downward by step (5-4-3), then returns to 5. The second phrase moves downward by step to the fifth tone of the scale (8-7-6-5). The third phrase, like the first, moves downward by step (5-4-3). In the fourth phrase the scale line is completed (2-1).

Example 113 - Love Came Down at Christmas

Christina Rossetti — Ron Sprunger

Love came down at Christ-mas,
Love all love-ly, love di-vine;
Love was born at Christ-mas-
Star and an-gels gave the sign.

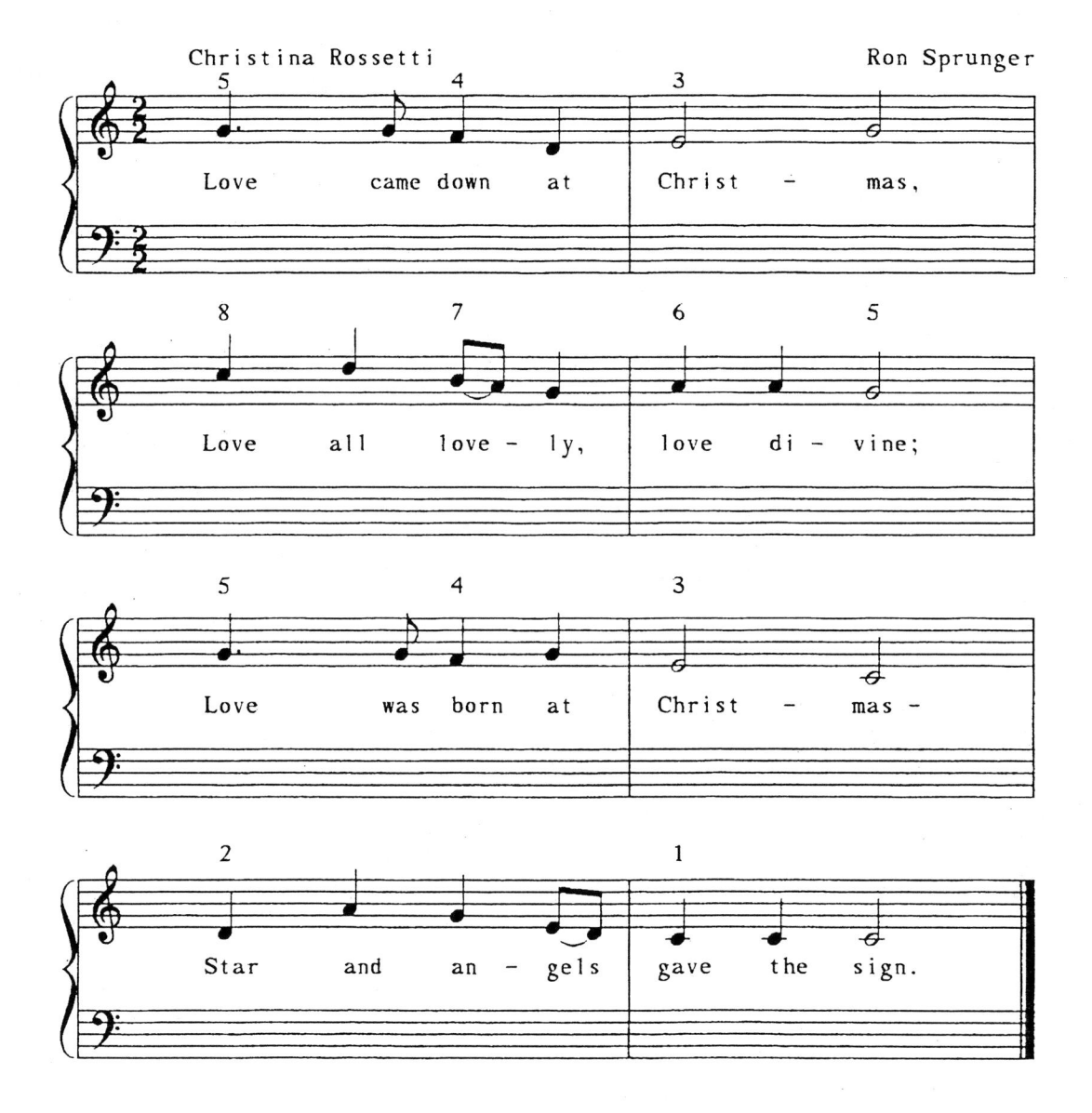

Chapter 7 – Harmonizing a Melody

Assignment 52

1. Harmonize "Love Came Down at Christmas" (Example 113) in keyboard style. Consider starting with a first inversion tonic chord (see Example 42A, m. 2). For the second line, a succession of fifths with an altered supertonic chord (II) would provide a strong cadence: vi-II-V-iii-vi-II (V of V) -V.
2. Transpose the song to Db and D.
3. Compose a short melody that progresses downward by step from 5 or 3, and add a bass line.

Work Space

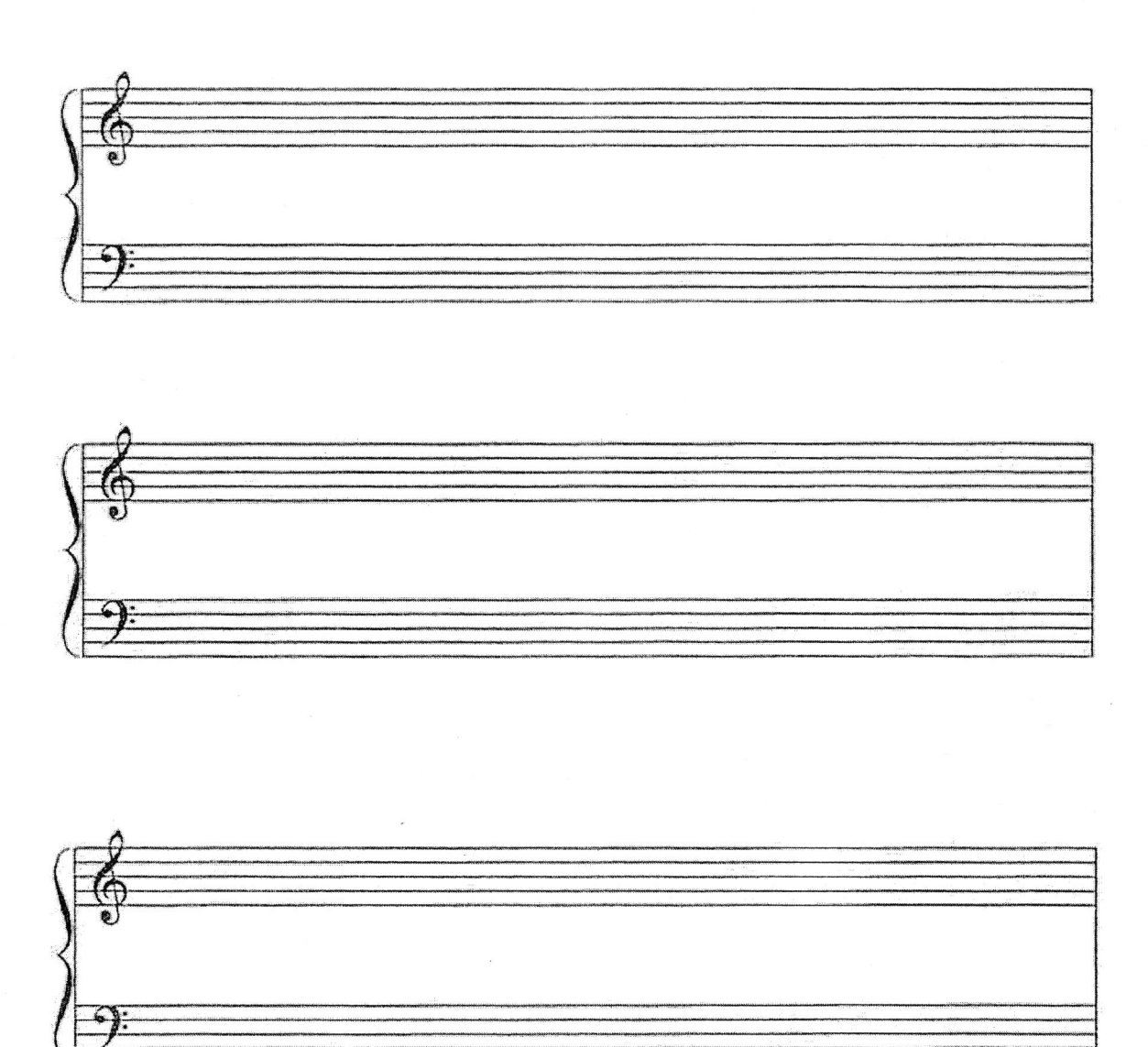

Chapter 7 – Harmonizing a Melody

Review: Harmonizing on the Basis of Chord Outlines and Scale Lines

After the disciplined work of this and preceding chapters, perhaps you've progressed to the point where you can harmonize a song such as "The Ash Grove" (Example 114) in an intuitive way. The disciplined use of a systematic approach will ultimately lead to freedom of expression, allowing one to harmonize melodies spontaneously.

Example 114 – Let All Things Now Living (ASHGROVE)

The above melody includes chord outlines and scale lines that could serve as guides for the selection of chords. Primary chords would suffice except for the phrase ending that includes the accidental (B natural). However, the harmony could be enriched by the use of substitute chords. The second half of the song, beginning with measure 9, is based on a descending scale line (5-4-3). This lends itself to the use of a succession of fifths (see Appendix H, p. 208, #3). The second half of "Give Thanks," p. 84, also illustrates the use of a succession of fifths with the scale line 5-4-3.

To conclude this chapter, let's consider the basic iambic (weak-strong, or short-long) rhythm pattern that characterizes the flow of this melody. The accompaniment patterns shown in Example 115 serve to accentuate the characteristic rhythm of the melody. Example 115B shows the effectiveness of a bass scale line. The repetition of a phrase should be viewed as an invitation to do something different. Example 115A could be used for the first phrase, and 115B on the repeat.

Chapter 7 – Harmonizing a Melody

Example 115 - Iambic Accompaniment for the Tune ASH GROVE

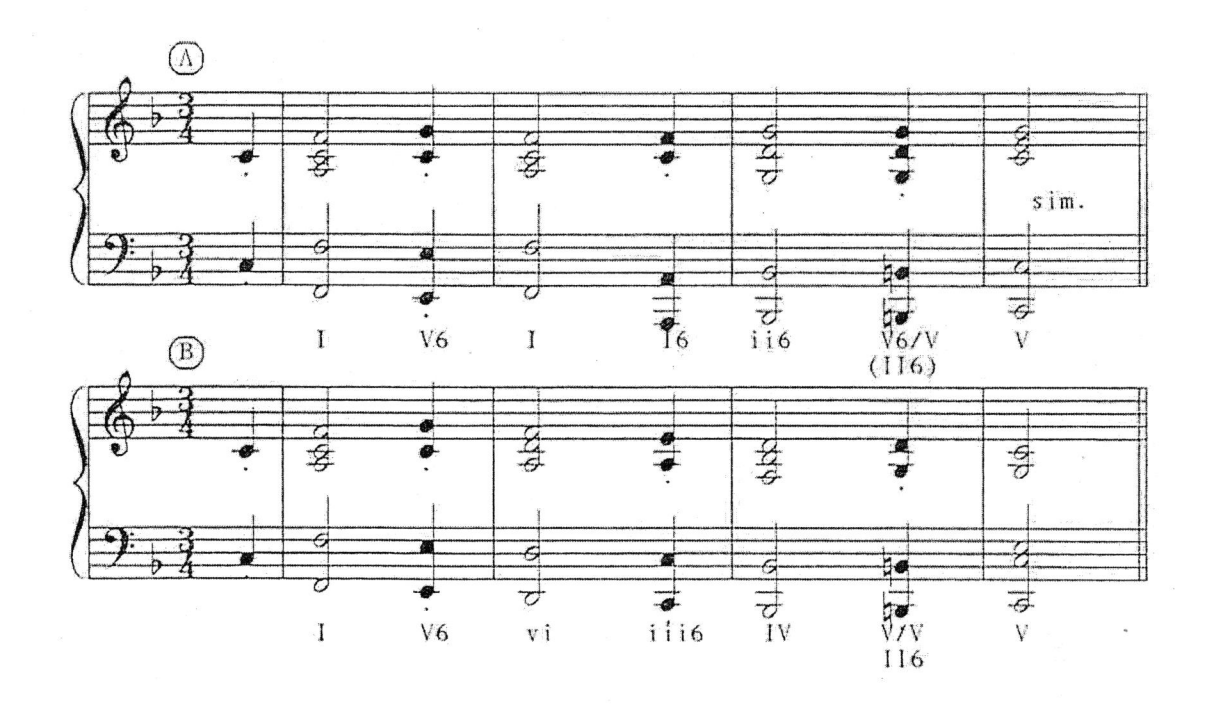

A

I   V6   I   I6   ii6   V6/V   V
            (II6)

B

I   V6   vi   iii6   IV   V/V   V
                           II6

Assignment 53

1. Listen to the tune ASH GROVE (**33.mid** or **CD 33**) and analyze it for:
   - scale degree (scale numbers or syllables)
   - phrase (types of cadences, e.g. complete or incomplete)
2. Circle chord outlines and mark underlying scale lines.
3. Use primary chords in root position.
4. Include inversions of primary chords.
5. Vary the harmony by including substitute chords.
6. Add seventh chords and altered chords.
7. Explore the use of successive fifths for the contrasting section.

Work Space

Chapter 7 – Harmonizing a Melody

Work Space

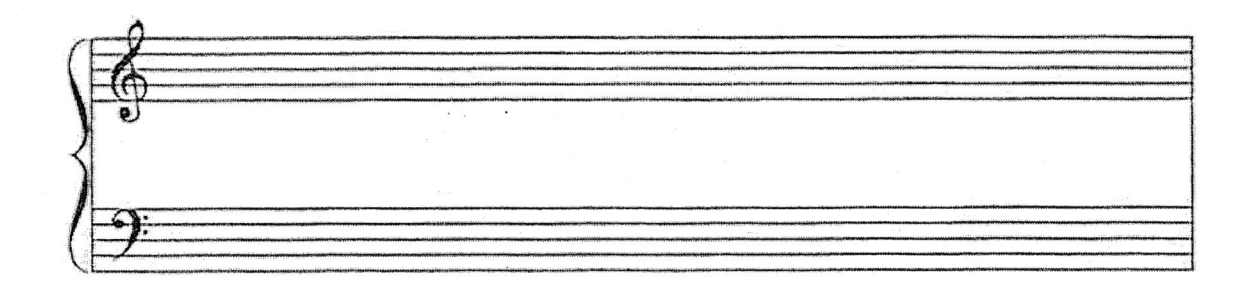

Chapter 8

MODULATION

Definition and Purpose

Modulation is a change of key within a composition. In service playing, the change of key between one musical selection and another is also regarded as a modulation. Changing keys serves as a means of...

1. emphasis for the final stanza of a hymn or the repetition of a chorus.
2. facilitating a flow of worship through the connecting of related songs.
3. leading worshipers to higher levels of expression.

Modulation has always fascinated me. Long before I even knew the word modulation, I delighted in the way our church organist was able to weave a meaningful connection between the offertory music and the singing of the "Doxology." Sometimes we forget the significance of experiences such as this that serve as inspiration later in life.

How Can Modulation Be Learned?

The study of modulation can be pursued in a variety of ways. First, the fundamentals of modulation are usually covered in a second-year college theory course. A higher level theory course that proved very helpful to me, personally, was eighteenth century counterpoint. In the study of Bach's Two-Part Inventions, one learns the art of using motivic material sequentially in the crafting of transitions to related keys.

Second, a person who is motivated to learn on his/her own will find many fine examples of modulation in the piano and organ music used in service playing. Another resource is church anthem repertory. Many of the accompaniments include well-crafted modulations which could be analyzed and adapted in different keys and styles of music. This is an excellent way to achieve greater mastery of modulation techniques.

Third, the ear is an excellent gateway to learning. An interesting modulation heard on a recording can be isolated for study. An inquiring mind serves as excellent motivation for learning, and opportunities for application help to keep learning relevant.

Sources of Motivation

The importance of modeling as a motivating factor has already been mentioned. Another essential ingredient in learning modulation is the kindling of a desire to explore. In our busy lifestyles, where one deadline or obligation follows another, we may think we're too busy to explore such things as key changes that would enhance worship. Unless the God-given spark of creativity that lies within us is rekindled, much of the creative potential that is ours to use will never be realized.

Another important factor for a learner is the practical application of that which is learned. The satisfaction this affords can be a strong motivating factor. Related to that is the positive feedback that comes from those who hear the difference that our efforts have made. If an idea

Chapter 8 - Modulation

that is presented in this chapter captures your imagination and delights your ear, go with it. Use or adapt it, even to excess, until it becomes a part of you. One word of caution, however, is in order. When you've mastered a concept such as modulation up by half step, restrain yourself, so that you don't modulate after each stanza of each hymn the following Sunday morning!

Guidelines

There are several things to remember when planning a modulation. Guidelines such as the following
will be observed throughout this chapter of instruction:

1. Begin with chord changes that do not interrupt the final sustained pitch of the previous stanza or song being sung.
2. Plan a chord progression that clearly establishes the new key.
3. Maintain a sense of pulse, meter and length of phrase.
4. Challenge yourself, whenever possible, to include a melodic pattern (motif) derived from either the song that is being sung, or the song that follows. To help the singers begin with a sense of confidence, the last phrase of the song to be sung may be used as closure to your modulation (see Example 117B).

Modulation Up a Half Step
The Simplest Way

The simplest means of modulating up a half step was used for the scale-like vocalises in Chapters 3-4 (Examples 40-41, 48-49). In these examples, there is a change in the function of the final pitch of the vocalise. More specifically, as the bass moves down <u>two whole steps</u>, the sustained soprano pitch <u>becomes the third of a major chord</u>. This chord is the <u>dominant</u> (V) of the new key, and the sustained soprano pitch is the <u>leading tone</u> (7, or Ti). An exercise for the mastery of this progression is provided in the example below, and a practical application is shown in Example 117A.

Example 116 - Modulation Up a Half Step by Means of the Dominant Seventh (V7) of the New Key

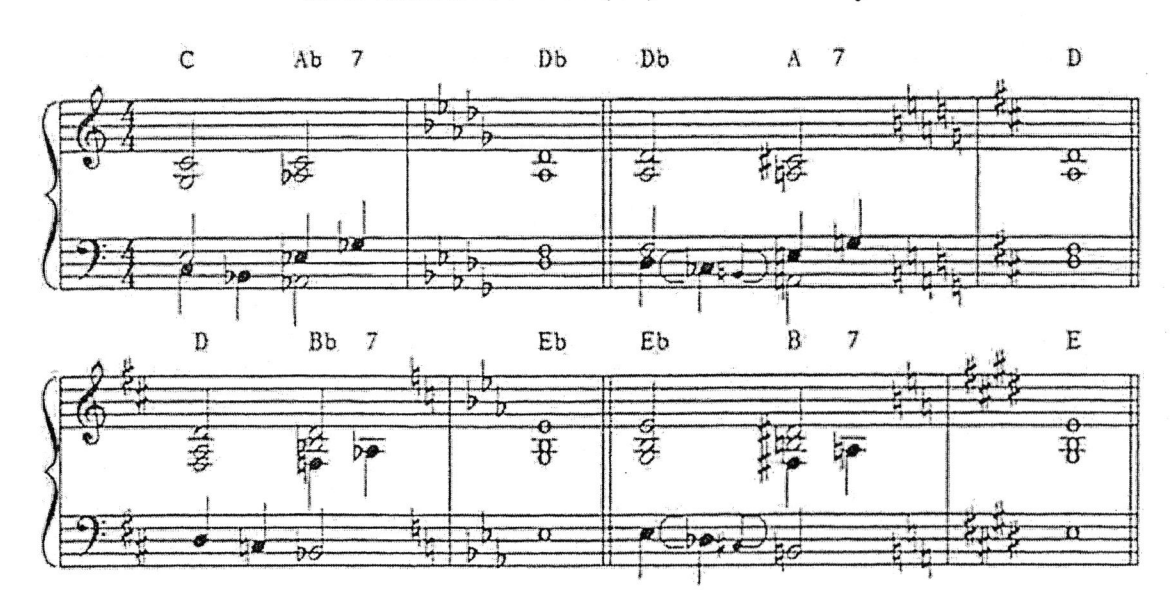

Chapter 8 - Modulation

Work Space

ASSIGNMENT 54

1. Continue Example 116 until all twelve major keys are played.
2. Repeat the exercise, resolving each dominant 7th chord to a minor chord (i).
3. Select a vocalise from Chapters 3 and 4 and lift it by half steps until it has been played in all twelve keys (see Examples 40-41, 48-49 and 52-53).
4. Select three familiar hymns and create a sense of lift for the final stanza by means of a simple half-step modulation (see Example 117A). Listen to the recorded example (**34.mid** or **CD 34**). **Note:** Keep in mind the range of the melody when considering whether or not to modulate.

Hymns for which the lifting of the final stanza would be effective:

-
-
-

Chapter 8 - Modulation

Example 117 - Four Different Half-Step Modulations

*See pages 121-122 for an explanation and examples of augmented sixth chords.

Extending Half-Step Modulations

For the sake of variety, and for a much-needed breath for some singers, a longer modulation may be used. The goal is to provide a sense of lift, and to clearly indicate *when* the next stanza begins, so that the singers can begin with confidence. The use of a motif (melodic fragment) from the hymn provides a sense of rhythmic flow that helps to keep the worshipers focused on the theme of the hymn (see Example 117B). In this example, the bass line moves downward by whole steps, but instead of leading to V in the new key, it leads to the tonic six-four chord (Eb/Bb).

Chapter 8 - Modulation

ASSIGNMENT 55

1. Play Example 117B several times, then start in Db and modulate to D.
2. Modulate from D to Eb, then from Db to D, for the final stanza of "Holy, Holy, Holy" (NICEA), using Example 117B as a model (**34.mid** or **CD 34**).

Half-Step Modulations Involving More Complex Chord Changes

Pivot Chord Modulation

Continuing with the half-step modulations, Example 117C also begins with whole-step movement in the bass. However, this time it leads to a G minor chord, which is an alteration of the subdominant chord from major (IV) to minor (iv). This chord, which belongs in both keys (D and Eb) is called a pivot chord, and the modulation is called a pivot chord modulation. The pivot chord (Gm/Bb) is iv$_6$ in the key of D, but in the key of Eb it is iii$_6$. As in Example 117B, the use of a motif taken from the hymn tune, along with the last phrase of the hymn, provides clear direction for the singer.

Half-Step Modulation Using an Augmented Sixth Chord

Example 117D is similar to the progression used in Example 117B, except for the half-step movement in the bass from C to B natural. The pitches that create the strong sense of lift are the bass pitch (Cb) and the tenor pitch (A natural) which is at the interval of an augmented 6th above the bass pitch. The above spelling, which is shown in the small notes of Example D, is the correct one, but it may be somewhat difficult to read. The augmented chord has been written first as B7 for the sake of ease in reading.

For study purposes, Example 118 (p. 122) shows the same augmented sixth chord placed within the context of a familiar chord progression. In measure 1 the flatted seventh in the bass leads to the third of the subdominant chord (major, then minor). Next the root of the subdominant chord (Ab), which is a sixth above the bass, is raised (augmented). This resolves to the tonic six-four chord (Eb/Bb). To locate the augmented sixth chord in any key, it helps to know that the bass pitch is a half step above the dominant. In Example 118 the different forms of the augmented sixth chord (Italian, French and German) are shown. In Example 119 the augmented sixth chord on count 3 of measure 3 is a German sixth. The note that follows (B natural) gives it a French flavor. This shift from a German to a French augmented sixth also occurs in Example 117D. The subtlety and beauty of this modulation is lost when it is played without some give and take in the tempo (*tempo rubato*).

Example 118 - Augmented Sixth Chords

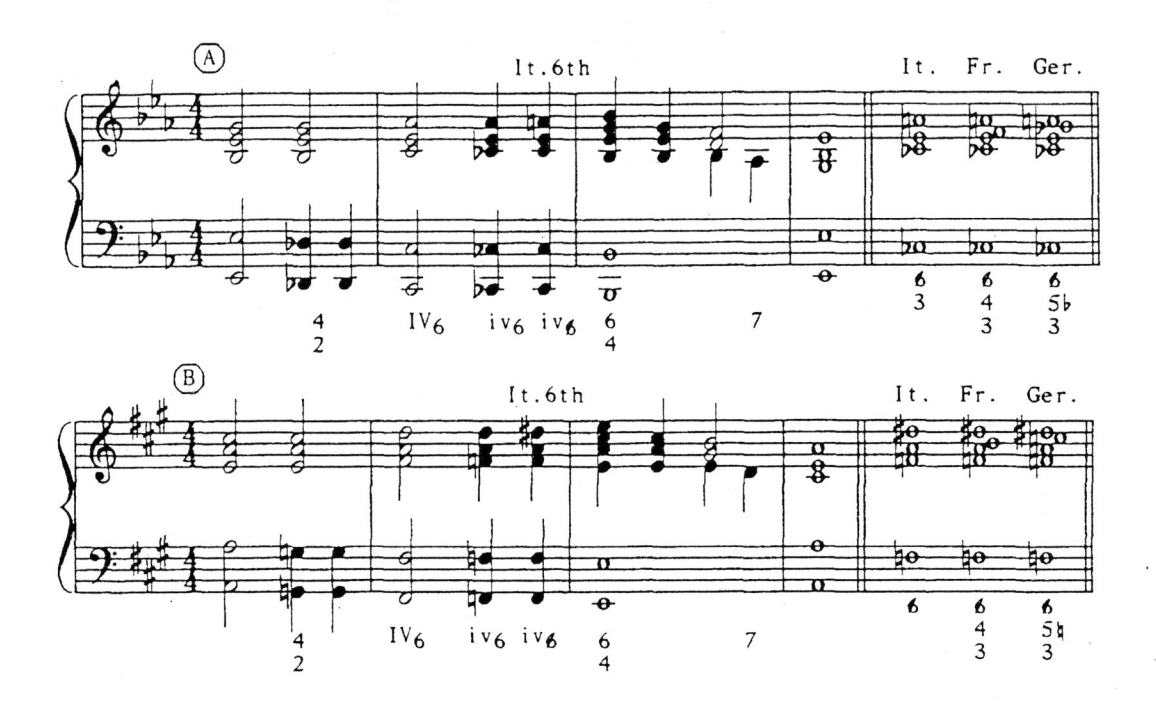

ASSIGNMENT 56

1. Play Example 118A and B. then transpose it to several keys.
2. Play Example 119, then transpose it down a half step, starting in G major.

Example 119 - MADRID (Modulation Using an Augmented Sixth)

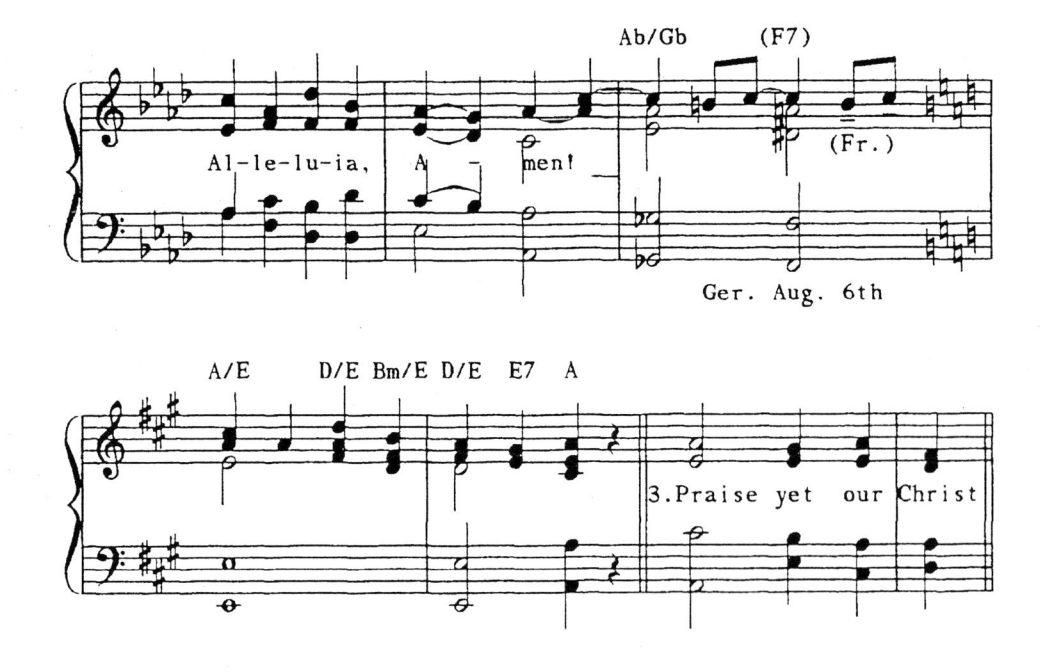

A quick and easy way to play a German augmented sixth is to play a dominant seventh chord a half step higher than the dominant (on the lowered sixth tone of the scale). In Example 119, the augmented sixth could be written as a flatted seventh (Eb). However, the correct notation is D#, because it is resolved <u>upward</u> to E. (The seventh of an F7 chord (Eb) would be resolved <u>downward</u> to D.)

Modulation Down a Half Step

We have become so accustomed to modulation up by half step that we tend to think of downward movement as anti-climactic. In Example 120A the chromatic movement upward to E minor (ii in the new key) creates the illusion of a lift to the next key. The second example (120B) moves in a slightly different manner to ii of the new key, then to a tonic six-four cadence.

Example 120 - Modulation Down a Half Step (Minor Second)

Modulation Up a Whole Step

One of the ingredients of an effective modulation that has been demonstrated in the preceding examples is the melodic/harmonic movement that is initiated as the last pitch of the melody is sustained. This alerts the singers to their need to delay the beginning of the next stanza. However, it is mandatory that this movement not interfere with the sustained pitch of the melody. In Example 121, which shows what **not** to do, the movement to the E major chord creates an undesirable clash between melody and harmony.

Chapter 8 - Modulation

Example 121 - Whole Step Modulation that Interrupts Final Pitch

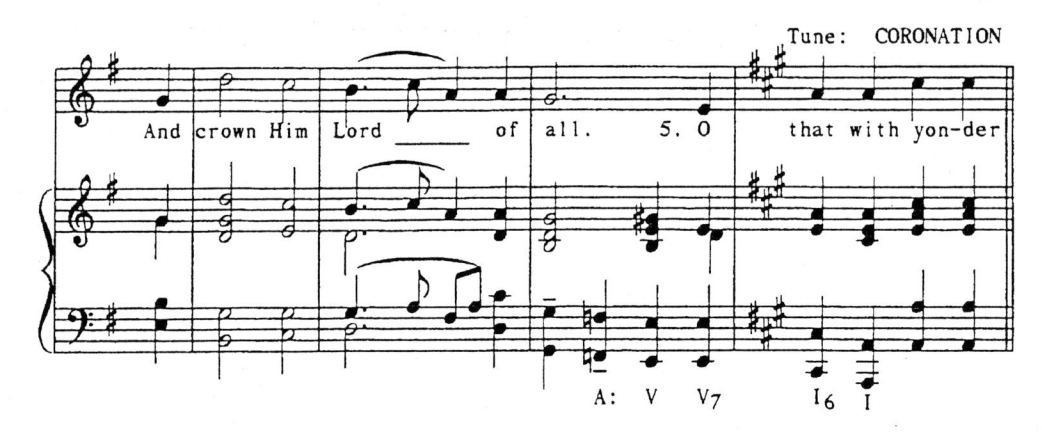

Tune: CORONATION

A: V   V7   I6   I

Pivot Chord Modulation

In the first example that follows (Example 122A), the connecting link between the keys of F and G is the pivot chord - A minor. This chord functions as Roman numeral iii in the original key and as Roman numeral ii in the new key (**35.mid** or **CD 35**). Example 122A ends with the tonic chord of the new key (G major), but it could end with a D major chord which is the dominant of the new key (see Example 123, m. 3). A simple application of the above modulation is shown in Example 123. For a more direct modulation without a pivot chord, see Example 122B.

Example 122- Pivot Chord Modulation Up a Whole Step

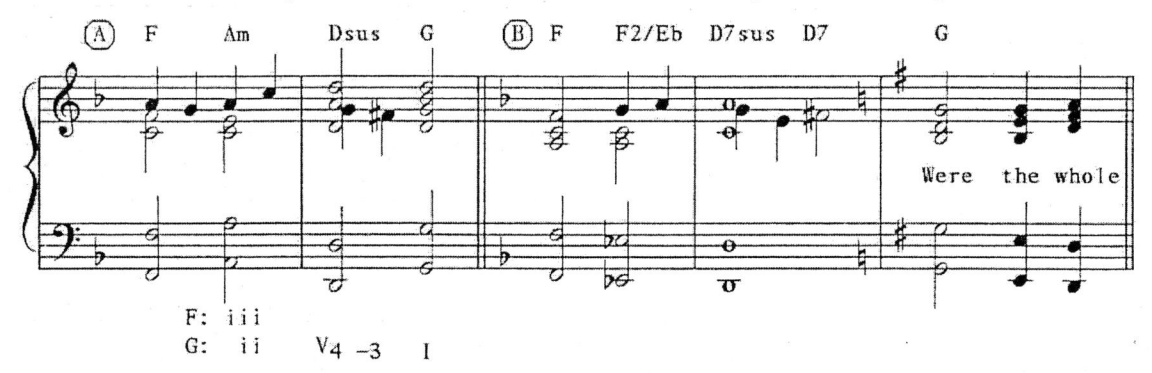

F: iii
G: ii   V4–3   I

Example 123 - SOLID ROCK (Pivot Chord Modulation)

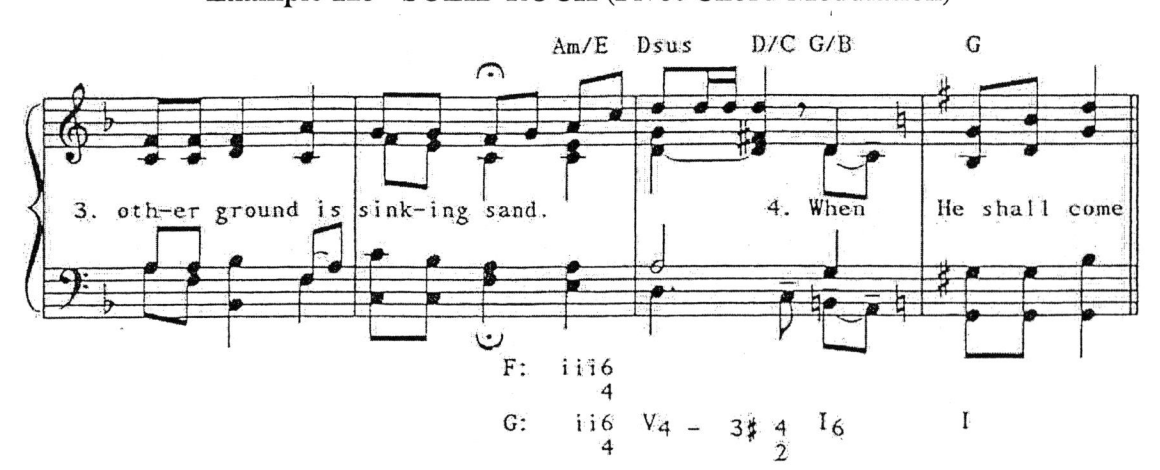

F: iii6/4
G: ii6/4   V4 – 3♯ 4/2   I6   I

In Example 124A the pivot chord (A minor), which is introduced in measure 4 and repeated in measure 5, is strongly reinforced by its use in measure 6 with the dominant pedal point of the new key (**36.mid** or **CD 36**). This modulation is even more effective when played on the organ, because of the organ's sustaining power (see Example 124B for an adaptation for organ).

Example 124 – Praise to the Lord (Pivot Chord over Dominant Ped. Pt.)
LOBE DEN HERREN

ASSIGNMENT 57

1. Modulate up a whole step from Db, Eb, Bb and C, using Example 122 as a model.
2. Use this progression for a modulation from F to G for the final stanza of "Hark! the Herald Angels Sing" (TWC 171) or D to E for the last stanza of "Joy to the World" (TWC 146). The motif from measure 12 ("heaven and nature sing") could be introduced as the last pitch of the tune is sung.

Chapter 8 - Modulation

In the final application of this principle (Example 125), the pivot chord is introduced by means of an augmented sixth chord, the bass of which descends by half step to the fifth of the chord (Fm/C). A diminished passing chord (B dim. 7) leads to the tonic six-four chord of the new key (Eb/Bb). Although the augmented sixth is usually resolved to a tonic six-four chord (see Examples 117 D, 118-119), there are other possible resolutions, including resolution to the mediant six-four. (**37.mid** or **CD 37**)

Example 125 – Crown Him with Many Crowns (Pivot Chord with Augmented 6th)

ASSIGNMENT 58

Play Example 125 as written, then use it for a modulation from D to E.

Modulation Down a Whole Step (Major 2nd)

Modulation down a whole step for a final stanza would likely be anti-climactic, but it can be used effectively between songs (**38.mid** or **CD 38**). The final chord of the original key is sustained for its full rhythmic value, or longer. It is then changed from major to minor, and this altered chord functions as the supertonic (ii) of the new key, moving to V, then I (see Example 126).

Example 126 – Go to Dark Gethsemane (Modulation Down a Whole Step)

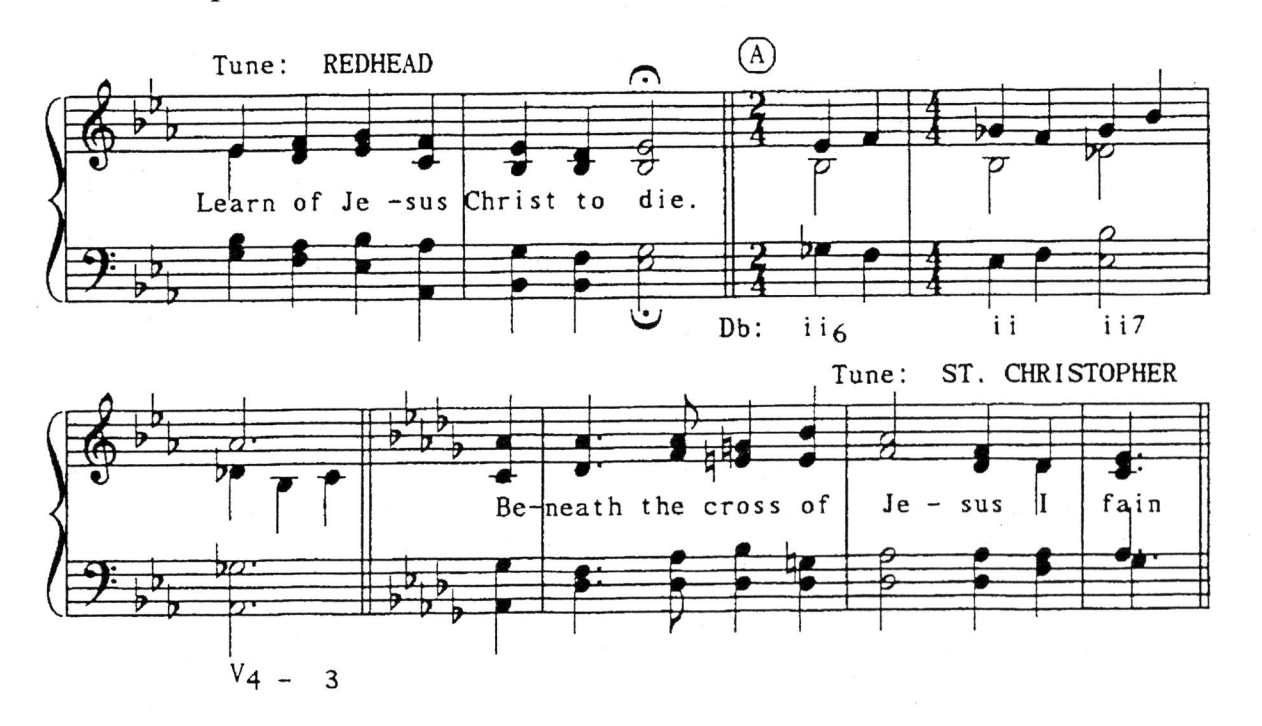

ASSIGNMENT 59

1. Connect the following songs with the progression ii - **V** - **I** used in Example 126.
   (a) My Jesus, I Love Thee (F) - Fairest Lord Jesus (Eb) (TWC 101 &115)
   (b) Have Thine Own Way (Eb) - I Surrender All (Db) (TWC 584 & 579)
   (c) Holy, Holy, Holy (D) and Holy, Holy by Owens (C) (TWC 2 & SPW 141)
2. Use the above progression for a transition from "Day by Day" (Eb) to "Near to the Heart of God" (Db) (TWC 367 & 542). Suggestion: Use the last phrase of "Day by Day" sequentially, starting with <u>Eb minor which is the ii chord in Db major</u> (see chart below).

Modulation Down a Minor Third
Shifts from Major to Relative Minor (Down a Minor Third)

A change from a major key to the minor key that has the same key signature is so natural that it can be done without any modulation. In Chapter Five ("Substitute Chords"), we noted that in shifting from the tonic chord (I) to the submediant chord (vi), two pitches remain the same. To experience this change within the context of a song, play "Love Divine, All Loves Excelling" (Example 127). The final pitch of the fourth phrase (Do, or 1) becomes the third pitch of the G minor scale, the submediant harmony (iii).

Example 127 - BEECHER (Shift from Tonic to Sub-Mediant Harmony)

The following list of songs shows how a shift from major to relative minor between songs can be used to facilitate an uninterrupted flow of worship in song:
1. Antiphonal Praise (Eb) and Sing Alleluia (Cm), (SPW 25 & TWC 771)
2. God Himself is With Us (F) and Let All Mortal Flesh (Dm), (TWC 799 & 167)
3. Hosanna (G) and King of Kings (Em), (SPW 82 and TWC 110)
3. My All in All (D) and You Are My Hiding Place (Bm), (SPW 215 and 230)
4. O Little Town of Bethlehem (F) and Let All Mortal Flesh (TWC 155 and 167)

Chapter 8 - Modulation

If a sudden shift of harmony is not desired, the progressions shown in the following examples could be used. In Example 128, a change of key is achieved through the use of a pivot chord. G minor, which is Roman numeral ii in the key of F major, functions as Roman numeral iv in the key of D minor.

Example 128 - Pivot Chord Modulation from Major to Relative Minor

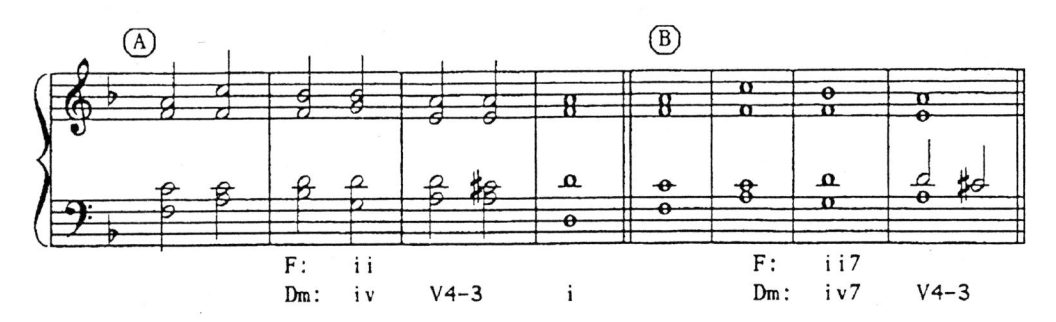

```
F:   ii                        F:   ii7
Dm:  iv    V4-3    i           Dm:  iv7   V4-3
```

Note: The progression in Example 128A could also lead to a major key (see Example 129).

Example 129 - Modulation Down a Minor Third to a Major Key (VI)

Tune: HAMBURG

De-mands my life, my soul, my all.

Tune: DUNCANNON

King of my life, I crown thee now

Modulation down a minor third can also be achieved by adding a flatted seventh to the tonic chord of the original key, which leads to the subdominant harmony (IV). Because the root of the subdominant chord is a half step above the dominant of the new key, an augmented sixth added to this chord leads to the tonic six-four of the new key (see Example 130). In Example 131 the same progression is used with a descending bass scale line (**39.mid** or **CD 39**).

Chapter 8 - Modulation

Example 130 - Modulation Down a Minor Third Via an Augmented Sixth

Example 131 – Down a Minor Third Using an Augmented Sixth Chord

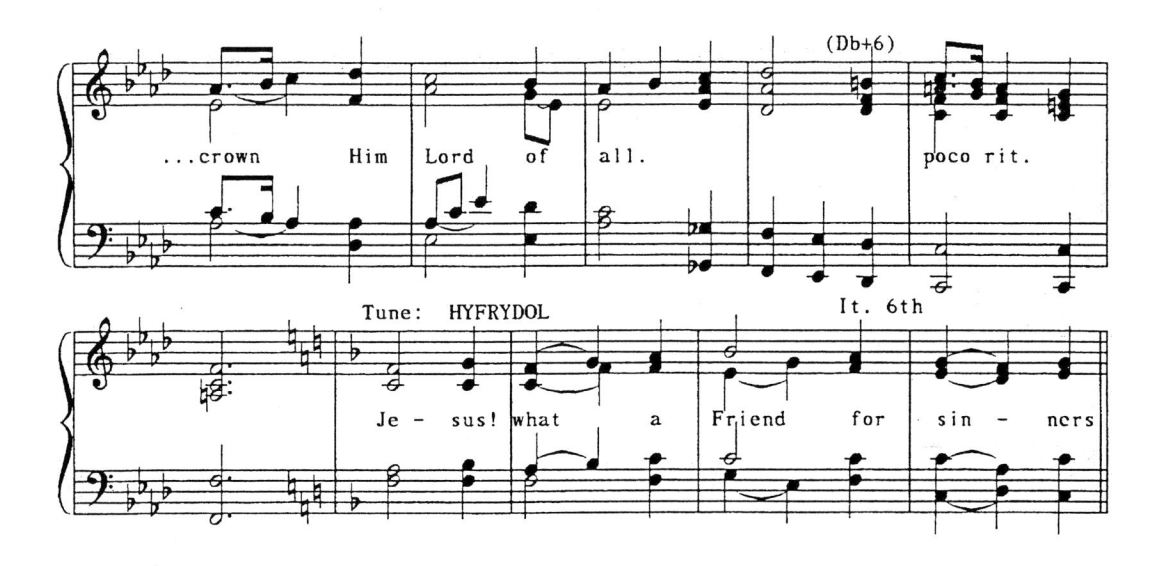

ASSIGNMENT 60

1. Adapt Example 128A for use in modulating from "Have Thine Own Way" (Eb) to "Change My Heart, 0 God" (C). (TWC 584 and SPW 195)
2. Study Examples 130 and 131, then adapt this progression for the following modulations:
   - Majesty (Bb) to All Hail the Power (G) (TWC 98 and 95)
   - Angels from the Realms (Bb) to Hark! the Herald (G) (TWC 174 and 171) (Note: Early editions of most hymnals have the latter hymn in G.)
   - In the Garden (Ab) to What a Friend (F) (TWC 242 and 622)

Modulation Up a Minor Third

A well-known example of this change occurs in the Epiphany hymn, "We Three Kings." After the stanza, which is in E minor, there is a sudden shift to G major for the refrain. When this shift to the relative major occurs between songs, there is no need for a modulation (see Example 132).

Chapter 8 - Modulation

Example 132 - From ABERYSTWYTH to JESUS, I COME (Em to G)

The following list of songs shows how a shift from minor to relative major can be used to facilitate an uninterrupted flow of worship in song:

1. Built on the Rock (Cm) and The Church's One Foundadtion (Eb), (TWC 705 and 689)
2. I Will Celebrate (Em) and I Will Sing of My Redeemer (G), (SPW 147 and TH 506)
3. I Want Jesus to Walk with Me (Dm) and 0 Jesus, I Have Promised (F) (TWC 642 and 648)
4. The Battle Belongs to the Lord (Em) and Be Strong in the Lord (G), (TWC 672 and 661)
5. What Child Is This? (Em) and Hark! the Herald Angels Sing (G), (TWC 150 and 171) (Note: Early editions of most hymnals have the latter hymn in G.)

Work Space

Modulation Up a Minor Third, Using Succession of Fifths

Modulation up a minor third, as from G to Bb, is quite easy when you realize that the final chord of the original key (G) leads strongly to Cm, which is Roman numeral ii (the supertonic) of Bb major (**40.mid** or **CD 40**). The progression ii -V -I (Cm F Bb) firmly establishes the new key (see circled chord tones in Example 133).

Chapter 8 - Modulation

Example 133 - Modulation Up a Minor Third, Using Succession of Fifths
All Hail the Power of Jesus' Name – with Change of Tune

ASSIGNMENT 61

1. Play CORONATION ("All Hail the Power") in F (stanzas 1-3, then modulate to Ab for DIADEM (stanzas 4-5). (TWC 95 and 93)
2. Use the above progression for a modulation from "When I Survey" (F) to "More Love To Thee, O Christ" (Ab). (TWC 213 and 555)

Modulation Down a Major Third

One of the most beautiful tonal relationships is that of a major third (**41.mid** or **CD 41**). In the following transition from "Take My Life and Let It Be Consecrated" to "I Surrender All," the final pitch of the first melody (F) is also the starting pitch of the next (Example 134A). This transition can be made without a modulation because of the common tone - F. Example 134B shows a modulation down a major third that could be used if time is needed to find the next hymn, or if the worship leader needs to hear the new key to find his/her pitch.

Chapter 8 - Modulation

Example 134 - From HENDON To SURRENDER (Down a Major Third)
Take My Life and Let It Be Consecrated to I Surrender All

[Musical notation: Tune: HENDON transitioning to Tune: SURRENDER, with lyrics "ev-er, on-ly, all for thee. All to Je-sus" and continuation "all for thee." with Transition to SURRENDER, ending "poco rit. All to Je-sus I sur-ren-der"]

Examples of Common-Tone Modulation

Other examples of modulations down a major third that could be accomplished by means of a common-tone are listed below. The song that follows must begin with the third tone of the scale (Mi or 3).

1. Joyful, Joyful, We Adore Thee (G) to Jesus, Name above All Names (Eb) (TWC 20 and 106)
2. God Will Make a Way (G) to Be Still, My Soul (Eb) (SPW 40 and TWC 530)
3. Be Still, My Soul (F) to Savior, Like a Shepherd, Lead Us (Db) (TH 347 and TH 462)
4. Take My Life and Let It Be Consecrated (F) to Lord, Be Glorified (Db) (TWC 568 and 537)
    Note: Change the key signature of the latter song from 2 sharps to 5 flats
5. Spirit of the Living God (F) to Open Our Eyes, Lord (Db) (TWC 297 and 536)
    Note: Change the key signature of TWC 536, as in #4 above.
6. Jesus Loves Me (C) to Oh, How He Loves You and Me (Ab) (TWC 470 and 479)
7. I Have Decided to Follow Jesus (C) to Precious Lord, Take My Hand (Ab) (TWC 576 and TH 463)

Chapter 8 - Modulation

For modulations down a major third, where there is no common tone in the melody, the following progression may be adapted (**42.mid** or **CD 42**):

Example 135 - Modulation Down a Major Third

Fm: iv
Db: vi   N6   I$_4^6$ V$_4$ - 3

Modulation Up a Major Third

Augmented sixth chords have been used in Examples 117D, 118, 119, 125, 130, and 131. In each case the augmented sixth chord resolves to a second inversion chord. In Example 136 the transition from Eb to G is accomplished by adding an augmented sixth (C#) to the Eb chord (**43.mid** or **CD 43**). As the C# resolves upward to D, the bass descends to D. The chord to which it resolves (G/D) is a second inversion of the tonic chord (I) in G major. This is the typical resolution of an augmented sixth chord.

Example 136 - Modulation from Eb to G by Means of the Augmented Sixth
Sing Praise to God Who Reigns Above to Praise Him! Praise Him!

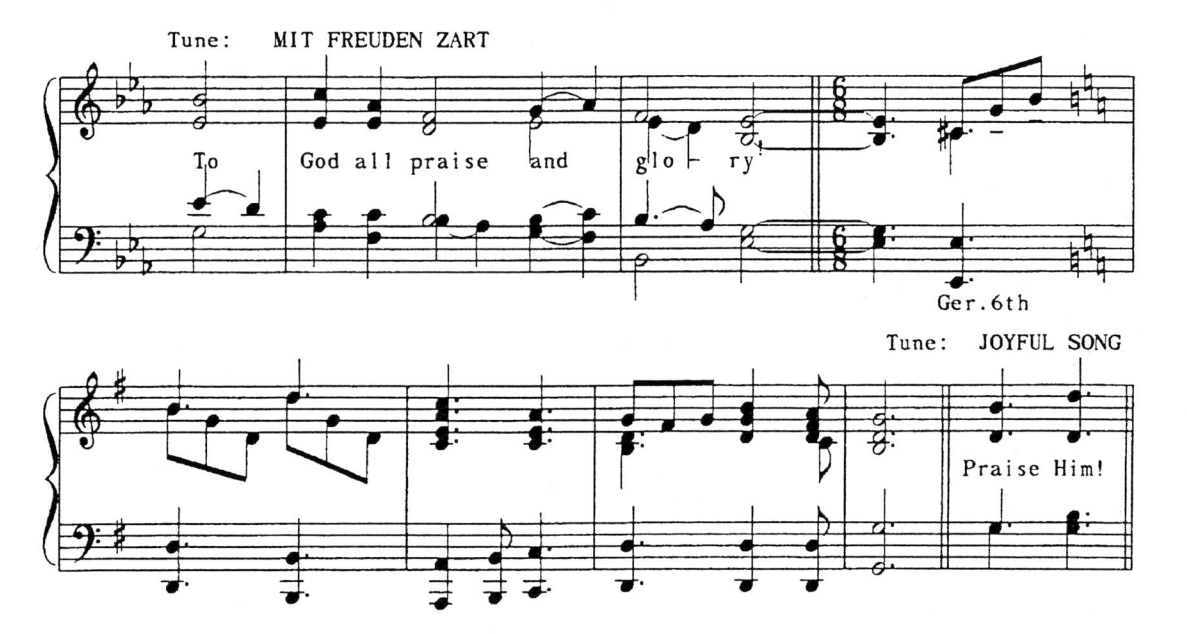

Tune: MIT FREUDEN ZART

To God all praise and glory

Ger.6th

Tune: JOYFUL SONG

Praise Him!

Chapter 8 - Modulation

In Example 137 there is a shift from Db to Fm, the mediant harmony (iii). As in the modulation shown in Example 136, the augmented sixth chord is used to modulate up a major third. Unlike the previous augmented sixth chord resolutions (except Example 125), this example resolves to a minor six-four chord (Fm/C). (**44.mid** or **CD 44**)

Example 137 - O HOLY NIGHT
(Modulation Up a Major Third to the Mediant Harmony - iii)

The Neapolitan Sixth - Another Shade of Subdominant

In Example 138 which follows, the shift to F minor that occurs in "O Holy Night" is used as a segue between two hymns: "Beneath the Cross of Jesus" (Db) and "Ah, Holy Jesus" (Fm). An augmented sixth is added to the final Db chord of the first hymn, and this resolves to Fm/C, which is the tonic six-four of the new key - F minor (**45.mid** or **CD 45**). The key of F minor is established by means of the following progression: Bbm - **Gb/Bb** - Fm/C – Csus - C7 - Fm (see measures 4-7). The chord highlighted by boldface print (**Gb/Bb**) is a Neapolitan sixth. This chord, which is an altered supertonic chord, was commonly used in the late 17th century in place of the subdominant chord (iv). Unlike the standard supertonic chord which, in minor keys, is a diminished chord (G Bb Db in this key), the Neapolitan chord is a major chord built on the lowered (flatted) second tone of the scale (Gb Bb Db). Another example can be found in Examples 84 and 135.

Chapter 8 - Modulation

Example 138 - Modulation from Db to F Minor

[Musical notation: Tune: ST. CHRISTOPHER with text "My glo-ry all the cross." with chord analysis Fm: Ger.6, i6/4, iv, N6, i6/4, leading to Tune: HERZLIEBSTER JESU with text "1. Ah, ho-ly Je-sus, how have you of-fend-ed,"]

Modulation Down a Fifth to the Subdominant (or Up a Fourth)

No segue is required when moving to a song related by succession of fifths. Just remember that a song in F (signature of one flat) leads naturally to a song in Bb (two flats), and Bb leads to Eb (three flats). With sharp keys, the number of sharps decreases as you move through the succession of fifths. A song in D (two sharps) leads to G (one sharp), and G leads to C. Several examples of worship segments linked by succession of fifths follow:

1. Shine, Jesus, Shine (A) to We Will Glorify (D) (TWC 721 & 118)
2. Come, Thou Fount (D) to Grace Greater Than Our Sins (G) and Wonderful Grace of Jesus (C) (TWC 45, 472 & 497)
3. When Morning Gilds the Skies (C) to I Exalt Thee (F) (TWC 99 & SPW 18)
4. Bind Us Together (F) to We Are One in the Bond of Love (Bb) (TWC 690 & 696)
5. Revive Us Again (F) to The Vision of a Dying World (Bb) (TWC 723 & 737)
6. *Christmas Medley (**46.mid** or **CD 46**)
   - Holy Night (SPW 160 in C)
   - Away in a Manger (SPW 149 in F)
   - Silent Night (SPW 164 in Bb)

Chapter 8 - Modulation

Modulation Down a Fourth to the Dominant (or Up a Fifth)

A simple way to move through the succession of fifths in the opposite direction is shown in Example 139A. The root of the F chord (1) becomes the seventh of G7 which is V7 in C major. In moving from C to G, the root of the C chord becomes the seventh of the D7 chord which leads to G. In a true modulation, the new key is suggested, then confirmed by means of a cadence. In Example 139B, the accidental (B natural) is used to suggest the new key. The key of C is then confirmed by means of the cadence – ii$_6$ - V7 - I (Dm G7 C).

Example 139 - Modulation to the Key of the Dominant

In Example 140 the new key is introduced by a half cadence, then confirmed by the first two chords of the succeeding hymn ("When Peace Like a River").

Example 140 - From WYE VALLEY to VILLE DU HAVRE
(Modulation to the Dominant Harmony)

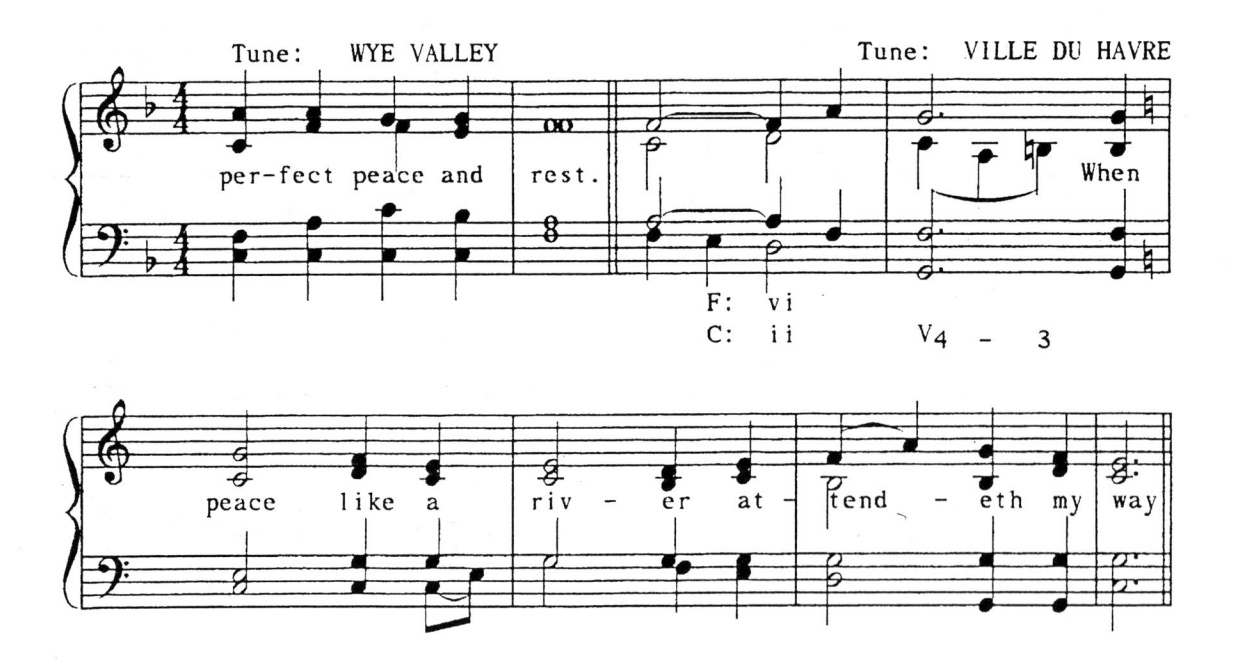

Chapter 8 - Modulation

ASSIGNMENT 62

1. Select and play several combinations from the list of common-tone modulations (p. 132), then return to the first key by using an augmented sixth (see Example 137 and 138).
2. Transpose Example 138 to C, then to Bb. Apply this in creating a modulation from "Angels from the Realms of Glory" (Bb) to "Joy to the World (D). (TWC 174 and 146).
3. Select and play several song combinations involving succession of fifths (p. 133).
3. Play Example 139A and continue through the entire <u>reverse</u> succession of fifths (modulation to the dominant).
4. Apply the progression used in Example 140 to modulate from "Grace Greater Than Our Sin" (G) to "Blessed Assurance" (D). (TWC 472 and 514).

Modulation Up or Down a Tri-Tone (Three Whole Steps)

Although this is not a common modulation, it is good to have a means of making this transition, in the event that someone without a knowledge of key relationships selects songs a tri-tone apart (e.g. Ab to D). The following progression is similar to that used for modulation down a half step. The difference is that the leading tone (G#) in this case leads to A major instead of A minor (compare Example 141A with Example 120B).

Example 141 - Modulations Down a Tri-Tone

D: V_2^4 ofV V_6 V $_2^4$ I_6 IV V_{4-3}

D: iii IV_{9-8} I_4^6 V_{4-3}^7 I

Modulations Up a Sixth and Up a Seventh

In that the intervals of a sixth and seventh are inversions of thirds and seconds respectively, modulations up a sixth and seventh have already been covered. For modulation up a minor sixth, see **Modulation Down a Major Third.** For modulation up a major sixth, see **Modulation Down a Minor Third.** For modulation up a minor seventh, see **Modulation Down a Major Second,** and for modulation up a major seventh, see **Modulation Down a Minor Second.**

Summary

As I conclude this chapter, I am reminded how long it has taken me to develop basic formulas for modulating to different keys. I realize, too, that this is not an exhaustive treatment of the subject. For me, personally, an essential factor in my progress has been a fascination with the delight that a well-crafted modulation provides. The motivation to develop more than a "skeletal" progression of chords that gets me to the next key continues to stimulate my God-given creativity. Necessity can also serve as motivation. For example, the current emphasis in worship on uninterrupted segments of song has caused many musicians to desire the ability to modulate effectively. Continual practice in creating musical segues will bring greater and greater enjoyment and mastery in this area of keyboard development. Keep trying!

Work Space

Work Space

Chapter 8 - Modulation

Work Space

138

The Chapter Nine

IMPROVISATION

My understanding of what improvisation is has been broadened through a number of experiences. The insights gained through these learning experiences have encouraged me in my efforts to make music in a creative, spontaneous manner. The following personal reflections are offered as encouragement as we embark on what, for some, may be a new musical journey.

First, I realized that I have creative potential by virtue of the fact that I am made in the image of God, Who is the Creator and Sustainer of everything. Then, too, there is safety in knowing that His love for the whole world includes me. This God-given confidence provides the freedom to venture beyond my comfort zone, to lean into life without the fear that could so easily stifle creative expression.

Second, there is encouragement in knowing that only God created *ex nihilo,* out of nothing. All of us who have been making music for any length of time have an inner storage bank of melodies, rhythms, and harmonies that are just waiting to be used in new ways. Slowly, then more rapidly, these can be recalled in a spontaneous way to express a part of me that might otherwise remain unknown, even to myself.

Third, I see a similarity between personal prayer and musical improvisation. Some of the most meaningful prayers that I have heard and used come from the hymnal and historical liturgies such as those in *The Book of Common Prayer.* However, to rely solely on the use of prayers that others have written would be to neglect a vital aspect of prayer, namely, the personal offering of the heart to God. Just as spontaneous prayer allows me to express my own thoughts to God, spontaneous music-making allows me to express my own musical "thoughts." The value of these experiences is not determined by the artistic merit of that which is expressed.

Fourth, I have been encouraged to learn that those who have excelled in the art of improvisation have worked to acquire their abilities. I stood amazed at the improvisatory skills of some of my teachers, people like Inda Howland, Bob Abramson, and Marta Sanchez. At one time I thought this all "just happened," but I suspect that even they had to work at it.

One of the great improvisateurs of all times was Marcel Dupré, a French organist and composer. In reading Michael Murray's biography of Dupré, I learned that he would spend hours doing counterpoint exercises in preparation for a competition in improvisation (Murray 1985). I was surprised to learn that something that appears to be spontaneous is, in fact, dependent upon rigorous discipline. To quote Murray,

> The word improvisation, with its connotations of looseness and unordered spontaneity, belies the skill, discipline and mental effort required to practice the art at its highest: to improvise well poses no less a challenge to competence than do the games of chess and certain exercises in higher mathematics. (Murray 1985, 38)

I began to realize that my analytical work, likewise, was freeing me to use chords and compositional devices more freely. However, more basic than analysis is the matter of nurturing one's instinctive desire to express thought and feeling through song and dance. This is at the root of music making. As a Christian musician, I have also found that spiritual attitudes such as praise, thanksgiving, adoration, and petition can serve both as motivation and as starting points for improvisation. I was encouraged to learn that the great Russian composer

Chapter 9 - Improvisation

Igor Stravinsky drew inspiration from things that might be regarded as commonplace. In a lecture at Harvard University, he gave this description of the creative process:

> The faculty of creating is never given to us all by itself. It always goes hand in hand with the gift of observation. And the true creator may be recognized by his ability always to find about him in the commonest and humblest thing, items worthy of note. He does not have to concern himself with a beautiful landscape; he does not have to concern himself with rare and precious objects. He does not have to put forth in search of discoveries: they are always within his reach. He will have only to cast a glance about him. Familiar things, things that are everywhere, attract his attention. The least accident holds his interest and guides his operations. If his finger slips, he will notice it; on occasion, he may draw profit from something unforeseen that a momentary lapse reveals to him. (Stravinsky 1947, 56)

Shortly after I had read the above lines, I was playing the piano and my finger slipped. I'm sure you know the feeling. Rather than cringe, I decided to delight in the sound that I played. Of course not all mistakes that we make are as delightful as this one was! Allow me to describe what happened. I was transposing the accompaniment of Kurt Kaiser's song, "Pass It On," from D to Eb. Instead of playing what is notated as Example 142A, my left hand slipped and I played the chord notated as Example 142B. The sound was delightful, so I played the mistake

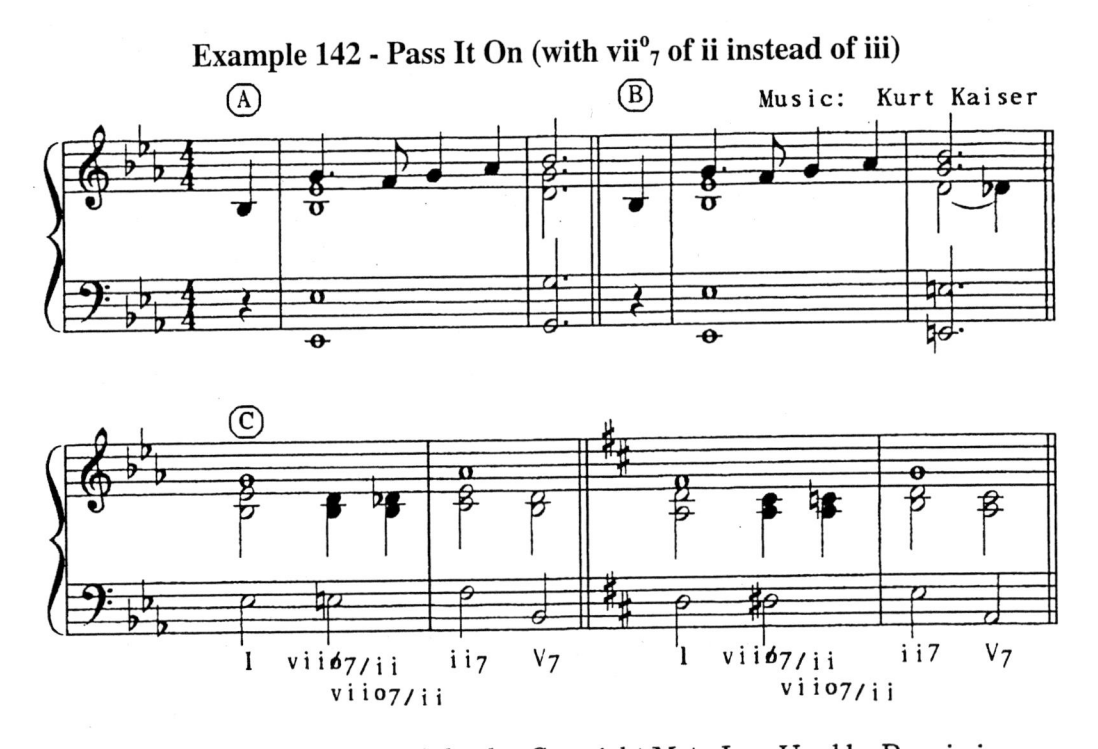

Example 142 - Pass It On (with vii°$_7$ of ii instead of iii)

Music: Kurt Kaiser

© 1969 Communique Music/adm. by Copyright Mgt., Inc. Used by Permission.

again, intentionally this time. It wasn't a chord that I had never played before, but the serendipitous nature of the experience gave a freshness to the sound. This reminded me of a progression used by many composers, including Irving Berlin in his song, "Give Me Your Tired, Your Poor." Although I hadn't played the song for years, I was encouraged to find that I could still play nearly all of it without referring to the music. After analyzing the opening progression as vii°$_7$ of ii, I remembered other songs that begin in a similar manner, songs like "Shepherd of Love" and "Mame." After transposing the beginning phrase of these songs to several keys, I started to search for other possible uses of this progression. I found it could be used with "Lord, Be Glorified" (TWC 537) and "Holy, Holy" by Jimmie Owens. When I used these variations in worship, a friend said that he had to make some alterations in the tenor part he was accustomed to singing. Too many alterations of the harmony might deter some people from singing in harmony. Most organists wait until the final stanza of a hymn to do a free harmonization, and the congregation is asked to sing unison.

Variations on the Submediant Chord

One day I was comparing my newly-discovered harmonies for "Holy, Holy" with the traditional chords, and I discovered something very interesting. I began to see more clearly how a simple chord progression can be varied through exploration. The following examples serve as illustrations of how the disciplines developed in Chapter Five ("Substitute Chords: The Changing Function of a Tone") can be used in improvising new harmonies.

Example 143 - Holy, Holy (with I and V)

Example 144 - Holy, Holy (with I, vi, ii and V)

Chapter 9 - Improvisation

Example 145 - Holy, Holy (with Altered Submediant, VI)
Step Three

Example 146 - Holy, Holy (Further Variations of Altered Submediant)

Step Four

© 1972 Lexicon Music, Inc./ASCAP. All Rights Reserved.
International Copyright Secured. Used by Permission.

Improvisation that involves the variation of harmonies, as in the above examples, requires an understanding of chords and how they function. Although this can be a source of delight for the experienced musician, it is not appropriate as a starting point in learning to improvise.

A Good Way to Begin: Improvising Pentatonic Melodies

Limiting yourself to the five tones of the pentatonic scale is a good way to begin improvisation. This scale is sometimes referred to as a "gapped" scale. Unlike the major scale, which consists of eight consecutive pitches (1 2 3 4 5 6 7 8, or Do Re Mi Fa So La Ti Do), the pentatonic scale does not include 4 and 7, or Fa and Ti, hence the term "gapped." A simple way to experience this scale is to play the black keys on the piano, beginning with Gb or F# and ending one octave higher.

Chapter 9 - Improvisation

ASSIGNMENT 63

1. To establish a feeling for the pentatonic scale, complete the following tunes, using only the black keys of the piano or other keyboard.
2. Review "Praise Him in the Morning" (Example 5C with **10.mid** or **CD 10**).

Example 147 - Pentatonic Melodies to Complete

An interesting way to begin black key (pentatonic) improvisation is to take a fragment of melody, more properly called a "motif," and create a melodic phrase through repetition and expansion of the motif. This experience may be enriched by the teacher's providing a chordal background as in Examples 148A and B (**47.mid** or **CD 47**). The rhythm patterns of a name (places, people or things) may be used as a starting point. Although the supporting chords may include pitches that are not in the pentatonic scale, the melodic improvisation is done on black keys only. This is almost certain to provide immediate success and a sense of amazement that creating new melodies can be so easy and rewarding!

Example 148 - Black Key Improvisation with Harmonic Background

Chapter 9 - Improvisation

(B) Additional accompaniment patterns

ASSIGNMENT 64

1. Select or create a motif and develop it while someone else provides an accompaniment or while listening to the recorded accompaniment (**47.mid** or **CD 47**).
2. Select one of the accompaniment patterns from Example 148 and play it while doing a vocal improvisation.

Creating Melodies from Basic Rhythm Patterns

A melody that is easily sung is often comprised of two or more recurring rhythm patterns. After looking through the ternary patterns listed in Example 149, note how they are combined in the melodies in Example 150. All of the ternary patterns (2-8) are equal in length to the dotted quarter note. The binary patterns are equal in length to the quarter note.

Example 149 - Ternary and Binary Patterns

A Fun Way to Do Dictation

A creative way of facilitating the mastery of basic patterns was developed by Dr. Marta Sanchez, Professor of Music at Carnegie-Mellon University. Dr. Sanchez used the following sequence: Listen, perform, analyze (**48.mid** or **CD 48**). The sequence is outlined below:

1. The students listen for the steady beat established by the left hand chord progression in Example 150, then to the improvised melodic phrase.
2. The phrase is sung, played or clapped in echo fashion.
3. The sequence of rhythm patterns is analyzed and represented by numbers.

Example 150 shows how rhythm patterns are introduced after the beat has been established with a steady progression of left hand chords.

Space for Practice of Dication Skills

1. _ _ _ _   6. _ _ _ _   11. _ _ _ _
2. _ _ _ _   7. _ _ _ _   12. _ _ _ _
3. _ _ _ _   8. _ _ _ _   13. _ _ _ _
4. _ _ _ _   9. _ _ _ _   14. _ _ _ _
5. _ _ _ _   10. _ _ _ _   15. _ _ _ _

Chapter 9 - Improvisation

The Example 150 - Binary Patterns Combined

The melody shown in Example 150 consists of binary patterns which would be analyzed as follows: 2 2 4 1 (see Example 149 for the list of binary patterns). A phrase of a song could be used for ear training. For example, the first two measures of "Wonderful Words of Life" (Example 151) could be played or sung, then echoed and analyzed. Using the list of ternary patterns in Example 149, the sequence of rhythm patterns would be analyzed as follows:

3 2 3 1   2 3 1 1.

Both of the melodies analyzed in Example 151 are very singable, because of the recurrence of basic patterns (see "What Child Is This?", the second tune).

Example 151 - Ternary Patterns Combined

The One -Two -Three Method of Melodic Development

Most of us are familiar with the expressions, "On your mark, get set, go!" and "Lights, camera, action!" A melody can be created in a three-step manner by: (1) playing a short motif ("On your mark"), (2) repeating it with or without variation ("Get set"), and (3) developing it ("Go!"). A classic example of this is the opening statement of *Symphony No. 5* by Beethoven. This approach could be used in something as simple as black key improvisation, or a melody improvised over a basic chord progression (see Example 152).

Example 152 - The One-Two-Three Method of Melodic Development

An excellent example of melodic development that involves the gradual expansion of a musical idea is shown in Example 73 (**28.mid** or **CD 28**). Unlike the above example which "takes off," or opens up on the third phrase, the development of Marcello's theme builds to a climax in the fourth phrase.

Through improvisation a student can gain rich insight into the inner workings of musical composition. Through an increased understanding of the intricacies of musical expression gained through improvisation, a performer is better equipped to interpret various styles of music, fulfilling his/her role as "co-author" of the music. This term denotes the team effort of composer and performer.

Embellishing Melodies and Harmonies with Non-Harmonic Tones

In Chapter Two (pp.16-18) the use of various non-harmonic tones (passing tones, neighbor tones and suspensions) were illustrated. In the following example the intervals of a third in the harmony parts (and occasionally in the melody) are filled in with passing tones (P.T.). Since it would be uncommon to use only one kind of embellishment, occasional use is also made of neighbor tones (N.T.) and suspensions (Sus.). Another device that may be used when others are not appropriate is that of moving to a different or related chord tone in order to maintain a sense of rhythmic flow (compare measure 4 of Example 153B with measure 4 of 153C).

Chapter 9 - Improvisation

Example 153 - Embellishing a Hymn Tune with Non-Harmonic Tones
ST. DENIO (Immortal, Invisible)

Chapter 9 - Improvisation

Example 153 (cont.) - Swedish Hymn

ASSIGNMENT 65

1. Improvise in the style shown in Example 150, using binary and ternary patterns from Example 149. (**Note**: For ternary patterns, play left-hand chords as dotted quarter notes.)
2. Improvise a melody using the one-two-three method of construction (see Example 152).
3. Continue the style of embellishment for each hymn in Example 153.
4. Add passing tones to the harmony parts of ASH GROVE (Example 154). After adding passing tones, it might be desirable to eliminate some of them to avoid overuse.

Chapter 9 - Improvisation

Example 154 - Exercise in Adding Passing Tones (ASH GROVE)

The Use of Suspensions

The adding of suspensions in improvisation is a means of increasing the intensity of a musical line. A well-known anthem that beautifully illustrates this is S.S. Wesley's "Lead Me, Lord" (Example 155). The suspensions in the alto part add intensity to the sustained pitches of the soprano line (measures 1-2). Another illustration of suspensions is the alto part of "God Himself is With Us" (Example 77). For more examples of suspensions, listen to **55.mid** and **56.mid** or **CD 55** and **56**.

Example 155 - Lead Me, Lord

Samuel S. Wesley

ASSIGNMENT 66

1. Study the use of suspensions in Examples 45B, 77 and 155.
2. Review the following musical examples, and look for notes in the inner voice parts that could be suspended (held or repeated) to create tension, then released.
   - Twinkle, Twinkle, Little Star (Ex. 42)
   - Angels We Have Heard on High (Ex. 69)
   - Sequential Bass (Ex. 76)
   - Give Thanks (Ex. 80)
   - Eternal Father, Strong to Save (Ex. 86)
   - Love Came Down at Christmas (Ex. 112)

Note: Remember that suspensions usually occur on strong beats and are resolved on weak beats.

Exploring Modal Harmonies
The Subtonic Chord (VII)

In this book the two modes, or scales, that are used the most are the Ionian (major) and Aeolian (minor). In exploring the other Greek church modes, one finds interesting arrangements of half steps and whole steps. For example, the subtonic chord (VII) used in Examples 79 and 80 is derived from the Mixolydian mode. A Mixolydian scale is easily created by playing the white keys from G to G. It is different from a G major scale in that there is a whole step between the seventh and eighth pitches. Another way to create the Mixolydian mode is to lower the seventh pitch of any major scale.

Composers and arrangers sometimes use the subtonic chord as a preparation for V, as in Examples 79 and 80. In Example 156, measure 3, it is used in place of V. In this arrangement there is a shift from ternary to binary rhythm (3 + 2), which will be explained later in the chapter.

Chapter 9 - Improvisation

Example 156 - Variation on Old MacDonald

ASSIGNMENT 67

Select at least two of the following familiar melodies, and explore the use of VII as a substitute or preparation for V. A recorded example is provided in Appendix H, the fourth variation on "What a Friend We Have in Jesus" (see selection D). **(60.mid or CD 60)**

1. Joyful, Joyful, We Adore Thee (TWC 20)
2. Fairest Lord Jesus (TWC 115)
3. Kum Ba Jah (TWC 630)
4. What a Friend We Have in Jesus (TWC 622)

Note: The most likely place to make this substitution is at a half cadence.

Bi-Modal Harmony: Combining Chords from Different Modes

The term "bi-modal" is used to describe the mixing of chords from different modes. In the variation on "Old MacDonald," **(51.mid or CD 51)** the F major chord in measure 3 is borrowed from the Mixolydian mode, and the Eb chord in measure 4 is borrowed from the natural minor scale (also known as the Aeolian mode).

In Example 157 there is an interesting juxtaposition of the minor tonic chord (i) and a major subdominant (IV). In the Dorian mode this is a natural occurrence (see measures 1-5 of Example 157). A Dorian scale can be created easily by playing the white keys from D to D. The Dorian scale is different from the D minor scale in that the sixth scale degree is not flatted (see m.1 of Example 157). For another example of the Dorian mode, play or listen to "What Child Is This" (Example 28, **19.mid or CD 19**). For a comparison of chords derived from the Dorian and minor scales see Example 157B.

Chapter 9 - Improvisation

Example 157 - Dorian Melody (NOEL NOUVELET)

If Example 157 were written with a signature of one flat (D minor), its distinctive Dorian quality would be lost. Another example of mixing minor and Dorian harmony is the harmonization of an excerpt from "Let All Mortal Flesh Keep Silence" (Example 158). Although the song is written in D minor, the major subdominant chord (IV) can be used to create an interesting effect (see m. 6 of Example 158). **Note:** The G major chord can be used only where there is not a Bb in the melody. **Note:** The G major chord could be used earlier, but its effectiveness is greater when delayed until the end of the song.

Example 158 - PICARDY (Minor Tune with Dorian Harmony)

ASSIGNMENT 68

1. Play the Dorian scale (the white keys from D to D).

    If, with a C major key signature, you begin one step higher on D, where would you begin with a signature of two flats?
2. In the work space below, write the Dorian scale with a signature of two flats, then with a signature of one flat.
3. Improvise a Dorian melody over the chord progression provided in Example 159.

Work Space

Chapter 9 - Improvisation

Example 159 - Dorian Improvisation

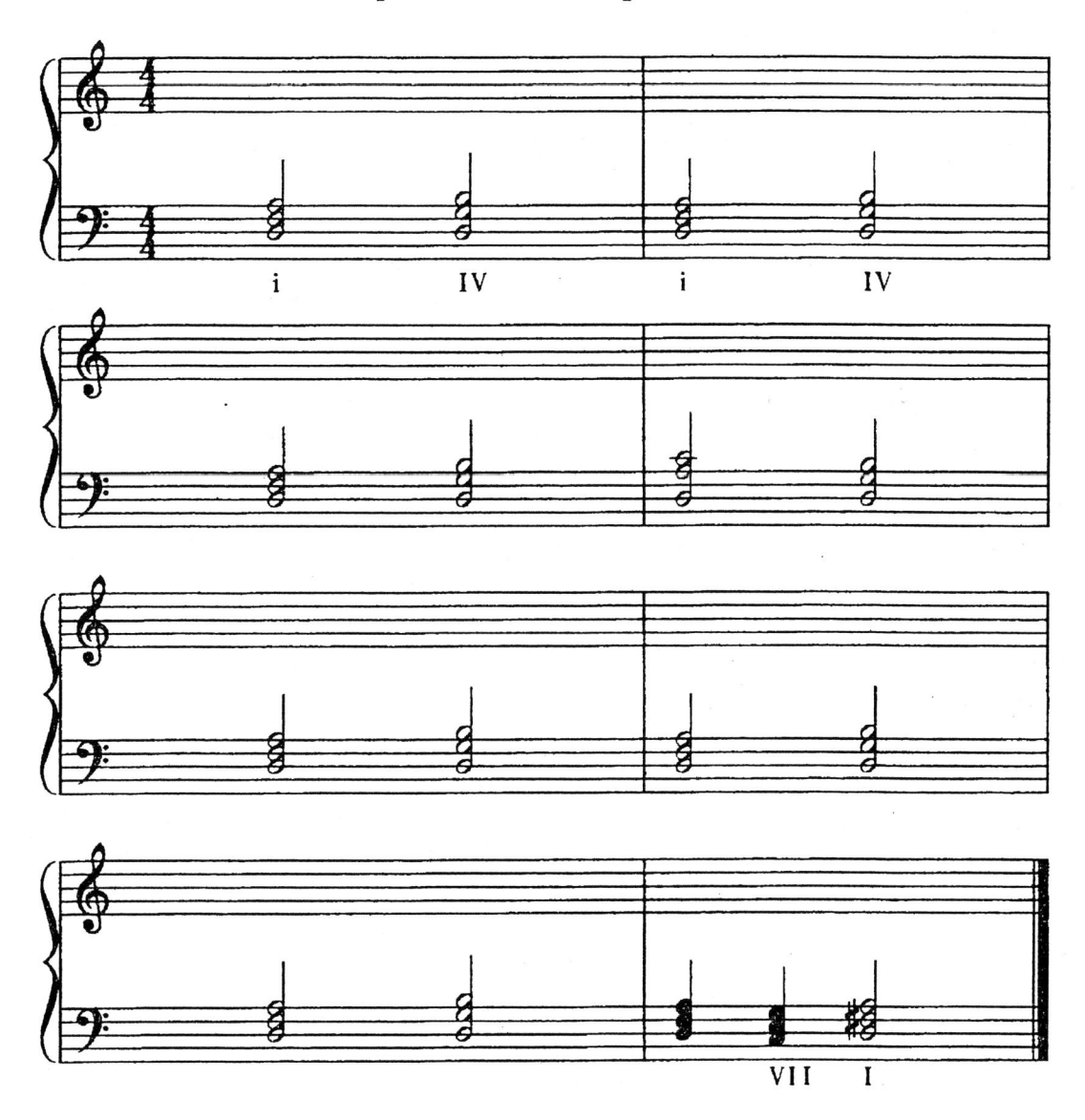

i   IV   i   IV

VII   I

4. Transpose the left hand chord pattern in Example 159 to Dorian with two flats.

Work Space

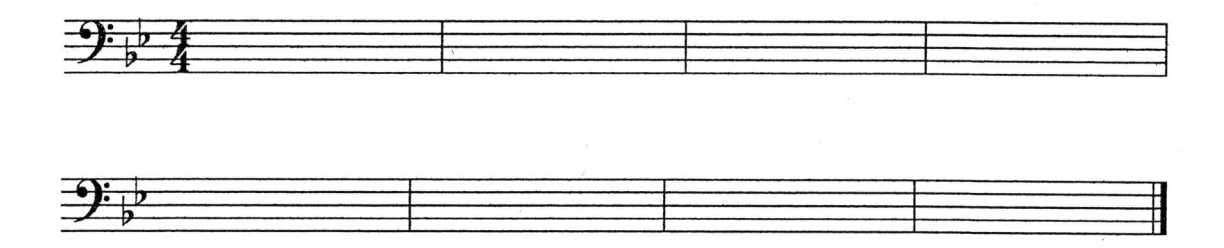

Chapter 9 - Improvisation

Combining Binary and Ternary Rhythms

In current musical practice, shifts of meter are common fare. In Example 160A there are shifts from 3 + 2 to 2 + 3 and vice versa. In Example 160B the pattern that is established in measure one (3 + 2 + 2) is continued. An excellent means of developing a command of such shifts is to change the rhythm of existing melodies, as in Example 156 and the following:

Example 160 - Shifts from Ternary to Binary Rhythm and Vice Versa

ASSIGNMENT 69

1. Sing "Old MacDonald" (Example 156), then play the accompaniment.
2. Complete Examples 160A and B. Establish a feeling for the meter and shifts of meter through rhythmic speech. For example, establish a feeling for 3 + 2 by saying, "quarter dot, quarter." For 2 + 3, say "quarter, quarter dot."
3. Sing each of the following songs to the suggested pattern: "Frere Jacques" (3 + 2), "Twinkle, Twinkle, Little Star" (3 + 2 + 2), "Deck the Hall" (3 + 2 + 2). The same pattern could be used for each measure of "Deck the Hall," but it might be desirable to change the grouping for some measures (2 + 2 + 3).

Chapter 9 - Improvisation

Renaissance Dance Rhythms

One day while playing early church tunes based on Renaissance dance rhythms, I began to explore various rhythmic possibilities for other tunes from this era. I discovered that "O-Sacred Head Now Wounded" could be played with a shift of meter on every other measure (Example 161). Although I thought I was being creative, I later discovered that the melody used for this hymn ("Mein Gmüth ist mir verwirret") was originally in mixed meter.

I should perhaps add that not everything that is done in personal exploration at the keyboard is necessarily appropriate for Sunday morning worship. Not too many congregations would want to sing "We Three Kings" or "O Sacred Head" in mixed meter, even though this version of the latter hymn was included in some hymnals. However, people might be accepting of such rhythmic variations if they were used occasionally as part of an instrumental prelude or offertory. Even modal harmonies, a delight to some listeners, may sound like wrong notes to others. That is part of the risk of exercising our God-given potential for creative expression. **Note**: For examples of early hymn tunes involving shifts of meter, including "A Mighty Fortress," see Alice Parker's excellent coverage of psalter tunes in *Creative Hymn Singing* (Parker 1975, 19-39).

Example 161 - Renaissance Tune with Shift of Meter

Chords That Never Made the Hymnal

There is a standard harmony for each hymn. Consequently, one can move from one hymnal to another and find the same progression of chords. Even when new chords are introduced, they are usually used in addition to the traditional ones, serving as enrichment for the final stanza. As illustrated, particularly in Chapters Five through Seven, the starting point for creative exploration is the standard harmony associated with a given hymn.

The modal harmonies discussed in the previous section, along with the chords that follow, could be used to provide enrichment for congregational singing. However, my primary goal is the use of different harmonies in improvising and in the arranging of preludes and offertories, accompaniments for solos, and other service music.

Tri-Tone Substitute Chords

The four-measure introduction to "What a Friend" (Example 162) concludes with a whole-tone scale. The chord that supports this scale could be viewed as a French augmented sixth with an added ninth. However, jazz musicians call this a "tri-tone substitute," because its root is a tri-tone (three whole steps) from the root of the chord for which it is a substitute. In measure four, for example, the most likely chord to use would be C7. However, instead of this, we have a chord based on Gb (**49.mid** or **CD 49**). This could serve as an effective introduction to a solo piece that includes deviant (non-traditional) harmonies.

To satisfy the appetite that has been whetted for chords that are different, another tri-tone substitute is used in measure 5. Since this chord, in function, leads to the subdominant chord

(IV), the easiest way to find and play it is to think of it as an augmented F chord with a flatted 7th. The bass pitch (Cb) is a half-step above the pitch to which it leads, or a tri-tone lower than the root of the F chord. The tri-tone substitute chord in measure 8 could be thought of as an augmented supertonic (G+), since its function is similar to that of II (V of V). (see circled chords)

Example 162 - What a Friend We Have in Jesus (with Tri-Tone Substitutes)

Chapter 9 - Improvisation

ASSIGNMENT 70

1. Study Example 162 and the explanation preceding it, then complete the hymn in the style that has been established.
   Alter the traditional harmonization of "Away in a Manger." Instead of beginning with C7, augment the C chord and play Gb in the bass (see first pitch marked with X). For the next marked pitch, play F+ instead of F7 and play a Cb in the bass (**50.mid** or **CD 50**.

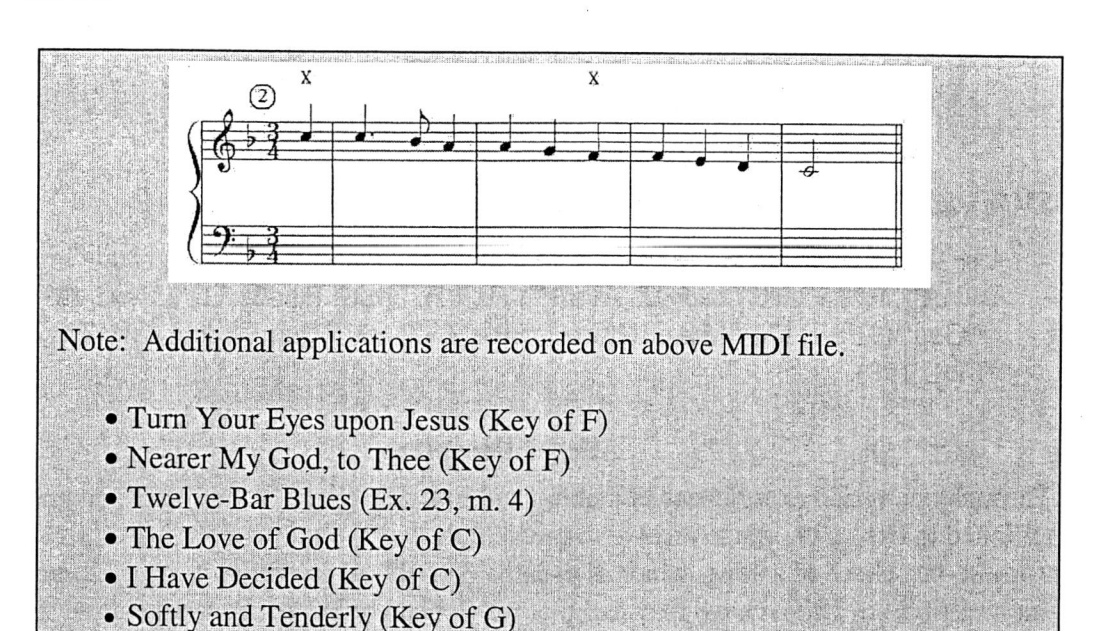

   Note: Additional applications are recorded on above MIDI file.

   - Turn Your Eyes upon Jesus (Key of F)
   - Nearer My God, to Thee (Key of F)
   - Twelve-Bar Blues (Ex. 23, m. 4)
   - The Love of God (Key of C)
   - I Have Decided (Key of C)
   - Softly and Tenderly (Key of G)

Another Chord That Didn't Make the Hymnal – The Altered Mediant Chord

Where the second (x) appears in the above example, an A+7 chord could be used. (Note: Even though the soprano pitch is written as F, the chord is analyzed as A+ (E# = F). As a rule this chord would lead to D minor, but in this case it resolves to Bb. Another option would be to harmonize all of measure 2 as A7. To hear this chord listen to variation F in Appendix H (**60.mid** or **CD 60**). This recording also includes "Turn Your Eyes upon Jesus," for which the altered mediant chord is used.

Altering the Chord Used for Notes of Anacrusis (Pick-up Notes)

In many traditional harmonizations of hymns beginning with a pick-up note (anacrusis), there is no change of chord over the barline. A greater sense of lift and forward movement can be provided by a change of chords. In the recording of "The Love of God" (**50.mid** or **CD 50**), a tri-tone substitute chord is used for the anacrusis. The example that follows shows a traditional song without, then with a change of harmony across the barline (Examples 163A and B).

Chapter 9 - Improvisation

Example 163 - Anacrusis Strengthened by a Change of Harmony

ASSIGNMENT 71

Use the above chord (IV/V) for the beginning of at least three of the following hymns and choruses: "God Leads Us Along" (TH 46), "Jesus Paid It All" (TWC 489), "Lamb of God" (SPW 112), "Make Us One" (SPW 137) and "Thou Didst Leave Thy Throne" (TWC 198).

Altered Deception

Through our varied experiences in making and listening to music, we have become conditioned to expect chords to resolve in predictable ways. For example, we expect the next-to-the-last chord of a song, which is usually V or V7, to resolve to I, as in Example 164A. When it resolves to Dm (vi), we may feel that we've been deceived, hence the term "deceptive cadence" (Example 164 B). When the deceptive chord is one that isn't even in the key of the song, our response may turn to delight, as in Example 164C. The Db chord is borrowed from the parallel minor (F minor) where Db is Roman numeral VI. This could be used effectively at the close of an improvisation in the style shown in Example 162. Listen to final variation on "What a Friend We Have in Jesus" which ends with this cadence (**60.mid** or **CD 60**).

Example 164 - Deceptive Cadences

Chapter 9 - Improvisation

The progression shown in Example 164C can be used (or varied) in numerous ways:

1. as harmonic support for the final pitch of a melody.
2. in place of the standard plagal (Amen) cadence at the close of a hymn (IV I).
3. as an alternative harmony for the three final chords of a melody that ends with repeated pitches, as Irish tunes sometimes do (see Example 165).

Example 165 - Be Thou My Vision (with Varied Cadence)

VI VII I

ASSIGNMENT 72

1. Transpose Example 165 to D major.
2. Play the hymn tune KINGSFOLD (TWC 559) and use the cadential chord progression in Example 165 in place of the last three chords. This would lead naturally to a Picardy 3rd (major chord) at the end.

To bring closure to this topic, which could go on in greater length, listen to the numerous variations on the hymn, "What a Friend We Have in Jesus" (**060.mid** or **CD 60**). The following guide might be helpful to the listener who needs help in identifying the various chords that are used.

- Basic chords (I, IV and V)
- Suspensions (2-1 and 4-3)
- Substitute minor chords (ii and vi)
- Sub-tonic chord
- Diminished chords
- Altered mediant
- Tri-tone substitute chords, also dominant chord with flatted 9th, and deceptive cadence.

The Values of Improvisation

One does not have to be a master of improvisation in order to benefit from creative expression. Although I am not a great improvisateur, I have gained much from my efforts to be creative. Consequently I urge others to begin. I would like to conclude by listing some of the values of improvisation. The reader may want to add others. Improvisation is:

- a means of nurturing God-given creativity.
- a means of mastering rhythmic and harmonic concepts.
- an antidote to sameness, which can become routine and even boring.
- useful in service playing.
- a means of gaining insight into compositional devices encountered as a performer.
- a means of freeing a performer from bondage to the printed page.
- fun and a source of immeasurable pleasure, if you are willing to overlook your mistakes.
- possibly a means of maintaining a youthful outlook and spirit!

Nurturing the Growing Process

Through the study of educational theory and pedagogy, and also through personal experience, I have learned that there are numerous factors that contribute to learning. Because of the uniqueness of each individual learner, it is important to realize that there is no one method or approach that fits everyone. I would offer the following as guidelines for those who fit the category of teacher, learner or a combination of both.

1. <u>Continuing Application</u> - Skill in the use of chords is the result of continuing application and transposition of that which is learned. Fortunately, muscles have a memory system (see "Muscles Have Memory," p.71). That which is acquired through painstaking effort eventually becomes easier.

2. <u>Learning Gap</u> - Essential to learning is the motivation that is provided by a gap between where learners are in their development and where they'd like to be. Learning may be viewed as a combination of persistence and pleasure. Although old-fashioned discipline may not be in vogue today, it seems only fair to remind the reader that a little "pain" is an integral part of gain.

3. <u>Goals</u> - At an impressionable time in life, you may have heard someone play an instrument and said, "Someday I'll play like that." I know a young man who enjoys playing guitar in a praise and worship band. When he was tempted to quit, he was motivated by the memory of an experience eight years earlier, when he heard someone play very well. Short-range goals and successes are also important, for they serve as continuing motivation for the learner.

4. <u>Perceived Relevance</u> - If one has a goal of playing by ear, that person is likely to become discouraged by a teaching approach that includes only the reading of notes. The student must perceive the learning activities, assigned by the teacher, to be relevant to his/her long-range goal of playing by ear.

5. <u>Nurturing Climate for Learning</u> - Another aspect of learning that serves as motivation for most of us is that of a learning environment that is nurturing. People of all ages tend to flourish in an atmosphere of love and acceptance. As learners, we must accept ourselves where we are and move ahead, taking time to compliment ourselves and each other for even the slightest improvements in understanding and skill development. Self-criticism and comparing yourself with others can be counter-productive and discouraging, causing many to quit.

6. <u>Slow, Steady, Relaxed Practice</u> - We are creatures of habit, so good practice habits must be established. The playing of harmonic progressions (or any repertory) slowly, in a relaxed manner, forms a habit that, when established, will carry over into the playing of the progression at faster speeds.

7. <u>Keeping the Play Instinct Alive</u> - The expression of emotion can and should be an integral part of all music-making, including chord study. Cognitive and affective development (thought and feeling) go hand-in-hand, unless we choose to separate the two. The spontaneity that is integral to jazz and gospel music can become a part of other styles of music, and improvisation is the means by which spontaneity is nurtured. Teachers and students who see the value of improvisation will carve out time for it both in lessons and in practice.

Notes on Chapter 9

Chapter Ten

READING FIGURED BASS

Throughout history keyboard musicians have used symbols to represent chords. By the time of J.S. Bach (1685-1750), there was a highly developed system called figured bass, sometimes referred to as *basso continuo* (continuous bass). Example 166A shows the melody and figured bass line of LOBE DEN HERREN ("Praise to the Lord, the Almighty"). Example 166B is the *realization* (written chords) for the figured bass, plus a Roman numeral analysis.

Example 166 - Figured Bass for LOBE DEN HERREN

The Inversions of Triads

In order to interpret the above symbols and translate them into sound, one must have some general information regarding their meaning:

1. **A bass note with no figure** (Arabic number) under it indicates a triad (chord of thirds) **in root position.** The figures 5 and 3 could be placed there to indicate pitches that are a fifth and a third above the bass pitch (chord root). **Note:** Example 166A includes only three bass pitches that are not chord roots. The Arabic number 7 indicates that the D chord is to include a 7th.
2. **The first inversion** of a chord is indicated by the numbers 6 and 3, but as a rule, only the number 6 appears. In Examples 166 and 167 there are several first inversion chords, and each of them is identified by Roman numeral. A careful examination of these first inversion chords in Example 168 will show that, regardless of spacing, **the third of the chord is always the lowest pitch.** The root of the chord lies a sixth above, or an octave and a sixth above the bass pitch.

3. **The second inversion** of a chord is indicated by the numbers 6 and 4. A careful examination of second inversion chords will reveal that **the fifth of the chord is always the lowest pitch**, and the root of the chord lies a fourth, or an octave and a fourth above the bass.

Example 167 - Triads and Their Inversions

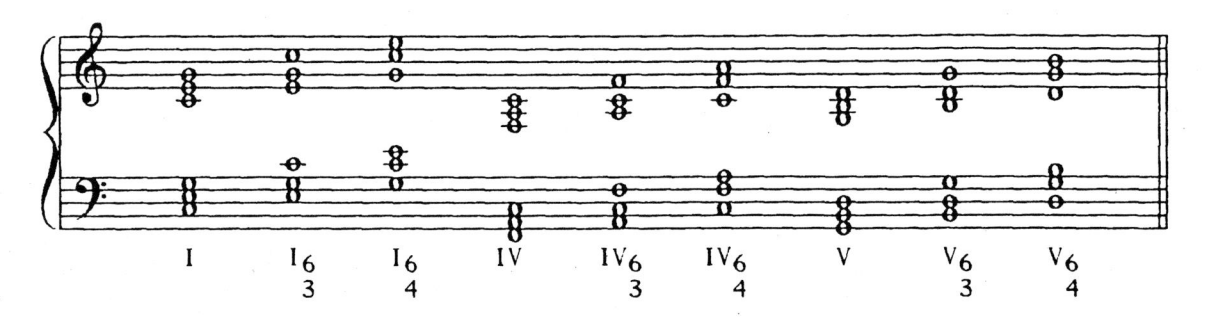

I   I$_3^6$ I$_4^6$ IV   IV$_3^6$ IV$_4^6$ V   V$_3^6$ V$_4^6$

Example 168 - Different Spacings of Chord Inversions

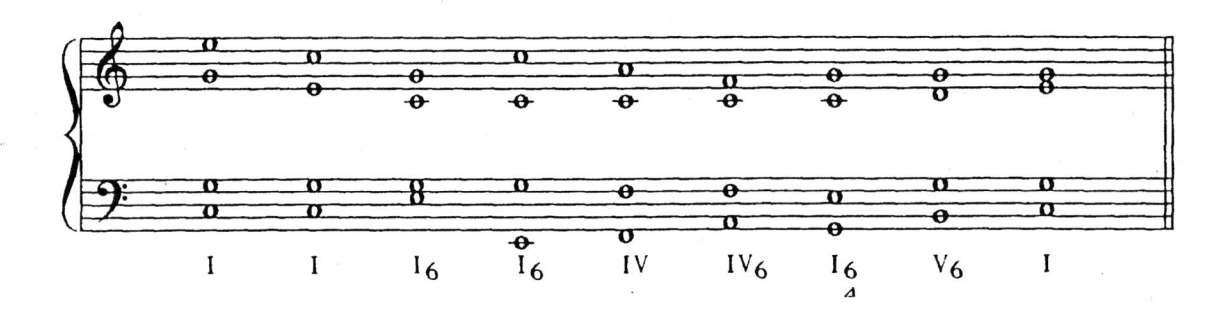

I   I   I$_6$ I$_6$ IV   IV$_6$ I$_6$ V$_6$ I

The Inversion of Seventh Chords

When a seventh is added to a triad, there are three possible inversions instead of two. In figured bass writing, the Arabic number 7 by itself indicates that the root of the chord is in the bass. It also indicates the presence of a pitch that is a seventh, or an octave and a seventh above the bass. Seventh chords in their various inversions are easily identified when written in close position (see first five chords in Example 169). In each inverted seventh chord (in close position), the root is one step (the interval of a second) above the seventh of the chord.

Chapter 10 – Figured Bass

Example 169 - Inversions of a Seventh Chord

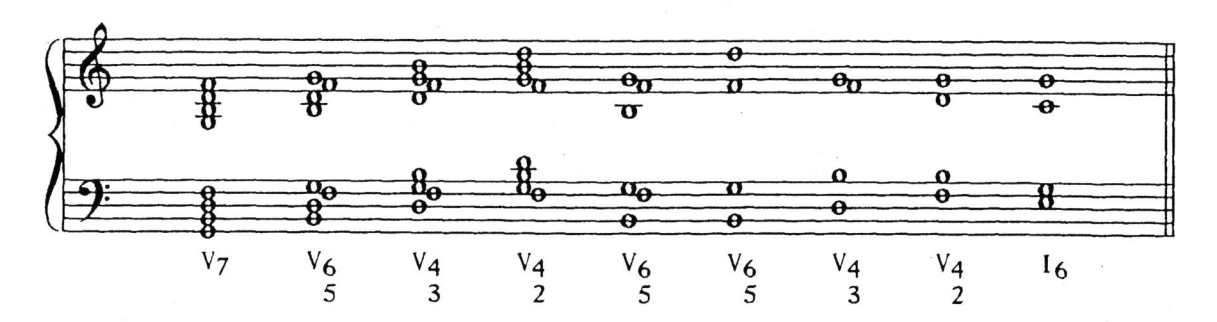

V7 V6/5 V4/3 V4/2 V6/5 V6/5 V4/3 V4/2 I6

A **first inversion seventh chord** is indicated by the Arabic numbers 6, 5 and 3, or just 6 and 5, and the **third** of the chord is always in the bass. A **second inversion seventh chord** is indicated by the Arabic numbers 6, 4 and 3, or just 4 and 3, and the **fifth** of the chord is in the bass. A **third inversion seventh chord** is indicated by 6, 4 and 2, or just 4 and 2, and the **seventh** of the chord is in the bass. With practice in chord analysis, it is possible to recognize the various chord inversions regardless of the spacing of pitches (see different spacings of chords in Example 169).

Additional information is carried by figured bass symbols, and competency in interpreting these symbols requires both study and practice. A few additional items of information are needed for beginning efforts in reading figured bass:

1. The resolution of suspensions is indicated by the numbers 4-3, 7-6, and 9-8 (see Ex. 170A).
2. A chromatic tone is indicated by an accidental placed next to an Arabic number. A raised pitch may also be indicated by placing a line through the number (see Example 170B). A sharp, flat or natural sign without an Arabic number denotes an alteration of the third of a root position chord (see Example 170A). Note: Each example is followed by a possible realization.

Work Space

Chapter 10 – Figured Bass

Example 170 - The Interpretation of Figured Bass Symbols

The art of interpreting figured bass symbols is called "realization," and there are numerous ways of interpreting the symbols. In Example 170 you will notice that the movement of the soprano line in relation to the bass is often characterized by oblique and contrary motion. This creates intensity.

In Example 171 ("Prelude in C" by J.S. Bach), chord symbols are also included. A comparison of the figured bass symbols with the chord symbols may contribute to our understanding of how these two musical disciplines are related. Fluency in reading both kinds of "musical shorthand" (figured bass and chord symbols) comes only with practice.

Chapter 10 – Figured Bass

Example 171- Prelude in C by J.S. Bach

Note: For an analysis of the above piece, a la Schenker, see Jonas (Reference List).

Work Space

Work Space

Chapter Eleven

Improvising Accompaniment to Enhance Praise and Worship

by Kathy Smith

A Word of Introduction

I became aware of Kathy Smith's excellent work in the area of hymn improvisation at the National Conference sponsored by the Lillenas Music Company. Her examples were well crafted, beautifully played and thoughtfully discussed. I suggested that she prepare these materials for inclusion as the final chaper of this book. Kathy teaches at MidAmerica Nazarene College in Olathe, Kansas, and also serves as a part of the keyboard ministry team at College Church in Olathe. I am grateful for her expertise in this area of keyboard ministry. (Ron Sprunger)

The material in the preceding chapters is presented in such a logical and orderly sequence that it leads naturally to a discussion of applying these concepts to the supporting and energizing of congregational singing. An understanding of scales, chord progression and chord substitution is invaluable knowledge. For the keyboard musician, this must also be hands-on information. We can train our fingers to respond to signals transmitted by eye and/or ear to the brain and on to the hands. It is rewarding to practice and make a practical application of music theory in communicating through God's wonderful gift of music.

Facility with scales enables our fingers to be "at home" in any key. Knowing the scale on which a song is structured, which involves the mental hearing of each pitch (internalization) as well as the mastery of fingerings, gives the keyboard musician a feeling for the pitches as they are played, and even before they are played. The establishing of good finger patterns allows a freedom that "pot-luck" fingering doesn't offer. Consistent practice of major, minor, chromatic and even whole-tone scales yields dividends in flexibility. Scales are good transitional material, serving both as "fills" and as integral parts of modulations.

Consistent practice of chord progressions will help our fingers develop a feel for chord functions while our ears are developing the ability to distinguish and identify the musical sounds. Playing a progression in several keys builds confidence in both transposition and modulation. Rarely, in congregational singing, would we accompany a song and abruptly begin playing it in a new key without a modulation to signal the arrival of a new tonal center.

Why Embellish the Voice Parts?

The hymn style notation for soprano, alto, tenor and bass provides a harmonic framework that allows each one to sing comfortably in his/her own vocal range. It is important to be able to play a hymn accurately and at a steady and appropriate tempo before providing embellishment. While it is far more important to have the original voice parts played accurately, musically, and with confidence than to have a random disarray of notes thrown together, an appropriate and tasteful embellishment from the keyboard can add lift and affirmation to the choir and congregation.

Chapter 11 – Improvising Accompaniments

What Makes a Supportive and Worshipful Accompaniment?

Good keyboard technique and an understanding of chord structure are foundational for improvising and providing a strong keyboard accompaniment. Much like an organist's adding of height and/or depth of tone through effective registration, a full sound from the piano, with added treble and bass octaves, can lift the confidence level of congregational singing and contribute to the momentum of praise and worship that continues right on through the ministry of preaching.

Melody Doubled with Full Chords

Perhaps the style of hymn playing we hear most often and think of as improvised involves doubling of the melody in the right hand and filling in the octave with chord members. Example 172 and 173 show how this style of accompanying can enhance the stately hymn, "Come, Thou Almighty King." Compare the four-voice setting with the fuller style. The left-hand octaves add depth as well as give stability to the rhythm. In the third measure, where the voices sustain the word "King," the moving keyboard part outlines an ascending F major chord, which keeps the rhythm flowing and provides a smooth change of register. In measure six, where the voices sustain the word, "sing," there is similar upward movement. In measure eight, where the voices sustain the word, "praise," the accompaniment is an imitation of measure seven, which is a descending F major chord outline.

Example 172 - Come, Thou Almighty King (Four-part Setting)

Chapter 11 – Improvising Accompaniments

Example 173 - Come, Thou Almighty King
(with Doubled Melody and Full Chords in Right Hand,
and Supporting Octaves in Left Hand)

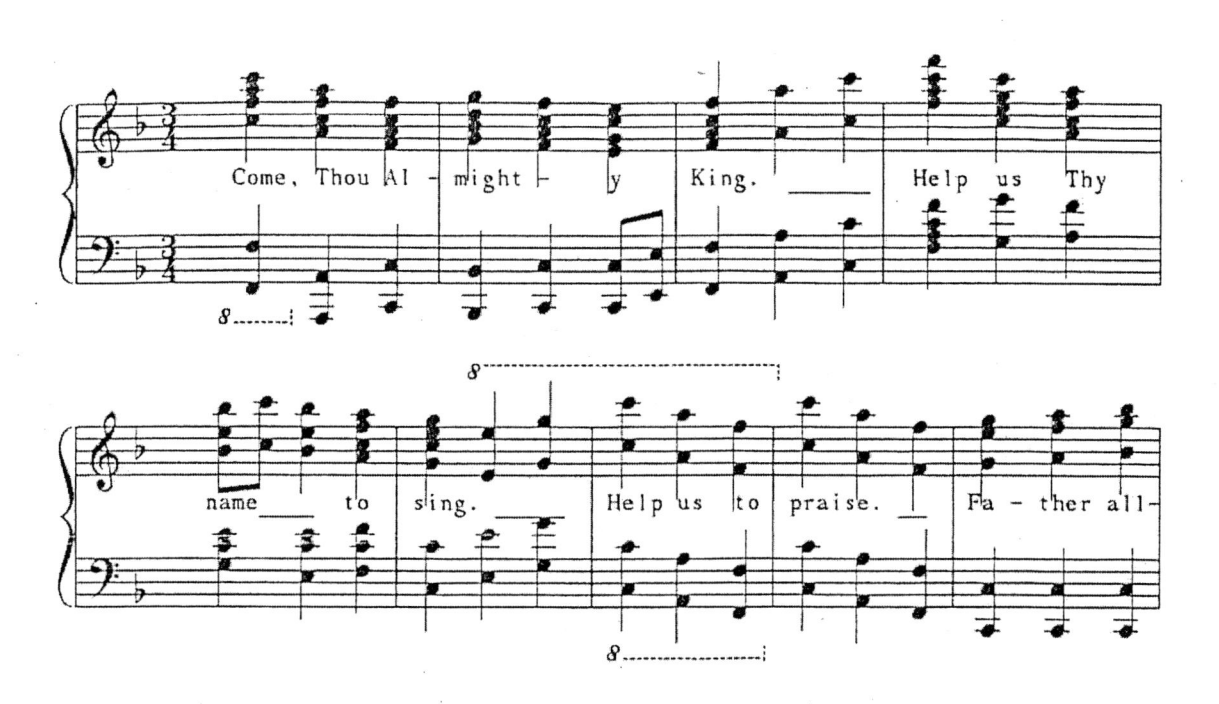

Come, Thou Almighty King. Help us Thy name to sing. Help us to praise. Father all-

Example 174 - Come, Ye Thankful People, Come (Four-part Setting)

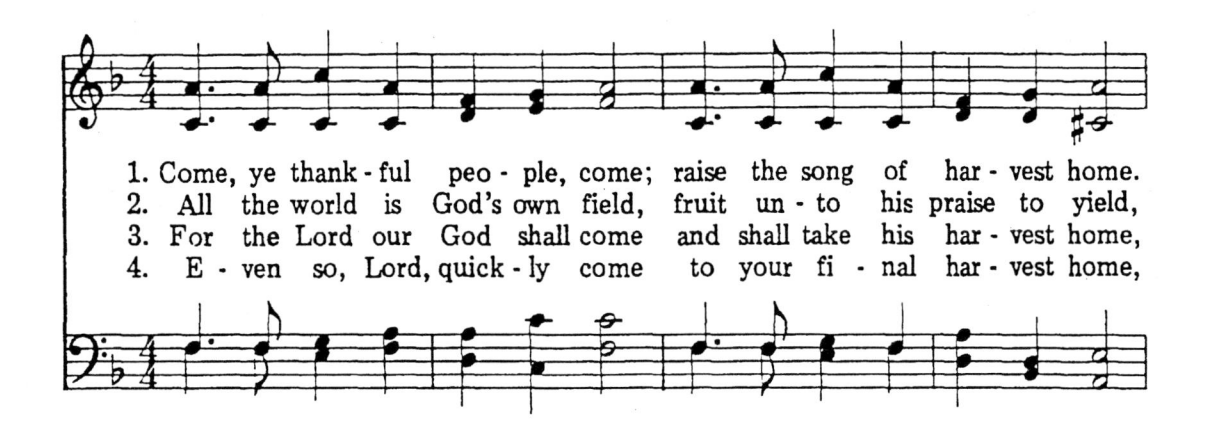

1. Come, ye thank-ful peo-ple, come; raise the song of har-vest home.
2. All the world is God's own field, fruit un-to his praise to yield,
3. For the Lord our God shall come and shall take his har-vest home,
4. E-ven so, Lord, quick-ly come to your fi-nal har-vest home,

Chapter 11 – Improvising Accompaniments

An embellishment of an excerpt from the four-voice setting of "Come, Ye Thankful People, Come" (Ex. 174) is shown in Example 175. In the first measure (Ex. 175) the right hand consistently plays complete chords, but only count three has a doubled melody note, which accounts for the fuller texture. It would be fine for the right thumb to double the melody in all of the chords, but since the hands begin close together, it doesn't sound incomplete with three notes in the right hand. At the end of measure two, the eighth note movement in octaves outlines the A major chord (from beat three of the four-voice setting). It incorporates a B natural passing tone, since the diatonic B flat isn't compatible with the A major secondary dominant. Ascending octaves moving in parallel motion enable the right hand to make a smooth transition while the left hand stays in the bass and tenor ranges, providing balance for the higher right hand register. The final measure shows the right hand doubling the melody with all chord members within the octave. By emphasizing the roots of the chords, the left hand supports the bass line of the vocal setting.

**Example 175 - Come, Ye Thankful People, Come
(with Fuller Accompaniment for Added Support)**

ASSIGNMENT 73

1. Using familiar hymns such as "What a Friend," "Praise to the Lord, the Almighty," "Rejoice, Ye Pure in Heart," and "Fairest Lord Jesus," practice doubling the melody in the right hand and filling in the octaves with chord members. Strive for a good supporting left hand. Incorporate some moving octaves.
2. Vary the accompaniment of "Fairest Lord Jesus" by including eighth-notes in the inner voices, as in Example 176. **Note:** Whether to begin the moving pattern with the alto or tenor pitch is determined by which chord tone (3rd or 5th) adds the most warmth. See the second phrase of Example 176, where the moving parts begin with the alto voice to avoid open sonorities in chords that follow. The absence of the third creates a sound that is not appropriate in this style of music.

Chapter 11 – Improvising Accompaniments

Example 176 - Fairest Lord Jesus (Four-part Setting)

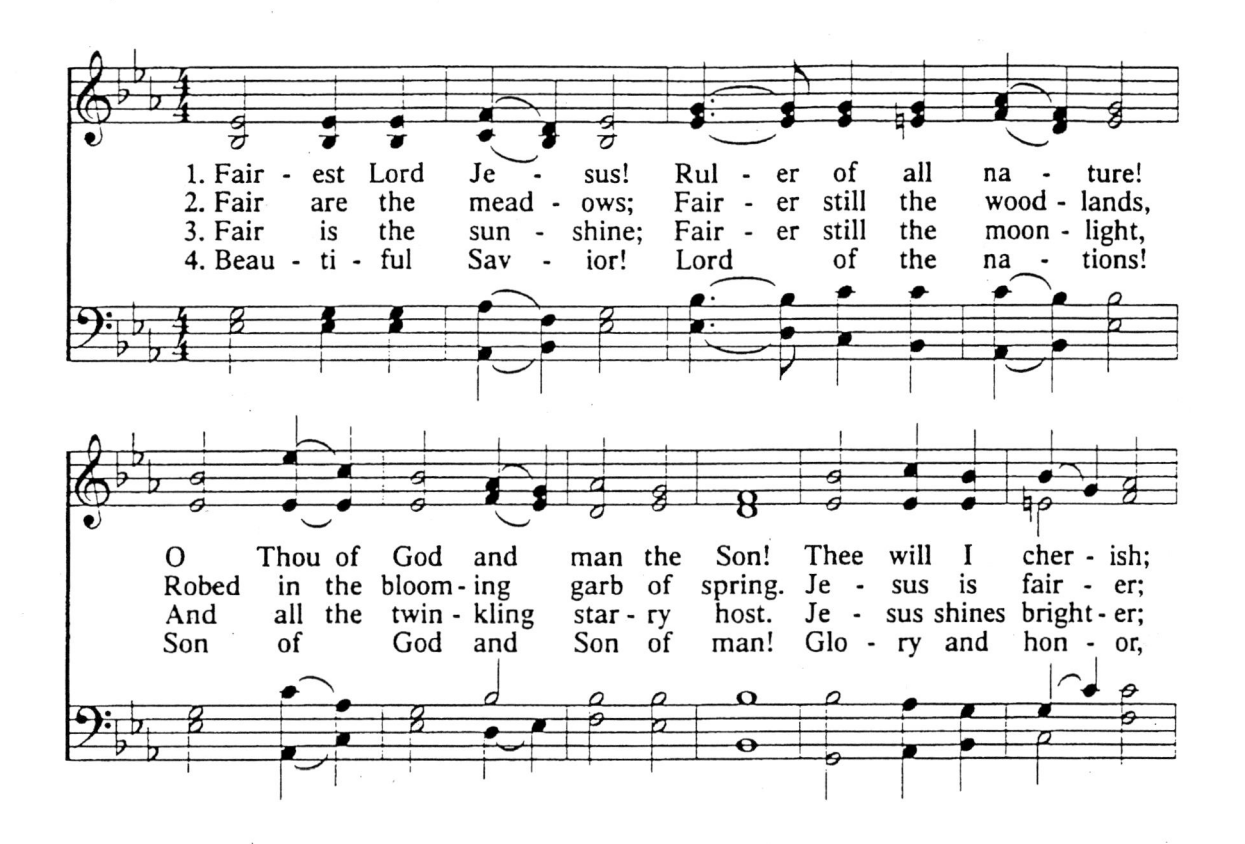

1. Fair - est Lord Je - sus! Rul - er of all na - ture!
2. Fair are the mead - ows; Fair - er still the wood - lands,
3. Fair is the sun - shine; Fair - er still the moon - light,
4. Beau - ti - ful Sav - ior! Lord of the na - tions!

O Thou of God and man the Son! Thee will I cher - ish;
Robed in the bloom - ing garb of spring. Je - sus is fair - er;
And all the twin - kling star - ry host. Je - sus shines bright - er;
Son of God and Son of man! Glo - ry and hon - or,

Example 177 - Fairest Lord Jesus
(Four-part Setting Varied through Use of Eighth-Note Movement in Inner Voices)

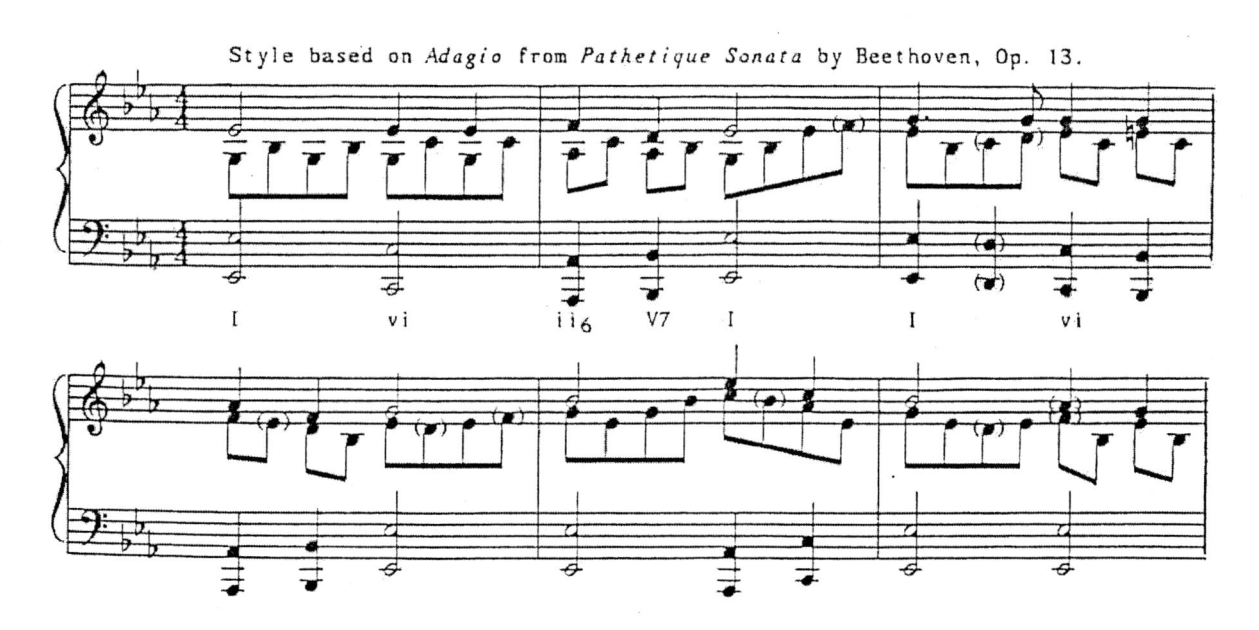

Style based on *Adagio* from *Pathetique Sonata* by Beethoven, Op. 13.

I   vi   ii$_6$ V7   I   I   vi

Chapter 11 – Improvising Accompaniments

Playing the two measure unison phrases of "Come, Christians, Join to Sing" in octaves adds height and depth to the vocal invitation to praise! Movement to a higher register for the descending scales in octaves serves to outline the melody and also embellish, while providing support for the four-voice structure (measure three). In measure four advantage is taken of the piano's range to emphasize the text's "Amen" and to provide variety to the line as well.

Example 178 - Come, Christians, Join to Sing (four-part setting)

Example 179 - Come, Christians, Join to Sing (melody and counter melody in octaves)

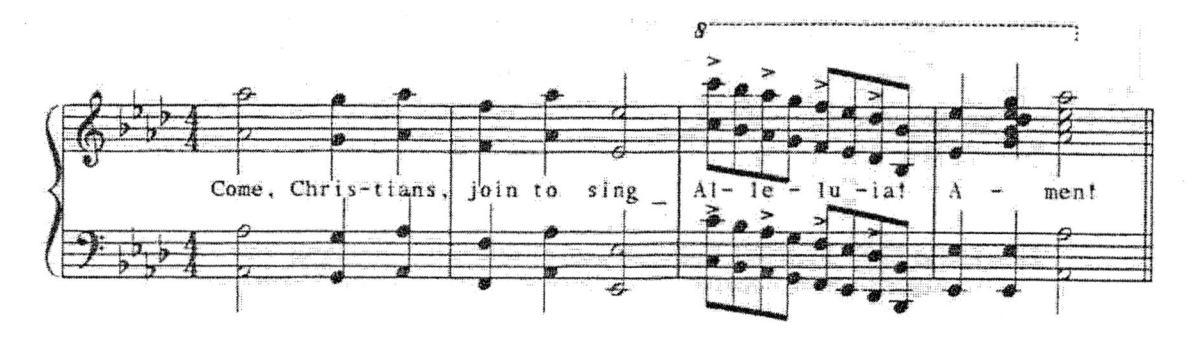

A similar parallel moving of octaves from high to low register in "Immortal, Invisible" seems appropriate to affirm the awesomeness of God's majesty and wisdom. Toward the end of the line some of the octaves are filled in with chord members to support voice parts in an otherwise octave-filled phrase. Since the next phrase is the same, the octaves could be repeated if desired. (**Note**: It is important to emphasize melody notes when using a moving octave accompaniment, as shown by the accent marks in Examples 179 and 181.)

ASSIGNMENT 74

1. Consider using descending octaves with "I Sing the Mighty Power of God," "How Great Our Joy" and "Onward, Christian Soldiers."
2. Explore possibilities of ascending octaves in one or both hands to add interest to the accompaniment for "He Lives."

3. Try a soft, subdued variation of moving octaves with Jerry Sinclair's "Alleluia" (Sing *to the Lord,* STTL 131) and "Lord, We Praise You" by Otis Skillings (STTL 135). There may need to be some rhythmic adaptation to accommodate harmonic and/or melodic changes which could provide enrichment.

Example 180 - Immortal, Invisible (Four-Part Setting)

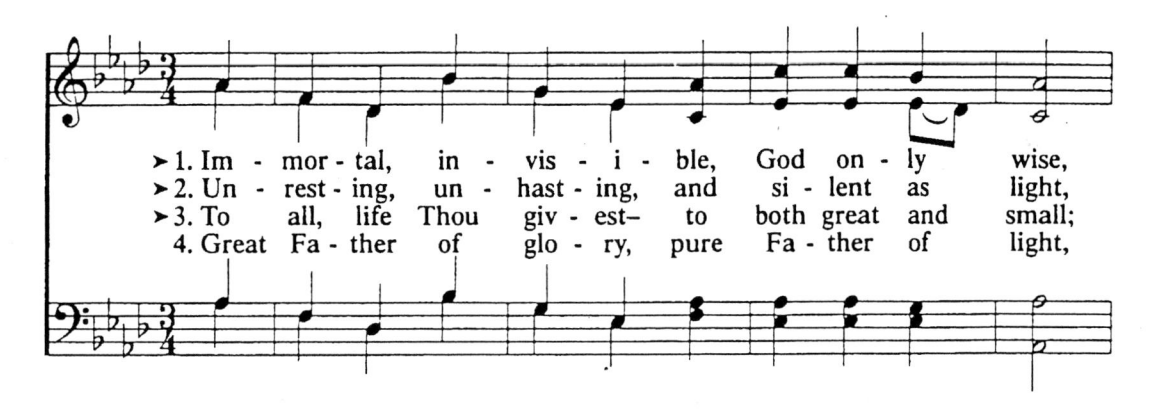

Example 181- Immortal, Invisible
(with Scale-wise Movement Emphasizing Chordal Outline of Melody)

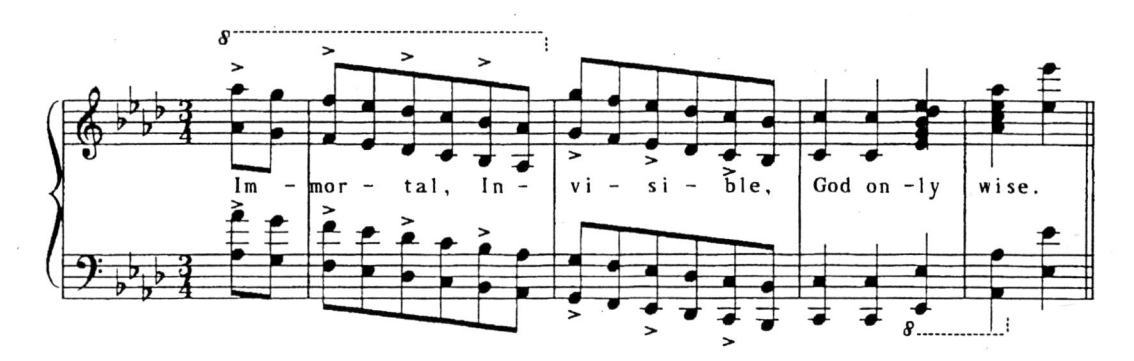

Outlining Chords with Scales

In Examples 179 and 181 descending scale movement in octaves was used. Scales or scale fragments provide pleasing filler, and they prepare the ear for harmonic change. In similar or contrary motion, scales that outline chords provide interest at points of cadence and at places where a melody note is sustained. Since a chord with a minor seventh resolves well to a chord whose root is a perfect fourth higher or perfect fifth lower (movement by succession of fifths), a scale pattern incorporating the minor seventh makes a nice progression from tonic to subdominant, supertonic to dominant, or dominant to tonic.

Example 183 is an excerpt from "Holy Spirit, Be My Guide," beginning with the fourth measure of the song. The incomplete cadence with the dominant Ab chord has a stronger pull onward when, in the four-voice setting, the alto moves to Gb, creating a dominant "pull" to the tonic. The embellishment demonstrates hands moving in contrary motion, with the right hand playing an ascending Db scale. The left hand outlines a descending Ab chord and then reverses its direction and outlines an ascending Db chord.

Chapter 11 – Improvising Accompaniments

Example 182 - Holy Spirit, Be My Guide (Four-Part Setting)

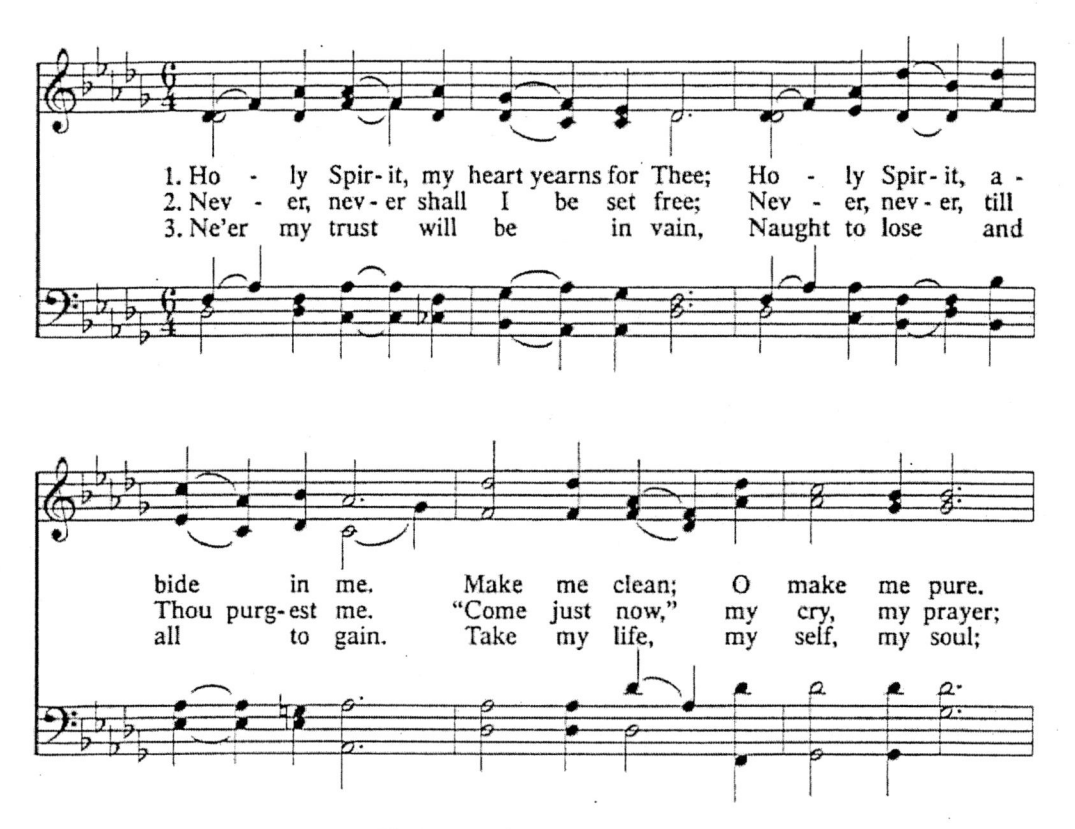

1. Ho - ly Spir- it, my heart yearns for Thee; Ho - ly Spir- it, a -
2. Nev - er, nev - er shall I be set free; Nev - er, nev - er, till
3. Ne'er my trust will be in vain, Naught to lose and

bide in me. Make me clean; O make me pure.
Thou purg- est me. "Come just now," my cry, my prayer;
all to gain. Take my life, my self, my soul;

Words and Music: Mildred Cope, 1963
© 1963 Lillenas Publishing Company (Administered by the Copyright Company. Nashville, TN)
All Rights Reserved. International Copyright Secured. Used by Permission

**Example 183 - Holy Spirit, Be My Guide
(with Ascending Scale and Descending Chord Outline**

a - bide in me. Make me

Example 185 begins with full right-hand chords and moving eighth note octaves in the left hand. The fourth measure changes dramatically with scales, first, in contrary motion, then in similar motion. I find this helpful to describe the marvelous freedom found in salvation as related in the third stanza. Musical devices we use should serve as tools to communicate the text.

Chapter 11 – Improvising Accompaniments

Example 184 - And Can It Be? (Four-Part Setting)

**Example 185 - And Can It Be?
(Full Chords in Right Hand and with Octave Movement in Bass)**

Chapter 11 – Improvising Accompaniments

In Example 187 ("O How He Loves You and Me") a descending scale passage spans two octaves as the final note of the phrase is sustained. This embellishes a very natural (and strong) progression, Ab (I) to Db (IV), as does Example 188 ("What a Day That Will Be"). While both examples show the use of a descending scale, they also demonstrate different rhythmic variations that may be used to make the musical device (a descending scale) compatible with meter, tempo, and number of beats available for the embellishment.

Example 186 - O How He Loves You and Me (Four-part Setting)

Words and Music by Kurt Kaiser © 1975 by Word Music. Used by permission

Example 187 - O How He Loves You and Me
(Descending Scale Serving as Fill and Preparation for Harmonic Change)

Example 188 - What a Day That Will Be (Four-Part Setting)

Words and Music by Jim Hill. © 1955 by Ben L. Speer. Used by permission.

Chapter 11 – Improvising Accompaniments

Example 189- What a Day That Will Be (Descending Scale in Triplets)

ASSIGNMENT 75

1. The verses of "Glory to His Name" (STTL 242) end with a tonic chord followed by a subdominant chord at the refrain. Use an ascending or descending scale to create a smooth transition from stanza to chorus.
2. Use a scale based on the dominant seventh chord to bridge the harmonic change from stanza to refrain of "Praise Him! Praise Him!" (STTL 117).

Chord Substitution

Chord substitution can add interest to an accompaniment, but it must be used with caution so that the notes added via a substituted chord don't conflict with the harmonic structure of the vocal setting. This is less of a concern if it is the final stanza of the hymn and the congregation has been asked to sing unison because of the free harmonization. Chords that share two common tones (e.g., tonic and submediant, subdominant and supertonic, and mediant and tonic) can be used compatibly in substitution. At the end of Example 189 (" What a Day That Will Be") a ii$_7$ chord substitution for IV is accomplished smoothly with a bass passing tone. Since the substituted ii$_7$ chord includes all the notes of the IV chord, it will not conflict with the vocal parts. Similar examples of substitution are shown in Examples 191 ("He Leadeth Me") and 193 ("Higher Ground").

Example 190 - He Leadeth Me (Four-part Setting)

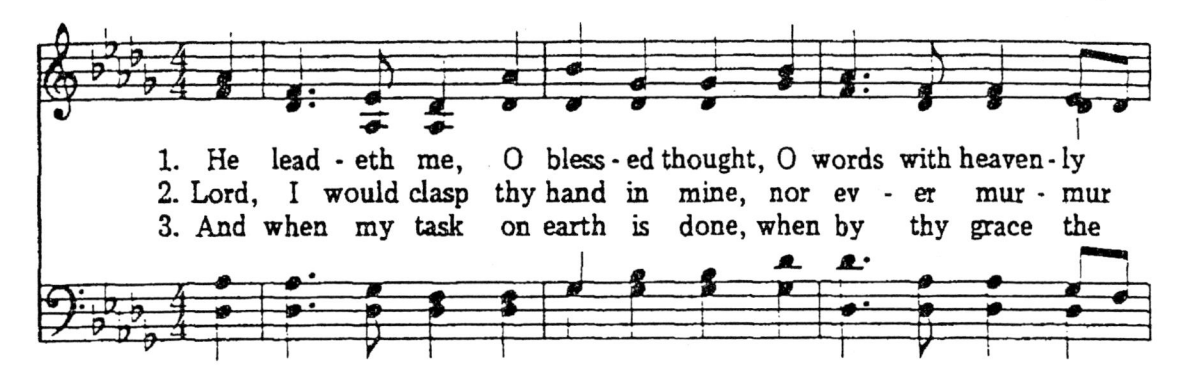

Chapter 11 – Improvising Accompaniments

Example 191- He Leadeth Me (with Substitute Chords)

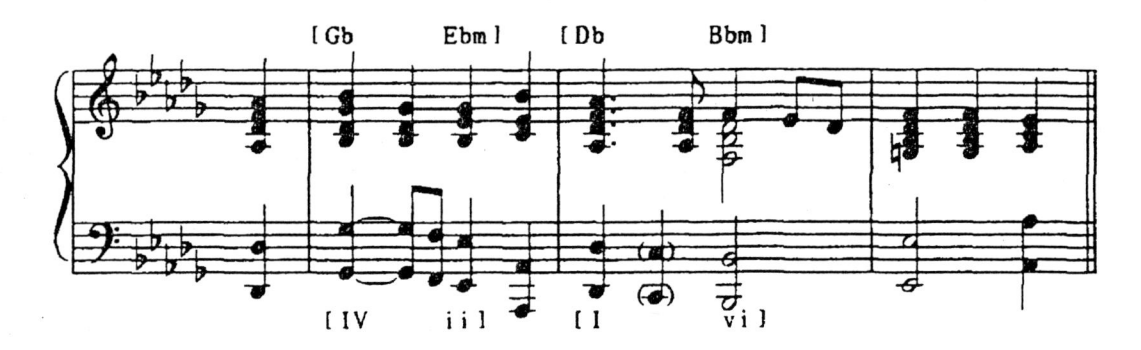

Example 192 - Higher Ground (Four-part Setting)

1. I'm press-ing on the up-ward way; New heights I'm
2. My heart has no de-sire to stay Where doubts a-
3. I want to live a-bove the world, Tho' Sa-tan's
4. I want to scale the ut-most height, And catch a

gain - ing ev - 'ry day, Still pray-ing as I'm on-ward
rise and fears dis - may. Tho' some may dwell where these a-
darts at me are hurled; For faith has caught the joy-ful
gleam of glo - ry bright; But still I'll pray till heav'n I've

Example 193 - Higher Ground (with Substitution of ii₇ for IV)

on the up-ward way; New heights I'm gain -

IV   ii₇   I₆   I

182

Chapter 11 – Improvising Accompaniments

ASSIGNMENT 76

1. Take the traditional chorus, "God is So Good," and incorporate chord substitution, including submediant (vi) for tonic and supertonic (ii7) for subdominant.
2. Analyze "I Give All to You" by Larnelle Harris (STTL 484), and consider possible chord substitutes that would not alter the basic harmonic structure.

Chord Inversions

The chord inversion drill (Appendix B) is excellent preparation for using this technique in improvising. Inverting a chord can help keep the rhythm steady where there are sustained pitches in the melody. While filling a gap that might even become awkward with regard to holding it long enough, the chord inversions can, in effect, help the singer "count" subliminally during the sustained sound. "Have Thine Own Way, Lord" (Example 194) offers several places where chord inversions may be incorporated. In Example 195 ascending chord inversions serve to fill in the dotted half notes of the melody. Example 196 shows the option of having chords ascend, then descend.

Example 194 - Have Thine Own Way, Lord (Four-part Setting)

Example 195 - Have Thine Own Way, Lord (Ascending Chord Inversions)

Example 196 - Have Thine Own Way, Lord (with Chord Inversions)

Broken Chords

Example 197 illustrates the use of broken (arpeggiated) chords to stabilize the rhythm during sustained sounds.

Example 197 - Have Thine Own Way, Lord (with Arpeggios)

The following excerpt from "I Will Serve Thee" and the improvisation that follows demonstrate how "broken chords" can direct the singers' focus on the melody, making them aware of the melodic line. This can also be seen in Example 197.

Chapter 11 – Improvising Accompaniments

Example 198 - I Will Serve Thee (Four-part Setting)

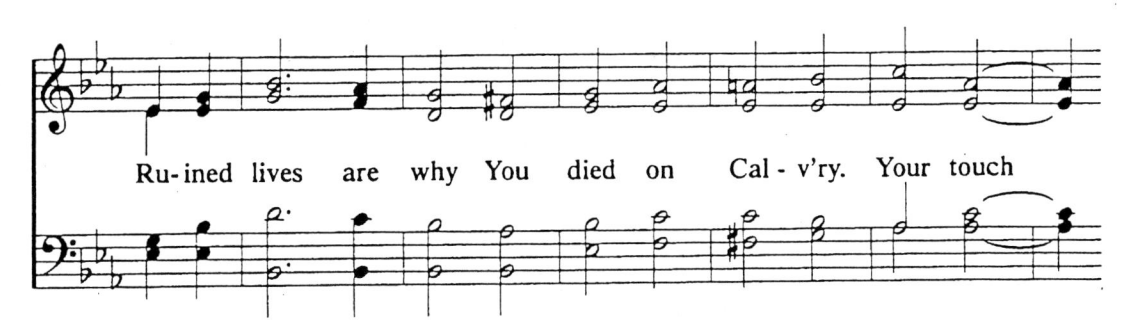

Ru-ined lives are why You died on Cal-v'ry. Your touch

Words by William J. and Gloria Gaither, 1969; Music by William J. Gaither, 1969
© 1969 by William J. Gaither. Used by permission.

Example 199 - I Will Serve Thee
(Ascending and Descending Arpeggios a Sixth Apart)

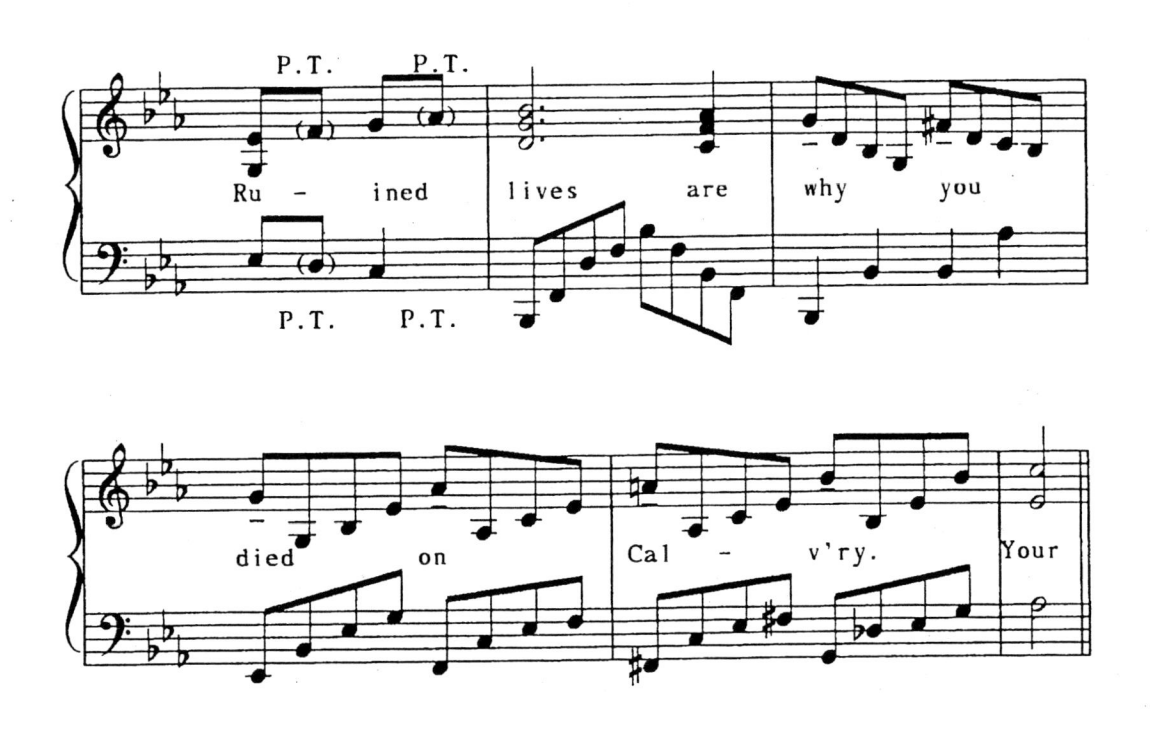

Ru - ined lives are why you died on Cal - v'ry. Your

Chapter 11 – Improvising Accompaniments

The next hymn, "Rejoice, the Lord Is King," is supported amid broken chords, with two measures of sixteenth notes followed by eighth notes.

Example 200 - Rejoice, the Lord is King (Four-part Setting)

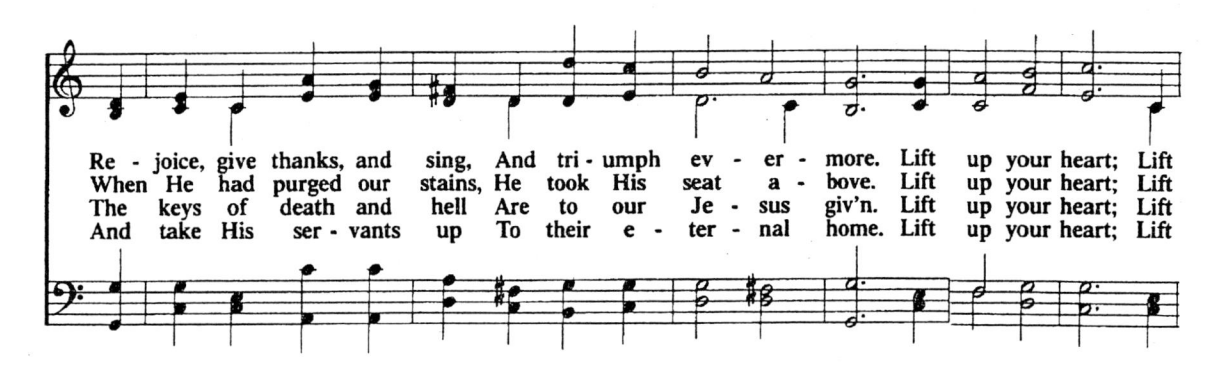

Re - joice, give thanks, and sing, And tri - umph ev - er - more. Lift up your heart; Lift
When He had purged our stains, He took His seat a - bove. Lift up your heart; Lift
The keys of death and hell Are to our Je - sus giv'n. Lift up your heart; Lift
And take His ser - vants up To their e - ter - nal home. Lift up your heart; Lift

**Example 201- Rejoice, the Lord is King
(with Broken Chords in Sixteenth and Eighth Notes)**

Re - joice, give thanks, and sing, and tri - umph ev - er - more. Lift up your heart; Lift

ASSIGNMENT 77

1. Incorporate broken chords in appropriate places for "Just As I Am" (STTL 343).
2. "Silent Night, Holy Night" lends itself to a flowing broken-chord accompaniment. Develop an expressive support for this lullaby with broken (arpeggiated) chords.
3. Use inverted chords to bridge sustained notes in the melody of "He Is Lord" (STTL 269).

Antiphonal Effect

The antiphonal effect, as in the next to the last measure of Example 201, is just one example of musical imitation that can be interesting and expressive. A more obvious imitation may involve a literal restatement, or echo of a motif while the voices are holding a note (see measure two of Example 203).

In measure five (Example 206) a brief antiphonal effect adds interest and contributes to the interpretation of the song. The final measure outlines the dotted half note chord with octaves in one hand, while the left hand outlines the tonic chord, moving in contrary motion.

Example 202 - We Bring the Sacrifice of Praise (Four-Part Setting)

Words and Music by Mark Dearman, 1984; arr. by David McDonald, 1992
© 1984 by John T. Benson Co./ASCAP. Used by permission of the Benson Company.

Chapter 11 – Improvising Accompaniments

Example 203 - We Bring the Sacrifice of Praise (with Melodic Imitation)

An imitation that is more subtle may be achieved by inverting an interval as in Example 204, where the initial interval of a major sixth in the melody becomes a minor third in a bit of imitative response. In the next phrase the melody leaps a minor sixth from F to Db and the keyboard response again inverts this to a major third, with the addition of a passing tone. In the last measure of the above example, eighth note octaves are used, first in parallel and then in contrary motion. This leads to a full chord for the proclamation, "Let all the people praise Thee."

Example 204 - Let All the People Praise Thee (Four-part Setting)

Words and Music by Lelia N. Morris, 1906

Example 205 - Let All the People Praise Thee
(with Inverted Melodic Intervals as Echoed Response)

In Example 206, "To God Be the Glory," we see again how a melodic motif can bring interest in imitative, responsive style.

Example 206 - To God Be the Glory (Four-part Setting)

Chapter 11 – Improvising Accompaniments

Example 207 - To God Be the Glory (Imitation Using a Melodic Fragment)

ASSIGNMENT 78

1. Bill Gaither's "Gentle Shepherd" (STTL 626) lends itself nicely to echo where there are sustained pitches in the melody. Consider how you might enhance this melody with some imitative additions in appropriate places. Locate these and incorporate imitations in the accompaniment at these points.
2. "I Have Decided to Follow Jesus" (STTL 468) offers several places for echo response. Incorporate imitative responses in the accompaniment.

Conclusion

The hymnal has been called the "handmaiden of the Word." Martin Luther said, "Next to the word of God, music deserves the highest praise." These words serve as an exciting challenge to keyboard musicians to practice and develop God-given abilities so that He can use them to bring honor and praise to Himself. The confidence that one gains through creative improvisation is just one of the rewards of consistent efforts. Another is realizing that effective keyboard ministry instills confidence in the people of God as they release their worship in song. An accompanist can make a positive contribution to corporate worship by playing skillfully, and with expression, in order to help people more fully express their love and adoration for the awesome Creator and Orchestrator of the universe, who is also their "Maker, Defender, Redeemer and Friend."

APPENDIX A

Common-Tone Chording with Basic Chords
(to be played in all keys)

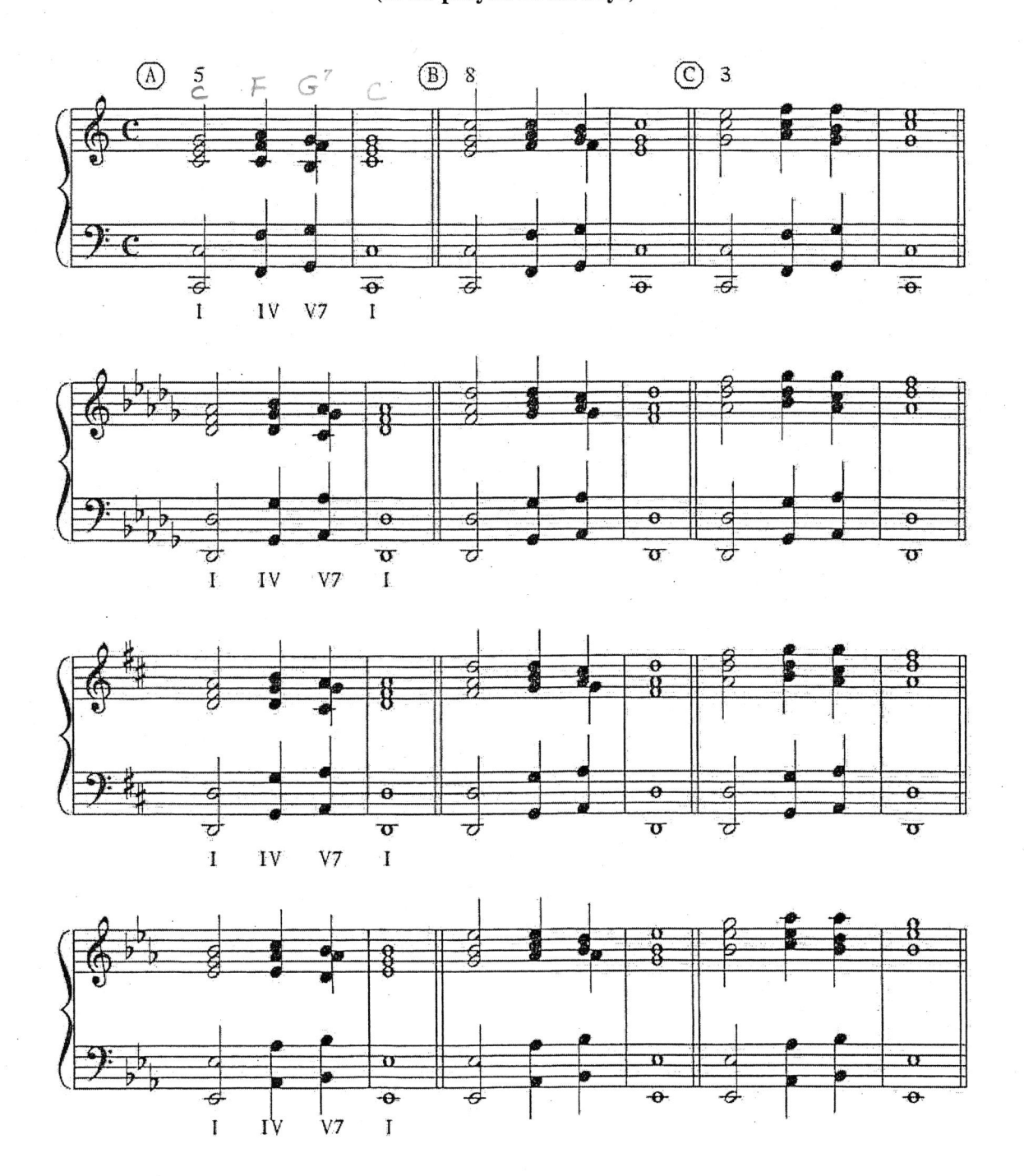

Appendeces

Common-Tone Chording with Basic Chords in Minor Keys
(to be played in all keys)

APPENDIX B

The Diatonic Triads of the Major Scale and Their Inversions

Continue through all major keys.

APPENDIX C

Common-Tone Chording with Basic Chords and V7 of V (II)
(052.mid or CD 52)

Note: The altered supertonic chord (V7 of V) is often preceded by the submediant chord (vi). The above progression could be varied by substituting the submediant chord (vi7) at the beginning of the second measure.

Application: Blessed Assurance (**053.mid or CD 53**)

Appendeces

APPENDIX D

A Review of Basic Chord Qualities: Major, Minor, Diminished, Augmented
(054.mid or CD 54)

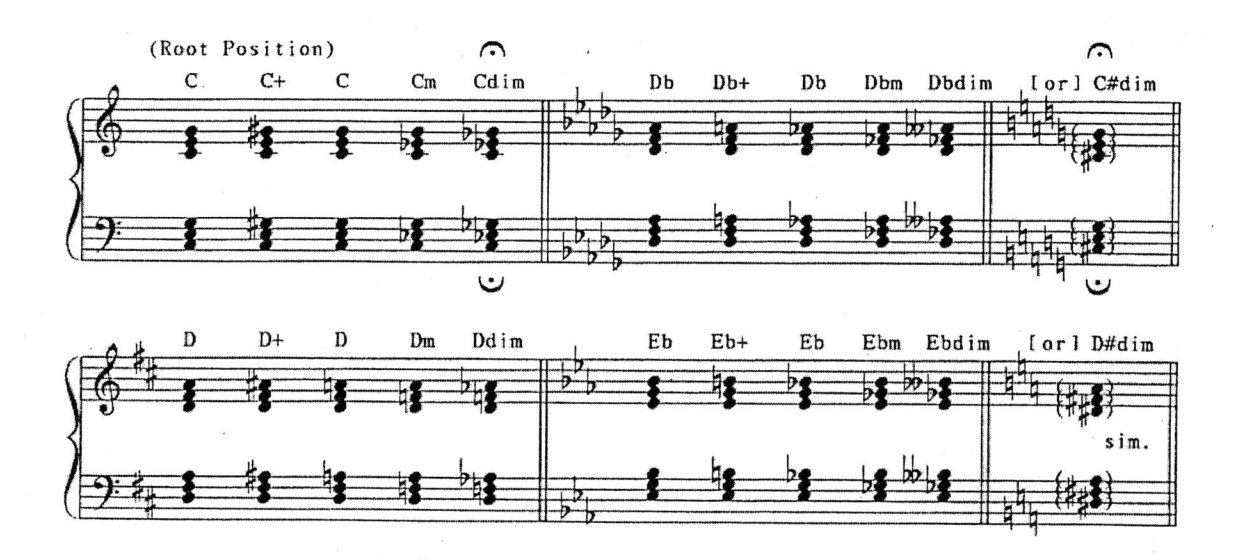

When the above chords are inverted, or spaced differently, it is sometimes difficult to determine which tone to alter when changing from one chord quality to another (e.g. major to minor). Starting the above progression <u>with a different inversion of the chord</u> is a means of gaining a command of these chords:

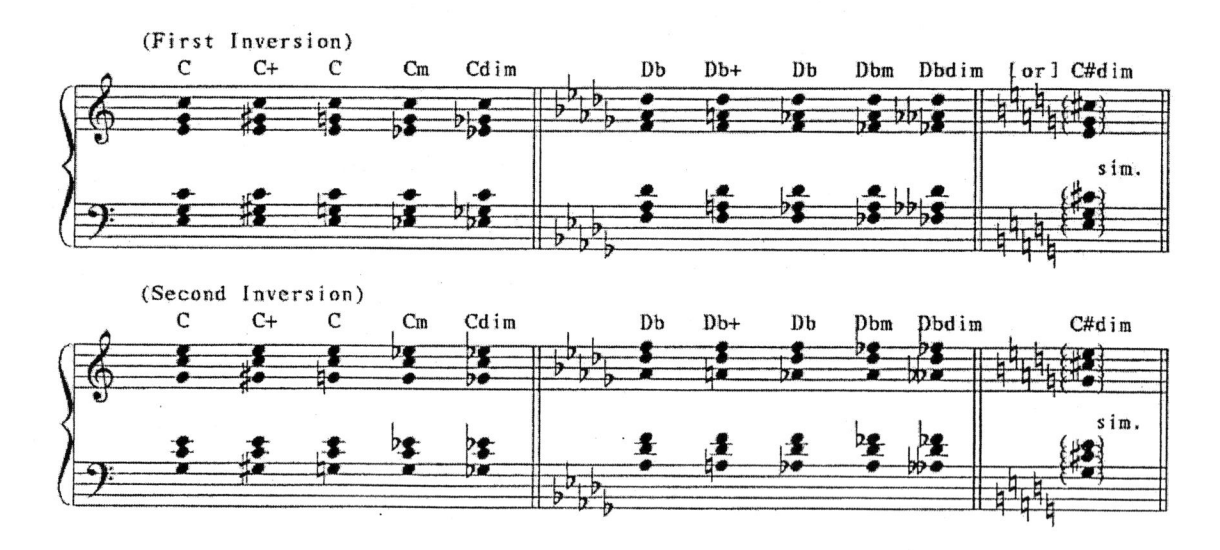

196

APPENDIX E

Diminished Chords

To realize the power (or pull) of the leading tone triad (vii°), all one must do is pause on the next-to-the-last chord in the following succession of chord.

The Pull of the Leading Tone Triad

I ii iii IV V vi viiO I   I ii iii IV V vi viiO I

Diminished chords often serve as dominant chords or as secondary dominants. When the root of a dominant seventh chord is removed, the remaining pitches constitute a diminished chord (see example below).

The Relationship of the Leading Tone Triad to V7

V7   viiO   V7   viiO

Each of the dominant seventh chord resolutions below is followed by a diminished chord that serves a similar function. In the key of C major, both the D7 and F#dim resolve to G (V). In a similar manner E7 and G#dim resolve to Am (vi).

Dominant and Diminished Chord Compared

V7 I   viio I   V7/V V   viio/V V   V7/vi vi viio/vi vi

The latter two diminished chords notated in the above example can be used effectively for the climax phrase of "Silent Night" (see next page).

Appendeces

Silent Night (with Diminished Chords for Climax Phrase)

G7	G#dim7	Am	F#o7	F7

Sleep in heav-en-ly peace,

V7 viio7/vi vi viiø7/V V7

The term "fully-diminished" is used to describe a diminished triad with a diminished seventh, as on the word "heavenly." The term "half-diminished" is used when a minor seventh is added, as on the word "peace." A fully-diminished seventh cannot be used here, because the E flat would clash with the E natural in the melody.

At the beginning of this discussion, a diminished triad was viewed as a dominant seventh chord with the root removed. For a really lush sound in measure 1 above, the pitch "E" could be played in the bass, along with the G# diminished seventh chord to create E7, flat 9 (see Example below). When I first used this chord for the climax phrase of "Silent Night," I found it delightful. Soon I was using it to excess, adding a flatted 9th to dominant and secondary dominant chords, just for the sake of gaining mastery. After a season of overuse, I began to tire of this lush sound, and I now use it much more sparingly. The secret of growth, however, is the application of newly-discovered chords, even at the risk of excess (but preferably during practice).

Silent Night (with the Addition of a Flatted Ninth)

G7	E7,b9	Am	F#o7	D9

Sleep in heav-en-ly peace,

Appendeces

Diminished Chords as Embellishment

Diminished Chords as Neighboring and Passing Motion

Diminished chords do not always serve a secondary harmonic function. In the first phrase of "O Little Town of Bethlehem" and "Beneath the Cross of Jesus," a diminished triad is used as embellishment (neighbor motion).

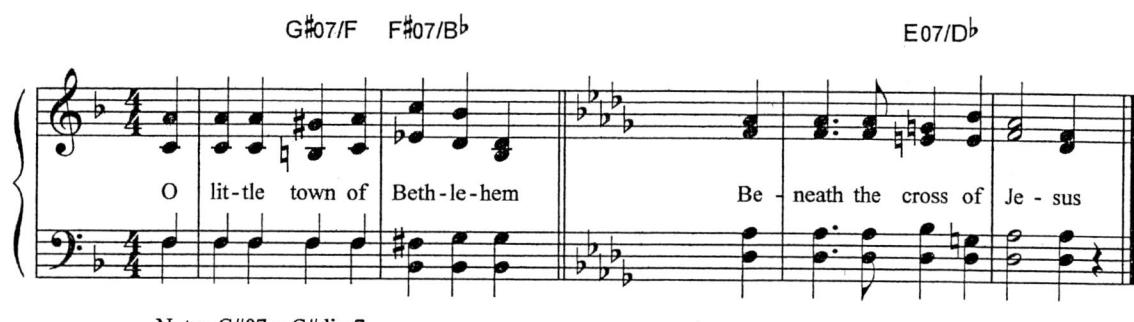

Note: G#o7 = G#dim7

A diminished chord may also be used as passing motion, as in the following harmonizations of familiar hymns:

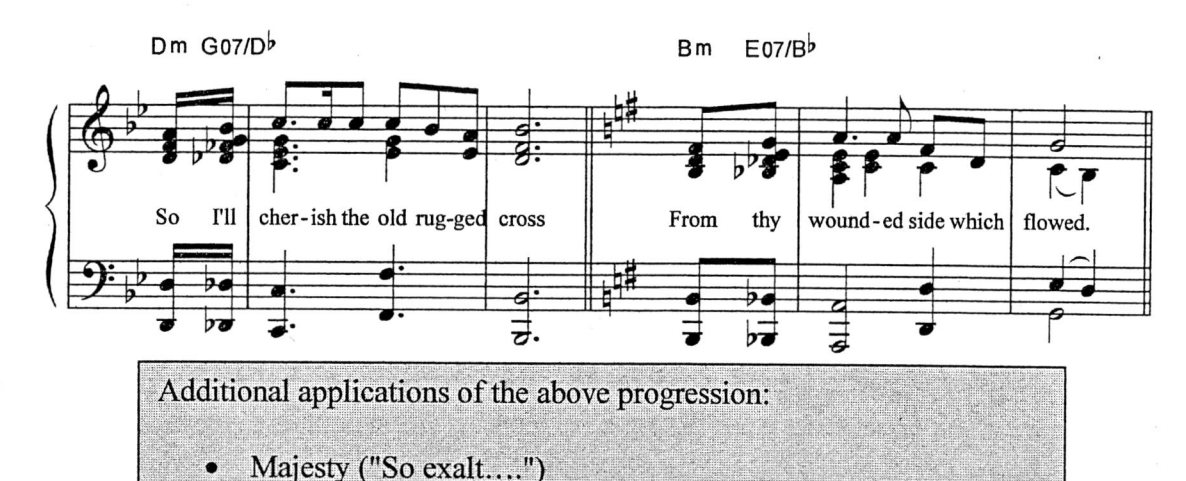

Additional applications of the above progression:

- Majesty ("So exalt....")
- He Is Lord (beginning pitches)

The Alteration of Fully-Diminished Seventh Chords to Create Dominant Seventh Chords

The ability to resolve dominant seventh chords should be regarded as a basic competency for keyboard musicians. Although most musicians have played these standard resolutions many times, there is a tendency for some to play them without really hearing them. The following drill in forming and resolving the various inversions of the dominant seventh chord is designed to engage the ear. I am indebted to Dr. Marta Sanchez, Professor of Music at Carnegie Mellon University, for this valuable ear training exercise.

Appendeces

Step One - Lowering the Root of a Fully-Diminished Seventh Chord
to Form a Root Position Dominant Seventh

Note: The root of a fully-diminished seventh chord is lowered one half step. This changes the bottom interval from a minor third (m3) to a major third (M3). The result is a dominant seventh chord in root position, with a major third between 1 and 3 (root and third), a perfect fifth between 1 and 5 (root and fifth), and a minor seventh between 1 and 7 (root and seventh). The same procedure can be applied to the incomplete examples below that begin with diminished chords built on F# and C#.

Bdim7   Bb7   Eb   F#dim7   F7   C#dim7

Step Two - Lowering the Seventh of a Fully-Diminished Seventh Chord
to Form a First Inversion Dominant Seventh

Bdim7   G7   C   F#dim7   D7   C#dim7

Step Three - Lowering the Fifth of a Fully-Diminished Seventh Chord
to Form a Second Inversion Dominant Seventh Chord

Bdim7   E7   A   F#dim7   B7   C#dim7

Step Four - Lowering the Third of a Fully-Diminished Seventh Chord
To Form a Third Inversion Dominant Seventh Chord

Bdim7   Db7   Gb   F#dim7   Ab7   C#dim7

Appendeces

Feeling the above changes is as important, or even more important than understanding the principles involved. The following explanation is offered as help in understanding the procedure more fully. In each of the alterations of the diminished seventh chord (Steps One to Four), the lowered pitch becomes the root of a dominant chord. Whereas a fully-diminished chord consists of a series of minor thirds, a dominant seventh chord consists of a major third between 1 and 3, and minor thirds between 3 and 5 and 5 and 7. The lower (bottom) pitch of the major third is the root of the dominant seventh chord, regardless of the inversion or chord spacing that is used.

APPENDIX F

Adding Suspensions to Basic Chords
(055.mid or CD 55)

Suspensions (4-3)

Appendeces

Seconds (or Ninths)

For practice is analyzing suspensions, listen to "Jesus Paid It All" (**56.mid** or **CD 56**).

APPENDIX G[1]

The Changing Function of a Repeated or Sustained Pitch
An Extension of Example 66 to Minor Keys
(057.mid or CD 57)

APPENDIX G²

Changing Function (with Different Resolutions)

(058.mid or CD 58)

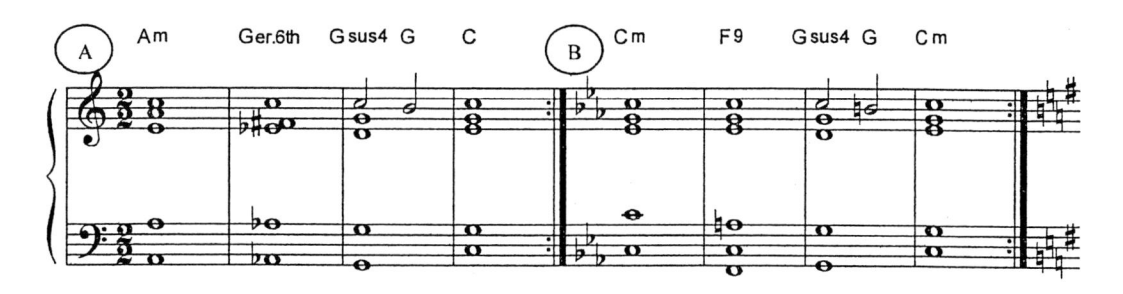

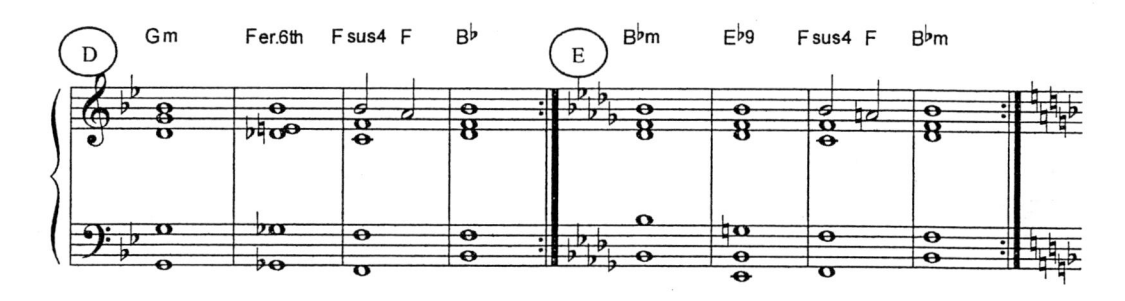

Appendix G³

Changing Function: More Changes and Resolutions
(059.mid or CD 59)

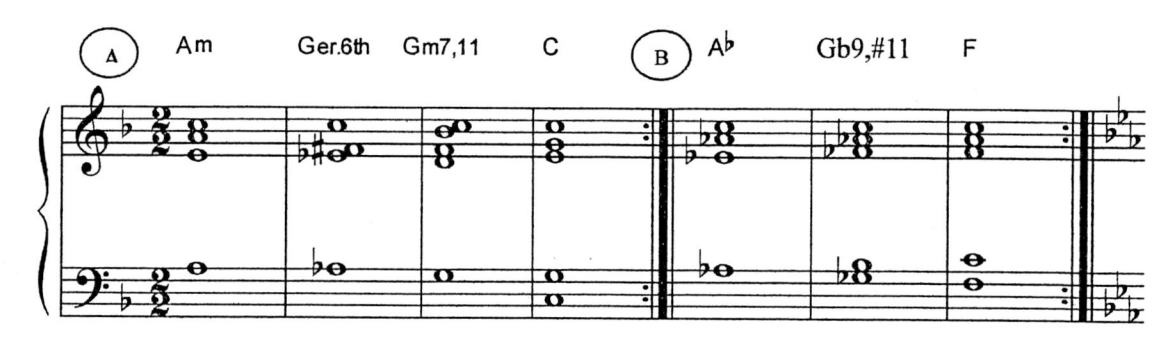

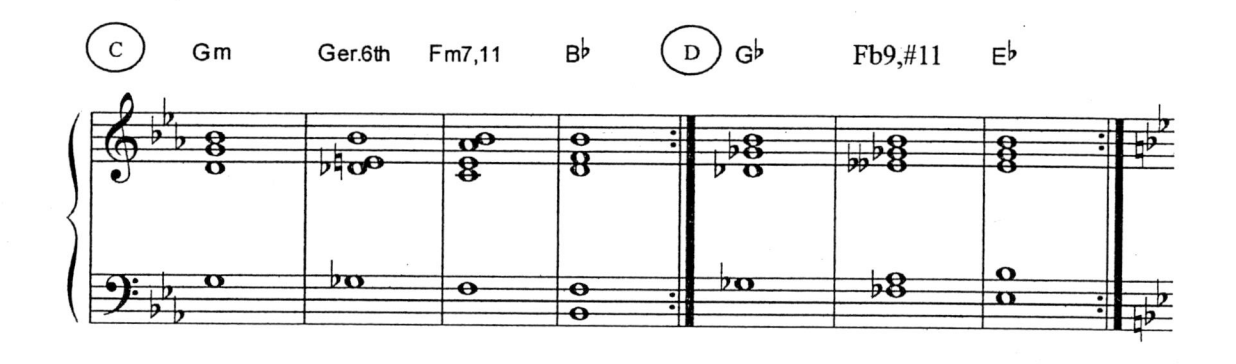

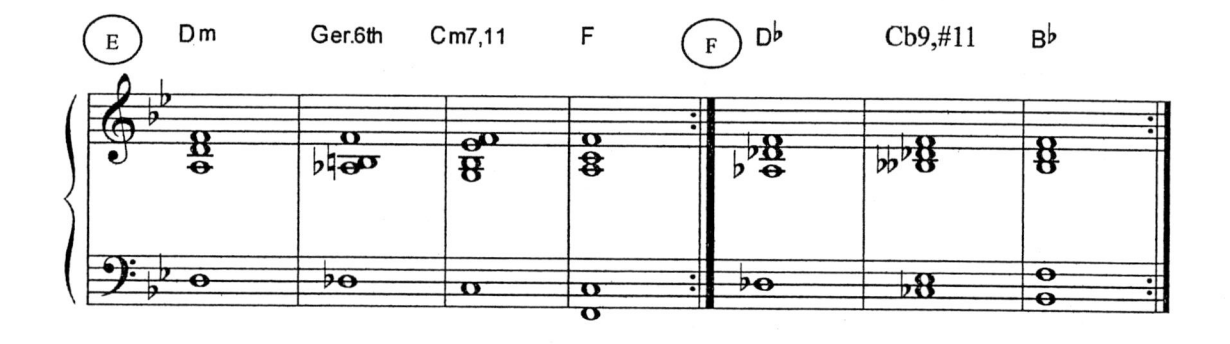

Note: To hear how the above progressions are used in a song, see "He's Everything to Me" by Ralph Carmichael (TH 516, m. 7-8 and 15-16).

Appendeces

APPENDIX H

Chords That Didn't Make the Hymnal: From Simple to More Complex Harmonies
What a Friend We Have in Jesus
(060.mid or CD 60)

A. F | B♭ | F | C7

B. F2 F | B♭2 B♭ | F2 F | Csus4 C

C. F | B♭ Gm | F/C Dm | Gm C

D. F | B♭ | F | E♭ C7

E. F | B♭ Bdim7 | F/C C7 | F

F. F | A+7 B♭ | F | Csus4 C

G. F2 | Cb9,#11 | F2 Dm | D♭9,#11 Csus4 C
    (or F+/Cb)   (or G+/Db)

Note: In Examples D, E and F, basic chords are used to both precede and follow the "featured" chord. In keyboard arranging, the other chords would also be varied, so that the new chord wouldn't seem inappropriate.

207

Appendeces

From Simple to Complex
Harmonizing a Descending Scale Fragment (5 4 3 2)

Note: Repeat the above phrases using each of the progressions that follow.

Other applications: Angels We Have Heard on High (refrain), Give Thanks (2nd half), Hyfrydol (3rd phrase)

For experience in moving from simple to complex, see pew edition of *Songs for Praise and Worship* (see REFERENCE LIST). The pew edition does not include chord symbols.

Appendeces

APPENDIX J

Lead Sheets

Turn Your Eyes upon Jesus

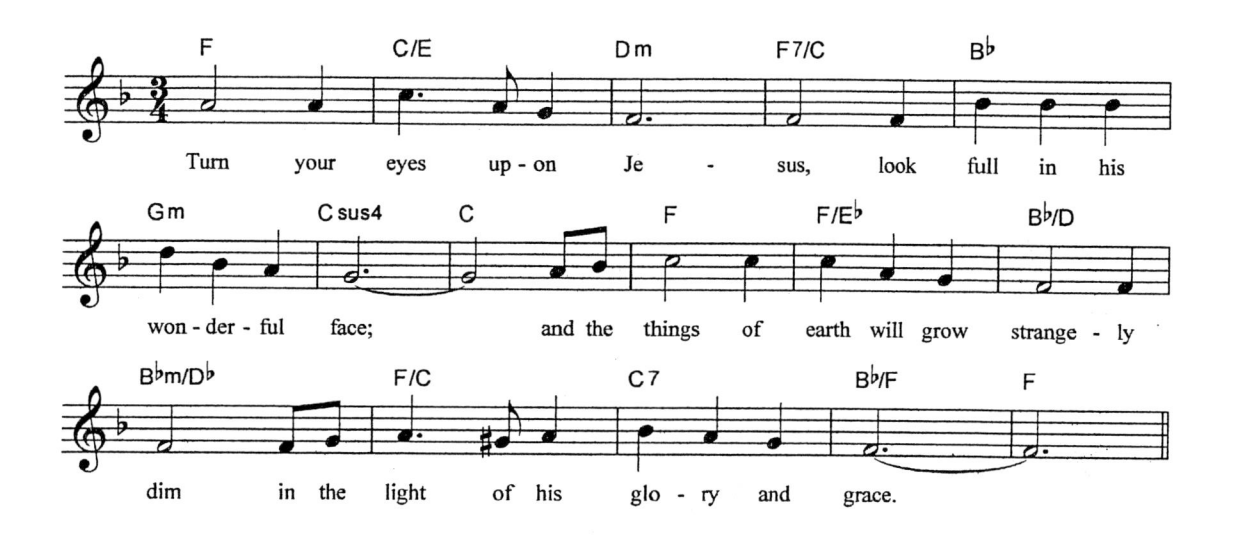

[Sheet music: first arrangement in 3/4 time with chords F, C/E, Dm, F7/C, B♭, Gm, Csus4, C, F, F/E♭, B♭/D, B♭m/D♭, F/C, C7, B♭/F, F. Lyrics: "Turn your eyes up-on Je-sus, look full in his won-der-ful face; and the things of earth will grow strange-ly dim in the light of his glo-ry and grace."]

Note: The following chart, which is more challenging than the above, is recorded as the final part of **60.mid** and **CD 60**. In measure 10 the melody pitch notated as C is analyzed as #9 (B#).

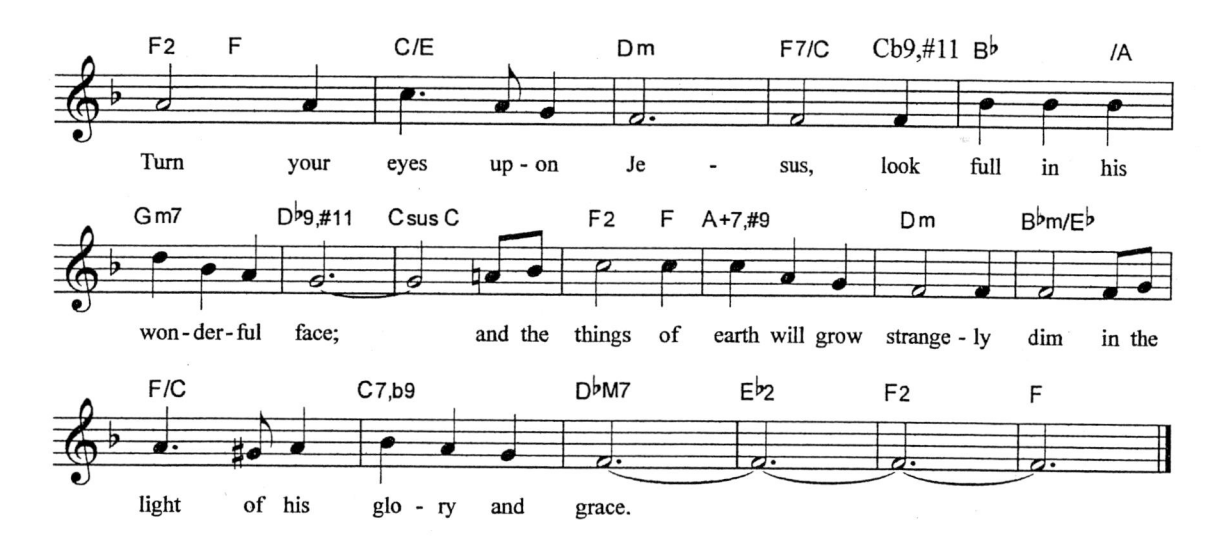

[Sheet music: second arrangement with chords F2, F, C/E, Dm, F7/C, Cb9,#11, B♭, /A, Gm7, D♭9,#11, Csus C, F2, F, A+7,#9, Dm, B♭m/E♭, F/C, C7,b9, D♭M7, E♭2, F2, F. Same lyrics.]

Words and Music by Helen H. Lemmel
© 1922. Renewed 1950 by H. H. Lemmel. Assigned to Singspiration Music. Used by permission.

For additional practice in reading lead sheets (chord charts) see *The Best of the Best*. The accompaniment edition can be used as a resource when having difficulty interpreting chord symbols. The accompaniment editions of *Sing to the Lord* and *The Celebration Hymnal* also include chord symbols which can be studied and compared with the notation (see Reference List).

Appendeces

O Holy Night

O ho-ly night! the stars are bright-ly shin-ing, it is the night of the dear Sav-ior's birth; Long lay the world in sin and er-ror pin-ing, till He ap-peared and the soul felt its worth. A thrill of hope the wear-y world re-joic-es, For yon-der breaks a new and glo-rious morn. Fall on your knees! O hear the an-gel voic-es! O night di-vine! O night when Christ was born! O night di-vine! O night, O night di-vine!

Words: John S. Dwight; Music: Adolphe Adam

210

Appendeces

Everything Was New One Day

Freely and Expressively   **Words and Music: Ron Sprunger**

1. There's a simple little truth that's so easy to-for-get, so I beg you to hear what I say. All the places we go and the people we know very likely were new to us one day. Yes, ev-'ry-thing was new one day: ev-'ry sound, ev-'ry sight, ev-'ry-thing that seems right, they were new one day.

4. So, if something's not your style, why not go the extra mile and consider the other person's view? Then, together we'll stand, joining hearts and hands, singing songs both old and new. In love we have un-i-ty. We'll not always agree on the song or the key, - but there's un-i-ty!

2. When you hear something that's new, that seems different to you, there's no need to turn away. Why not give it a change, decide in advance that this could be the day when something new becomes yours? A new sound, a new sight could soon seem right; it could soon be right.

3. When you hear something that's old, perhaps you have been told that is has no relevance today. Well, the old can be new and meaningful, too, no matter what they say. For every thing was new one day: Every sound, every sight, every thing that seems right; they were new one day!

©2001 by Ron Sprunger

Everything Was New One Day

Freely and Expressively

Words and Music: Ron Sprunger

There's a simple little truth that's so easy to forget, so I beg you to hear what I say. All the places we go and the people we know very likely were new to us one day. Yes, ev'rything was new one day: ev'ry sound, ev'ry sight, ev'rything that seems right, they were new one day!

© 2001 by Ron Sprunger 408 Keen Ave. Ashland, OH 44805

REFERENCE LIST

Baker, Ken, ed. *Songs for Praise and Worship: Worship Leader's Edition.* Waco: Word Music, 1992.
Note: The pew edition, which includes only the melody, is recommended for assignments in harmonizing melodies. It is available at approximately one-fourth the cost of *The Worship Leader's Edition.* The latter is a rich resource for the worship leader, and it includes the harmonization of each melody.

Bible, Ken, ed. *Sing to the Lord: Accompanists'/Pulpit Edition.* Kansas City, MO: Lillenas Publishing Co., 1993.

Clough, John and Joyce Conley. *Scales, Intervals, Keys, Triads, Rhythm and Meter.* New York: W.W. Norton Co., 1983.
This programmed learning text is recommended for the keyboard musician who is motivated to acquire a knowledge of music theory on his/her own.

Fettke, Tom, ed. *The Celebration Hymnal: Songs and Hymns for Worship.* Word/Integrity, 1997.

_____. *The Celebration Hymnal: Accompaniment Edition.* Word/Integrity, 1998.
This edition includes the chord symbols above the written music.

Forte, Allen. *Tonal Harmony in Concept and Practice.* New York: Holt, Rinehart and Winston, 1979.
This book would serve as an excellent review of theory for professional musicians with a background in theory.

Haron, Larry. *Great Songs for God's Kids.* Ed. Ken Barker. Waco: Word Music, 1992.
This is a rich mixture of classic hymns and choruses, old and new. Because there is neither accompaniment nor chord symbols, the keyboard musician is free to explore chords, applying the principles presented in *Want to Play by Ear?*

Hustad, Donald P., ed. *The Worshiping Church.* Carol Stream: Hope Pub. Co., 1990.
The Worship Leader's Edition of this hymnal serves as an excellent resource for the musician who wants to explore the rich scriptural content of the hymns. It provides some interesting biographical material as well.

Hymns and Folk Songs for Guitar. Carol Stream: Hope Publishing Company, 1971.
This collection of hymns and folk songs notated as lead sheets is an excellent resource for the keyboard musician who needs practice in interpreting chord symbols.

Jonas, Oswald. *Introduction to the Theory of Heinrich Schenker.* Trans. and ed. John Rothgeb. New York: Schirmer Books, 1982.
This is an excellent presentation of Schenker's method of analysis for the student of theory.

Liesch, Barry. The New Worship. Grand Rapids: Baker Book House, 1996, 2001. (www.worshipin
On-line tutorials on keyboard improvisation are available (www.worshipinfo.com).

Murray, Michael. *Marcel Dupre: The Work of a Master Organist.* Boston: Northeastern University Press, 1985.

Palmer, Willard A., Morton Manus and Amanda Vick Lethco. *Intermediate Musicianship, Book Two.* Alfred Pub. Co., 1988.
>This keyboard theory book provides a review of scales, primary chords in each inversion, arpeggios, and diatonic triads and their inversions. All of the above are notated in each key, except for the diatonic triads, which are only in C.

Parker, Alice. *Creative Hymn Singing.* Chapel Hill: Hinshaw Music, Inc., 1976.

Sprunger, Ron and Linda Sprunger. *Worship the King.* Kansas City: Lillenas Music, 1994.
>This collection and the ones listed below are piano and organ arrangements that include examples of the various concepts presented and discussed in *Want to Play by Ear?*

_____. *Holy, Holy, Holy.* Kansas City: Lillenas Music, 1997.

_____. *Seasonal Duets.* Kansas City: Lillenas Music, 2000.

_____. *Rejoice!.* Kansas City: Lillenas Music, 2002.

Sprunger, Ron. *Organ Praise and Worship.* Kansas City: Lillenas Music, 2001.

Stravinsky, Igor. *Poetics of Music in the Form of Six Lessons.* Trans. by Arthur Knodel & Ingolf Dahl. NewYork: Vintage Books, 1974.

Vegh, Michael. *Maranatha! Music Praise Hymns and Choruses.* Maranatha! Music, 1997.

Zehnder, Mike. *The Best of the Best.* Fellowship Publications (Distributed by Maranatha! Music through Word Music, 2000).
>This collection of praise and worship songs, printed as lead sheets (chord charts), is suggested as a resource for the development of skill in interpreting chord symbols.

_____. *The Best of the Best: Accompaniment Edition.*
This collection includes chord symbols above the printed accompaniment for each song.

INDEX OF MUSICAL EXAMPLES

Page

ABERYSTWYTH (Jesus, Lover of My Soul)	128
Adagio by A. Marcello	77-78
All Creatures of Our God and King	118
All Hail the Power (CORONATION)	122,129
All Hail the Power (DIADEM)	129
All through the Night	90
Amazing Grace	5
And Can It Be That I Should Gain	179
Angels We Have Heard on High	74,92
ARNSBERG (God Himself Is with Us)	80
ASH GROVE (Let All Things Now Living)	112-113,150
Away in a Manger	93,159
Bach: March in D	91
Bach: Prelude in C	169
Be Thou My Vision	161
BEECHER (Love Divine of)	125
Beneath the Cross of Jesus	124,133,199
Binary Patterns	144
Binary Patterns Combined	146-147
Blues (Twelve-Bar)	23-24
Calypso Style	22,25
Canon in D (progression)	80-83
Children of the Heavenly Father	149
Christ, We Do All Adore Thee	53-54
Come, Christians, Join to Sing	120,176
Come, Thou Almighty King	172-173
Come, Thou Long-Expected Jesus	73
Come, Ye Thankful People, Come	173-174
Comfort, Comfort, Now, My People	95-97
CONVERSE (What a Friend We Have)	158,160,207
CORONATION (All Hail the Power) of	122,129
Crown Him w/Many Crowns	33,90,106-108,118,124
DARWALL (Rejoice, the Lord Is King)	4, 186
DIADEM (All Hail the Power)	129
DIADEMATA (Crown Him)	33,90,106-108,118,124
Dorian Improvisation	154-155
DOXOLOGY (Praise God from Whom....)	64
DUKE STREET (Jesus Shall Reign)	47
DUNCANNON ((King of My Life)	126
Eternal Father, Strong to Save	91
Everything Was New One Day	211
Fairest Lord Jesus	61-62,65,67,175
Father, Lead Me Day by Day	98-103
FOUNDATION (How Firm a Foundation)	143
FREU DICH SEHR (Comfort, Comfort, Now)	95-97
Give Thanks	82-84
Go to Dark Gethsemane	124
God Himself Is with Us	80
God Is So Good	2,34,37
GREENSLEEVES (What Child Is This?)	30-31
HAMBURG (When I Survey)	126
Have Thine Own Way	183-184
He Is Lord	34-35,92
He Leadeth Me	181-182
HENDON (Take My Life....)	130
HERZLIEBSTER JESU (Ah, Holy Jesus)	133
Higher Ground	182
Holy, Holy (Jimmie Owens)	141-142
Holy Spirit, Be My Guide	178
How Firm a Foundation	143
HYFRYDOL (Come, Thou Long-Expected Jesus)	73
HYFRYDOL (Jesus, What a Friend for Sinners)	127
I Have Decided to Follow Jesus	160
I Surrender All	130
I Will Serve Thee	185
If You're Happy and You Know It	63
Immortal, Invisible	33,148,177
In My Life, Lord	2,87
In Our Church We Have a Band (Old MacDonald)	152
It Is Well with My Soul	134
ITALIAN HYMN (Come, Thou Almighty....)	172-173
Jesus, I Come	128
Jesus, Lover of My Soul (ABERYSTWYTH)	128
Jesus Shall Reign	47
Jesus, What a Friend for Sinners	127
Jingle Bells	22
Joy to the World	33
Joyful, Joyful, We Adore Thee	2,14-16,64
JOYFUL SONG (Praise Him! Praise Him!)	131
King of My Life	126
Kum Ba Yah	10-13
LASST UNS ERFREUEN (All Creatures of....)	118
Lead Me, Lord	151
Let All Mortal Flesh Keep Silence	154
Let All the People Praise Thee	188-189
Let All Things Now Living	112-113,150
Like a River Glorious	36,134
LOBE DEN HERREN	85,123,165
Lord, Be Glorified	2,87
Love Came Down at Christmas	110
Love Divine, All Loves Excelling	125
MADRID (Come, Christians, Join to Sing)	120,176
MELITA (Eternal Father, Strong to Save)	91
MIT FREUDEN ZART (Sing Praise to God)	131
My Hope Is Built	122
NOEL NOUVELET (Sing We Now of Xmas)	153
O Come, Little Children	20,27
O Holy Night	132,210
O How He Loves You and Me	180
O Little Town of Bethlehem	199

INDEX OF MUSICAL EXAMPLES

O Sacred Head, Now Wounded	157
ODE TO JOY (Joyful, Joyful, We Adore)	2,14-16,64
OLD HUNDREDTH (Praise God from Whom)	64
Old MacDonald	152
On Christmas Night (SUXXEX CAROL)	15
One Two Three Method of Melodic Dev.	146-147
Pachelbel: Canon in D (progression)	80-83
Pass It On	140
PASSION CHORALE (O Sacred Head)	157
PATRICIA (O How He Loves You and Me)	180
PICARDY (Let All Mortal Flesh Keep Silence)	154
Praise God from Whom All Blessings Flow	64
Praise Him in the Morning (Spiritual)	5
Praise Him! Praise Him!	131
Praise to the Lord	85,123,165
Prelude in C - J.S. Bach	169
REDHEAD (Go to Dark Gethsemane)	124
Rejoice in the Lord Always	21
Rejoice, the Lord Is King	4, 186
Rock of Ages	103-105,199
ST. CHRISTOPHER (Beneath the Cross)	124,133,199
ST. DENIO (Immortal, Invisible)	33, 148, 177
ST. GEORGE'S WINDSOR	173-174
SAGINA (And Can It Be?)	179
SCHOENSTER HERR JESU	61-62,65,67,175
Sarabande by Johann Pezel	88
Set My Spirit Free	26-27
Silent Night	28-29,198
Sing Praise to God Who Reigns Above	131
Sing We Now of Christmas	153
SLANE (Be Thou My Vision)	161
SOLID ROCK (My Hope Is Built)	122
STILLE NACHT (Silent Night)	28-29,198
SURRENDER (I Surrender All)	130
SUSSEX CAROL (On Christmas Night)	15
SWEDISH HYMN (Children of the Heavenly)	149
Swing Low, Sweet Chariot	143
Take My Life and Let It Be Consecrated	130
Ternary Patterns	145
Ternary Patterns Combined	146
To God Be the Glory	189-190
TOPLADY (Rock of Ages)	103-105,199
Trust and Obey	90
Turn Your Eyes upon Jesus	209
Twelve Bar Blues	23-24
Twinkle, Twinkle, Little Star	3,42
Venite Adoremus	109
VILLE DU HAVRE (It Is Well with My Soul)	134
Vocalises	41,49-52,55-58
We Bring the Sacrifice of Praise	187-188
We Three Kings (mixed meter)	156
WELSH AIR (All through the Night)	90
What a Day That Will Be	180-181
What a Friend We Have in Jesus	158,160,207
What Child Is This?	30-31
When I Survey the Wondrous Cross	126
When Peace Like a River	134
Wonderful Words of Life	146
WYE VALLEY (Like a River Glorious)	36,134

INDEX OF RECORDED EXAMPLES

MIDI = Standard MIDI File (SMF)
CD = Compact Disc

Note: In some MIDI players the songs might not appear in this exact order. Also, the names might be slightly different for some selections. It is suggested that any variances be notated in the user's copy.

File	Title	Time
001.mid (CD1)	Five-Finger Pattern	01:43
002.mid (CD2)	Lord, Be Glorified	00:52
003.mid (CD3)	God Is So Good	01:40
004.mid (CD4)	Joyful, Joyful	01:25
005.mid (CD5)	Twinkle Little Star	01:28
006.mid (CD6)	The First Noel	01:50
007.mid (CD7)	Joy to the World	01:13
008.mid (CD8)	Jingle Bells	01:58
009.mid (CD9)	Jingle Bells (w/o Melody)	01:06
010.mid (CD10)	Praise Him in the Morning	01:05
011.mid (CD11)	O Come, Little Children	00:33
012.mid (CD12)	Rejoice in the Lord Always	00:40
013.mid (CD13)	Jingle Bells w/o Chords	01:08
014.mid (CD14)	Jingle Bells w/o Bass	01:08
015.mid (CD15)	Boogie Woogie Bass with Blues Progression	00:58
016.mid (CD16)	Boogie Woogie Bass (w/o Chords)	00:55
017.mid (CD17)	Boogie Woogie (w/o Bass)	00:55
018.mid (CD18)	Silent Night	01:05
019.mid (CD19)	What Child Is This?	00:57
020.mid (CD20)	Do Re Do (1 2 1)	02:52
021.mid (CD21)	Do Re Mi (1 2 3)	01:07
022.mid (CD22)	Do Re Mi Fa (1 2 3 4)	02:07
023.mid (CD23)	Descending Scale	01:38
024.mid (CD24)	Ascending and Descending Scale	01:29
025.mid (CD25)	Changing Function	01:55
026.mid (CD26)	Hyfrydol (basic chords, then w/ succession of 5ths)	01:35
027.mid (CD27)	Angels We Have Heard on High	00:42
028.mid (CD28)	Adagio by Marcello (succession of 5ths in minor key)	00:31
029.mid (CD29)	Pachelbel Progression	00:40
030.mid (CD30)	Pachelbel w/scale in bass	00:25
031.mid (CD31)	Lord, Be Glorified	01:42
032.mid (CD32)	Venite Adoremus	01:08
033.mid (CD33)	Ashgrove	01:05
034.mid (CD34)	Crown Him with Many Crowns (half-step modulations)	00:33
035.mid (CD35)	Whole-Step Modulation	00:24
036.mid (CD36)	Praise to the Lord, the Almighty (whole-step modulation)	00:25
037.mid (CD37)	Crown Him with Many Crowns (whole-step w/pivot chord)	00:30
038mid (CD38)	Go to Dark Gethsemane (modulation down a whole step)	00:20
039mid (CD39)	Diadem to Hyfrydol (down a minor third)	00:23
040mid (CD40)	Coronation to Diadem (modulation up a minor third)	00:21
041.mid (CD41)	Take My Life to I Surrender (down a major third)	00:37
042.mid (CD42)	Modulation Down a Major third (Ex. 135)	00:40
043.mid (CD43)	Sing Praise to God to Praise Him! Praise Him! (Up a major third)	00:24
044.mid (CD44)	O Holy Night (modulation up a major third to mediant harmony)	00:43
045.mid (CD45)	Beneath the Cross to Ah, Holy Jesus (N6) (up a major third)	00:31

INDEX OF RECORDED EXAMPLES

MIDI = Standard MIDI File (SMF)
CD = Compact Disc

046.mid (CD46)	Christmas Hymns grouped by Succession of 5ths	00:45
047.mid (CD47)	Pentatonic Improvisation	00:37
048.mid (CD48)	Combining Binary Patterns	00:37
049.mid (CD49)	What a Friend We Have in Jesus (tri-tone substitutes)	00:47
050.mid (CD50)	Tri-Tone Substitute Applications	05:07
051.mid (CD51)	Old MacDonald (mixed meter modal harmonies)	00:42
052.mid (CD52)	Appendix C (basic chords plus II (V of V), the altered supertonic)	01:12
053.mid (CD53)	Appendix C2 Blessed Assurance (w/common-tone chording)	00:48
054.mid (CD54)	Appendix D (Review of Chord Qualities)	03:28
055.mid (CD55)	Appendix F (Suspensions)	01:43
056.mid (CD56)	Appendix F2 Jesus Paid It All (w/basic chords, then w/suspensions)	02:09
057.mid (CD57)	Appendix G1 Changing Function of a Repeated Pitch (minor scale)	01:52
058.mid (CD58)	Appendix G2 Changing Function (with Different Resolutions)	01:05
059.mid (CD59)	Appendix G3 More Changes and Resolutions	00:50
060.mid (CD60)	Appendix H From Simple to Complex	03:05

TOPICAL INDEX

Accompaniment Styles 19-31, 87, 90, 156, 158, 172-190
Altered Chords (see Secondary Dominants)
Augmented Sixth Chords 119-120, 127, 132, 152
Basic Chords
- Applications 10-29, 96, 99
- Basis for Selection 10-13, 103-104, 112
- Blues (see Twelve-Bar Blues) 23-24
Cadences
- Authentic and Plagal 93
- Deceptive 160
- Half 11, 92
Changing Function of a Tone (also see Substitute Chords) .... 60-70, Appendix G
Chord Functions 9-29, 73-93, 95-110, 151-161
Chord Qualities (major, minor, diminished, augmented) .... Appendix D
Circle of Fifths (see Succession of Fifths)
Common-Tone Chording .... 20-29, Appendix A and C
Diatonic Triads of the Major Scale and Their Inversions .... Appendix B
- I   tonic .... 10-16, 69, Appendix A and B
- ii   supertonic 34-35, 67
- iii   mediant .... 65-66, Appendix B
- IV   subdominant .... 13, 17-18, 24, 28, 37-40, Appendix A and B
- V   dominant .... 10-17, 20-21, Appendix A and B
- vi   submediant 60-64, 68, 80, 160
- vii^0 leading tone .... Appendix B and E
Diatonic Triads of the Minor Scale 77
Diminished Chords .... 92, Appendix E
Dominant Seventh with Flatted Ninth (-9) 93, 198, 209
Dorian Mode (Scale) 153-155
Drones 14-15
Figured Bass 16, 165-169
Five-Finger Melodies to Complete by Ear (also Melodies with a Wider Range 1-6
Harmonizing a Melody 97-115
- A Six-Step Approach 95-102
- On the Basis of Chord Outline 10-13, 103-104, 112
- On the Basis of Underlying Scale Line 106-110
Harmonizing the Scale (see Scale Harmonization)
Hymn Improvisation (see Improvising Hymn Accompaniment)
Improvisation 139-163
- Anacrusis with Change of Chords 160
- Combining Binary and Ternary Patterns to Create Melody 145-147
- Deceptive Cadences 160
- Embellishing Melody and Harmony with Non-Harmonic Tones .... 147-151(16-18)
- Mixed Meter 156-157
- Modal Harmonies 151-155

TOPICAL INDEX

- Nurturing the Growing Process 162-163
- One-Two-Three Method 146-147
- Pentatonic 142-144
- Tri-Tone Substitute Chords 156-159
- Values of Improvisation 162
- Variations on the Submediant Chord 141-142

Improvising Hymn Accompaniments 171-190
- Chord Inversions 183-184
- Chord Substitution 181-182
- Doubling of Melody (Full Chords in Right Hand with Octaves in Bass) 173-174
- Eighth Note Movement in Inner Voices 175
- Imitation 187-188, 190
- Inversion of Intervals as Fill 188-189
- Rationale 171
- Scale-Wise Movement in Octaves as Embellishment of Triadic Melody 177
- Scales as Fill 176-181

Independent Accompaniment Styles 19-31
- Arpeggios 26-31
- Broken Chords 20, 25-31
- Calypso 25
- Salsa 22
- Walking Bass 21-22

Inversions of Chords (see Chord Inversions)
Key Signatures (Arranged by Succession of Fifths) 79
Meter (Mixed) 58, 156-157
Modal Harmonies 151-155
Modulation 115-137
- Definition and Purpose 115
- Guidelines 116
- Up a Half Step 116-121
- Down a Half Step 121
- Up a Whole Step 121-124
- Down a Whole Step 124-125
- Up a Minor Third 127-129
- Down a Minor Third 125-127
- Up a Major Third 131-133
- Down a Major Third 129-131
- Down a Fifth (Up a Fourth) 133
- Up or Down a Tri-Tone 135
- Down a Perfect Fourth (Up a Perfect Fifth) 134
- Up a Sixth and Up a Seventh 136

Motivation for Learning (Educational Principles) 162-163
Muscle Memory 70-71
Neapolitan Sixth Chord 88, 132-133

TOPICAL INDEX

Non-Harmonic Tones..16-18, 147-151
Parallel Harmonies...30-31, 153
Pivot Chords...122-125
Relative Major/Relative Minor..125, 128
Scale Harmonization (Ascending and Descending)
- Applications (see Scale-Based Melodies below)
- Complete Scale 47, 49-52, 55-56
- Scale Fragments
- Do-Re 34-35
- Do-Re-Mi (1-2-3)...36-37
- Do-Re-Mi-Fa (1-2-3-4) 37-39
- Do-Re-Mi-Fa-So (1-2-3-4-5) 40-41
- Do-Re-Mi-Fa-So-La) 1-2-3-4-5-6..42
- Re-Mi-Fa (2-3-4)..44-45
- Mi-Fa-So (3-4-5)..46
- Scale-Based Melodies 33-34. 37, 42, 50, 53, 73-79, 80-84

Secondary Dominants (Altered Chord)
- II (V of V)...90, 92, 108
- (vii° of V)..197-198
- III (V of vi) 159, 209
- (vii0 and vii^{o7} of vi)...197-198
- VI (V of ii and V7 of ii) 74, 76, 92
- (vii° of ii and vii^{o7} of ii)...92

Sequential Harmonies 73-92
- Pachelbel Sequence (I V vi iii IV I from "Canon in D") 80, 83, 85, 87-88, 109
- Pachelbel Sequence with Scale-Wise Movement in Bass......................81, 83, 87-88
- Succession of Fifths (iii vi ii V I) 73-79, 84, 112
- Succession of Fifths (Shorter Segments)....................................35, 92, 100-101, 129
- I IV ii(II) V iii (III) vi 90-91
- V I vi (VI) ii 91

Substitute Chords
- Changing Function of a Tone 61
- Mediant Chord (iii) - a Substitute of the Tonic Chord...65-66
- Submediant Chord (vi) - a Substitute for the Tonic Chord (I)......................................61-64
- Supertonic Chord (ii) - a Substitute for the Subdominant Chord (IV).....................26, 67
- Subtonic Chord (VII) - Substitute for the Dominant (V) 82-84, 151-152
- Tri-Tone Substitute ....157-159, Appendix H

Vocalises Based on Scale..49, 51-52, 55-58